D1075445

Don't Get a Job, Get a Life!

FlexLife®
The New Way to Work and Live

By Erik Vonk

ᴎꞏ randstad

While you were busy, the workplace changed. Traditional employment dissolved. "Flexible employment" caught on. FlexLife® emerged as the workplace trend for the next 25 years. Employment security replaced job security. Productivity improved. And employees and employers alike saw that it was good.

— *Erik Vonk*

Published by:
Randstad North America
2015 S. Park Place
Atlanta, GA 30339

Copyright © 2001 Erik Vonk

All rights reserved. No part of this book may be reproduced in
any form or by any means without the prior written permission of
the Publisher, excepting brief quotes used in conjunction with
reviews, written specifically for inclusion in a magazine or newspaper.

Printed in the United States of America.

Editing by Yow Editorial.

Book design by Shock Design, Inc.

Printing and binding by Sheridan Books.

1 2 3 4 5 6   2006   2005   2004   2003   2002   2001

Library of Congress Catalog Number: 00-130053

ISBN: 0-9678316-0-1

Contents

Prologue

I hope you enjoy *Don't Get a Job, Get a Life!* Much of the book's terminology is familiar to many within the Randstad organization, yet it is not a book "about" Randstad nor is it designed solely for company personnel. Consequently, readers may recognize subtle differences in the *"FlexLife"* portrayed in the book and that espoused in corporate training. This is not an inconsistency, but the nature–and strength–of *FlexLife®*.

FlexLife® is much more than a catch-phrase employed for the moment by a single staffing organization. Rather, it is a mode of work and a way of life that I and others believe is the major trend in employment far into the future. *Don't Get a Job, Get a Life!* is one man's effort to draw the outer parameters of the subject so that all parties to the workplace–not just Randstad–have a framework to operate within. Many variables are possible within the context of the bigger picture, including the approach prescribed by Randstad North America.

The management team of Randstad North America offers *Don't Get a Job, Get a Life!* as a guidebook to its personnel, customers and talent pool. While the company enjoys the benefits of launching the concept on a major scale, *FlexLife®* is not our exclusive domain. Indeed, we expect to see it materialize under various names throughout the labor exchange industry and the workplace. This bodes well for the future of work. We at Randstad can take some small measure of pride in advancing a workplace trend that promises so much for so many segments of society.

Erik Vonk

Preface

Employment is as basic to modern life as eating and sleeping. Gone are the days when more than a few people can literally "live off the land." Somewhere, some way, people need the first fruit of employment—income. In many ways, the single greatest struggle around the world today is for sustained employment. In nearly all developing economies, gainful employment falls far short of the needs of society. And in advanced economies, traditional employment is no longer the sure thing it used to be. In his book *Beyond Workplace 2000*, Joseph H. Boyett writes, "In the last five years, almost everything about working in America has changed. The places Americans work, the way they work, the relationships they have with their boss and peers, the security of their jobs—all of these things and many, many more have changed." Those changes have produced a lot of heartache, pain and disappointment, notes Mr. Boyett. Indeed, most Americans see themselves as survivors of a revolution they hope is surely coming to an end. *"But it isn't,"* exclaims Boyett. "America's workplace revolution isn't over. It has only just begun."

Mr. Boyett could just as easily have been referring to the European community of nations or to Japan, Canada or any other country deemed an "advanced economy." Everything about working nearly anywhere seems to have undergone tremendous change in recent years.

So what's the future of employment, and what does it mean for those who work for a living and those who rely upon the skills and labor of others to produce and deliver products and services?

For starters, change—even dramatic change—is not necessarily bad. It's just change. The basics of employment have not changed. People still need jobs, jobs are still available, talent and skills and initiative and reliability still have value, employers still pay "the going rate" for the product of employee. What's changed are the traditions of employment as workers have known them for most of the 20th century. Career-long jobs. Security. Health insurance. Seniority. Automatic pay raises. Steady advancement. Paid vacations. Pension income upon retirement. "I'm the boss and you're not" management style. Loyalty to the company. Employer as benevolent benefactor. Government as protector of the status quo.

The dismantling of these workplace traditions is unsettling, *especially for those who have known nothing else.* But they only mark the end of an era and the beginning of another. A new reality is afoot in the modern workplace, one loosely termed "flexible employment." At Randstad, we have another name for it—*FlexLife®*, a contraction of "flexible lifestyle." It reflects the very real progression from the traditional workplace of early Baby Boomers and their parents to the capricious workplace of today where the Internet makes waste of time-honored employment practices, "job-hopping" is viewed as valuable experience, employees can fire their bosses and continue to work, and "staffing" plays an integral role in the plans and operations of business and the lifestyles of employees.

FlexLife® is the dawning of a new era in how people work and live. Whether employee or employer, the more you know about *FlexLife®* the better prepared for the 21st century you will be. That's the motivation for writing *Don't Get a Job, Get a Life!* It is also the motivation for reading it. Enjoy.

About the Author

Erik Vonk is the CEO of Atlanta-based Randstad North America and a member of the Executive Board of Randstad Holding nv of The Netherlands, the third-largest staffing organization in the world with 1999 revenues in excess of $4.65 billion. An international banker and acquisitions specialist before joining Randstad, the 46-year-old Vonk took the lead in the company's bold entry into the highly competitive U.S. staffing market in 1993.

Via acquisition, Randstad established a presence in the states of Georgia and Tennessee. But there would be no "easing" into this totally new foreign market. Prodded by Vonk, the company signed on with the 1996 Centennial Olympic Games in Atlanta as the "Official Staffing Sponsor"—a position never before known in the annals of Olympic organization.

Then began a furious three-year run that culminated in 1996 with the largest peacetime recruiting and staffing initiative ever undertaken—the 16,000 paid employees that comprised the principal workforce of the 1996 Summer Olympics. Along the way, Randstad opened 80 branch offices in five states. At the close of the Olympic year, the company placed an average of 13,000 staffing employees in gainful employment every working day. In 1998, Vonk engineered the $850 million acquisition of Strategix Solutions, Inc., extending Randstad's reach into 36 states. By the onset of the new millenium—after little more than six years of operation—Randstad North America was the ninth-largest staffing organization in the U.S. From more than 450 offices in the U.S. and Canada, the company places an average of 100,000 people on job assignments each business day.

Against this backdrop and Randstad's four decades of staffing experience in Europe, Erik Vonk writes with unusual insight and clarity about one of the most important workplace developments since World War II—FlexLife®, Randstad's term for the logical evolution of "flexible employment." Every person who works for a living and every person who hires the skills, talent or labor of others owes it to himself to see the workplace through the eyes of Erik Vonk. The view is most rewarding.

Acknowledgements

After many years in finance and acquisitions, my total immersion in the staffing business starting in 1991 proved a profound eye-opener for me. To my chagrin, I soon realized how typical of society were my views of the staffing business—mostly superficial. I knew the industry was strong, with a great tradition and an exciting future. But I didn't understand the pervasiveness of *employee* desires to gain some parity in the traditional employee-employer relationship. Nor did I fully appreciate *employer* desires to gain some control over rigid personnel costs that hindered competitiveness in a global market.

I learned these things firsthand from innumerable discussions with staffing employees, employers and various experts on every nuance of employment. To these people goes the credit for the education of Erik Vonk. And I am deeply appreciative. In particular, I want to acknowledge the support and encouragement of my mentor Frits Goldschmeding, founder and former CEO of Randstad Holding nv. He has been an unflappable tower of strength as Randstad makes its way amidst the formidable challenges of the U.S. workplace.

Special thanks are due John Thompson for his steadfast assistance with this book project, Joey Reiman, CEO of BrightHouse, for the depth and quality of his thinking on the new role of work in society, professor Jeffrey Rosensweig of Emory University for his thoughtful editing and publishing guidance, and Walker Smith, author and managing partner of Yankelovich Partners, for opening my eyes on the defining characteristics of current generations.

Dr. Joseph Boyett, author of *Workplace 2000 and Beyond Workplace 2000,* and Peter Yessne, Editor in Chief of *Staffing Industry Report,* have provided valuable insight and support. George von Stamwitz, President of OmniCorp, helped with workplace statistics.

The relentless support and encouragement of Karin Schippers, my partner, kept me on course with this project. Dawn Coley and Roger Milks of BrightHouse have also contributed large doses of inspiration. And I am grateful for the support of colleagues like Fred van Haasteren, Professor Hans Junggeburt and Diane Krabbendam who helped with proofreading and editorial suggestions, Mar Kuhlkin and Don Hopper who chipped in with research assistance, and Daryl Evans and Rebecca Johnson who provided design and marketing oversight.

Chapter One

Great T-shirt, man.
What does it mean?

Introduction to a workplace revolution

Don't Get a Job, Get a Life! The phrase came out in a brainstorming session back during the feverish run-up to the 1996 Centennial Olympic Games in Atlanta. Randstad Staffing Services, the company I head, had signed on as the Official Staffing Sponsor for the games, and we were scrambling to deliver the 16,000 paid employees needed to run the biggest show on Earth. We needed lots of good people in a hurry, but mostly for very intense weeks and months, not permanently. And it wasn't the best of times to find them. The booming economy in the southeastern United States had absorbed nearly all the available workforce, and we were trying every conceivable angle to pry loose the people we needed.

One of our tactics—a minor one, admittedly—was to print T-shirts with the message, *Don't Get a Job, Get a Life!* The idea was to challenge people to use the Olympic Games as a sampling of *FlexLife®*, a term we coined for a quiet revolution catching hold throughout the workplace. Obviously, we were doing other things on a grander scale to get our name out into the populace with the message, "Hey, come work at the Olympic Games." There were national advertising campaigns, media activities that generated unprecedented press coverage, a converted Winnebago dubbed the Randstadebago to recruit students on college campuses, even a garishly painted Cadillac—*the Randstadillac*—that I drove everywhere for over a year. Anything to spread the word.

But with all that went on in that magical and trying time between September 1994 and August 1996, those T-shirts remain vivid in my mind. People actually came up to those of us who wore them, wherever we went, and commented on the message and inquired about its meaning. In a world of endless T-shirt messages, who takes time to stop someone and talk about what's printed across his or her chest or back? I was flabbergasted by the interest. And therein lies the root of this book.

Don't Get a Job, Get a Life! conjures up very appealing images for a great many people. But is it possible? Who wouldn't want a life free of the traditional constraints of a job? Perhaps the very rich have that freedom. But nearly everyone else has to work if they want to live decently, right? Right. But they no longer have to bend their lives and their family's lives into such distortions to acquire the rewards of gainful employment.

Much more than people realize, the workplace has changed dramatically in recent years. Respected observers like British author Charles Handy foretold of the change back in 1989 with his best-selling book *The Age of Unreason*. Of the 1990s and the approaching millennium, he wrote, "It is a time for new imaginings, of windows opening even if some doors close. We need not stumble backward into the future, casting longing glances at what used to be; we can turn around and face a changed reality. Some people, however, do not want to keep moving. Change for them means sacrificing the familiar, even if it is unpleasant, for the unknown, even when it might be better. Sadly for them . . . standing still is not an option, for the ground underneath is shifting. For them, more than for the movers and the shakers, it is essential that they understand what is happening, that they begin to appreciate that to move and to change is essential, and that through change we learn and grow, although not always without pain." Eight years later, Angel Martinez, CEO of Rockport Co., confirmed Handy's prediction. "The one constant factor in business today is we live in a perpetual hurricane season," he said. "A leader's job is less about getting through the current storm and more about enabling people to navigate the ongoing series of storms."

The changes to which Handy and Martinez refer now make it pos–sible for a person to "get a life" where the job adjusts to the lifestyle of the employee and employers find the situation much to their liking. That's right, neither side has to lose in today's workplace. Both parties can escape the drawbacks of contemporary employment that have been in place for most of the 20th century. For employees, it's freedom from things like a dead-end job with too much pressure, not enough pay, too little time for personal interests and the nagging fear of downsizing. For employers, it's relief from the need to retain expensive employee skills year-round when they are needed only now and then. It's not having to neglect new markets or R&D because labor costs are too high, or putting off technological improvements or management talent because margins can't bear the cost, or curbing investment in expansion because overhead takes too big a slice of the revenue pie.

FlexLife® for employees is a self-managed, full-time career of short-term job assignments strung together by an agent, resulting in all the benefits of permanency and few of the drawbacks.

Yes, employees can "get a life" that's more than a faintly wagging tail on an all-consuming job. Yes, employers can move from the "fixed cost of labor" to the "variable cost of flexible human resources" and be assured of the talent, skills and other competencies required—when, and only when, they are required. What's good for employers (the ability to shrink or expand labor costs as market conditions dictate) and what's good for employees (job security, good pay, health insurance, etc.) are not neces-sarily incompatible.

Sit back, if you will, and let me focus the view on "flexible employ-ment," especially the emerging trend called *FlexLife®*. When you see the picture, I think you will be excited about the possibilities. *FlexLife®* is the beginning of a new employment tradition that is apt to find a great many admirers in the workplace once people adjust to the new order of things.

What exactly is *FlexLife®*? It is literally a new way to work and live, both for employees and employers. Not to be confused with temporary work, or "temping," *FlexLife® for employees is a self-managed, full-time career of short-term job assignments strung together by an agent, resulting in all the benefits of permanency and few of the drawbacks.* FlexLifers are paid the going rate or more for the skills, experience, education and value they

The Terminology of Flexible Employment

Temporary worker or "temp"
> *Traditional emergency or special project employee hired for short periods of time for relatively low-skilled assignments. Normally, temps do not have employee benefits and do not see their work as a career pursuit.*

Assignment personnel
> *Employees who work on an assignment basis and are subject to re-assignment by the employer or a third-party labor exchange service.*

Contract worker
> *Personnel hired under the stipulations of a written contract for a particular task, a specific length of time, at a specified price.*

Independent contractor
> *Self-employed workers who normally find their own job assignments, manage their own careers and provide their own benefits.*

Freelancer
> *An independent contractor by another name.*

Free agent
> *Those who work outside the realm of traditional permanent employment. Free agents are as diverse as hired mercenaries, top financial consultants or self-employed plumbers.*

Just-in-time worker
> *A generic term applied to personnel dispatched to accomplish a specific task when the need arises and only for as long as the need exists.*

Contingent worker
> *U.S. Bureau of Labor Statistics terminology for employees who work under non-traditional employment arrangements.*

Staffing employee
> *Personnel placed in job assignments by a staffing agency. These employees generally work for the agency when on assignment but may operate as free agents otherwise.*

Management consultant
> *Often the best and brightest from top business schools, hired by major accounting and management firms, then placed in large companies to solve problems and bolster management. Many consultants are FlexLifers and earn big salaries and employee benefits.*

Telecommuter
> *Employees who work from home all or part of the time and may be free agents or permanent employees working from their places of residence instead of the office.*

Part-time employee
> *These may be permanent employees (with or without benefits) who work part of a day or week, usually the same time on each occasion. FlexLife® employees may also schedule themselves so as to be part-time.*

FlexLifer
> *FlexLife® for employees is a self-managed, full-time career of short-term job assignments strung together by an agent, resulting in all the benefits of permanency and few of the drawbacks. FlexLife® represents the high end of the flexible employment spectrum.*

bring to the job. In the best of arrangements, the gamut of employee benefits are provided by the FlexLifer's agent, including retirement provisions, paid vacations, sick leave, training and the other perks of full-time employment. A job doesn't define a FlexLifer's worth or identity. Rather, job assignments are but an extension of one's lifestyle. Downsizing doesn't apply to *FlexLife®* careerists because just-in-time employees are not a fixed cost of doing business; full-time employees are. Indeed, just-in-time personnel—hired when needed and only as long as needed—are one of the principal ways employers cut operating costs. *FlexLife®* is how downsizing can proceed without the loss of productivity. There is no fear that competencies will fail to measure up in the marketplace—because FlexLifers are immersed in the marketplace much more than traditional full-time employees could ever be. As a result, the experience level of FlexLifers increases. Their value to employers rises. "Employment security" improves. And they—not some manager—control their lives and careers. Unlike permanent employees, FlexLifers are not "stuck" with the jobs they have—stuck because convention says you don't change jobs; stuck because the job is the source of health insurance and retirement provisions. In *FlexLife®* relationships, neither are employers stuck with employees they don't need or those of limited skills or wearisome idiosyncrasies. Like an accordion, *FlexLife®* organizations compress around a core staff of key people to reduce costs and increase options, then expand quickly "as and where" needed with assignment personnel to capitalize on opportunity.

FlexLife® for employers means a value-added gain in skills from the employment of seasoned assignment personnel. It means an intermediary (e.g., a staffing agency) takes on the headaches and employment risks

The Spectrum of Flexible Employment

Temp 0 1 2 3 4 5 6 7 8 9 10 **FlexLife®**

The flexible workplace is comprised of a broad range of skills, pay scales, employment security and lifestyles. On one end of the flexible employment scale traditional temps often work uncertain hours for low wages and no benefits. Earnings fill an immediate need and enable employees to pursue other interests, including the search for a permanent job. On the other end of the scale, high-priced FlexLife® careerists stay as busy as they wish through the efforts of staffing agents who protect their clients with traditional employee benefits. Between the two extremes lies every gradation of just-in-time skills, talent and labor. All are "temps," but some have it better than others.

associated with finding and developing productive workers. Bottom line, *FlexLife*® means maximum employer flexibility and control of labor costs, substantially enhancing organizational performance in an increasingly competitive world market. The agent, last element in the FlexLife® equation, already exists in certain industries and gains ever wider acceptance in the general workplace.

Employee skills, high-tech or low, matched with employer needs, simple or sophisticated, by an agent specifically groomed for the role— that's *FlexLife*®. It is the logical progression of employment. What used to be a real job was a permanent job with security where the employer managed your career and retained your services with health benefits, pay raises, advancement, paid vacation, a pension plan and the like. Those jobs were mostly about where you worked and who you worked for. To the inevitable question raised in any social engagement, "So, what do you do?" people typically answered: "I work for IBM," or AT&T, Philips, Nissan, Daimler-Benz, Barclay, Samsung, the Lippo Group or some other high-profile organization. With such responses, people acknowledged that they identified themselves to a large extent by the jobs they held. Jobs construed as good and prestigious carried a certain air of elitism and the presumption of stability and longevity. All other jobs were somehow inferior. Talented young people rushed off campuses into the arms of these "elite" organizations ready and eager to work for less just to be on the team. Such

Employment today has little to do with where you work or who you work for, and nearly everything to do with what you do and the skills you possess.

was the prestige and long-range promise of these jobs that new hires accepted the detachment of their competencies from their compensation. "Oh, we'll have to train you in the ways of the company," went the recruiter's rationalization. "But you'll make up for it (lesser pay) later." Unstated was the notion that one's education and competencies didn't really mean all that much. And very capable people bought into the thinking. That was the mindset then. Life for all but a few was fairly predictable. Growth and development came in familiar blocks of time. Kindergarten. Elementary school. Middle school. High school. College, perhaps. Maybe graduate school. Then you took a job. And the employer managed your career. Six months as a trainee. Perhaps a small pay raise. A year or so as someone's assistant. A modest pay raise. Advancement to assistant manager and another year or two learning the ropes. Training programs. A relocation to a more responsible position. Better pay and, sometimes, a company car. Three years making the grade, then on to somewhere else. Incremental pay raises along the way. To break from the mold, you quit and took a better position with someone else. But you didn't do it much. The corporate elite didn't like job-hopping. By playing to this cultural mindset in their human resources practices, the elite companies enjoyed a competitive advantage in the critical category of labor costs for decades.

Of course, all this was before the insecurity of downsizing, right-sizing, outsourcing and the other norms of today's workplace intruded on the sense of well-being. Rarely in those typical social encounters did people inquire about what skills or competencies a person possessed. That you might be a dedicated oboist in the local symphony or a mountain climber or herbal gardener was thought to be a novelty, not what you really did. People, after all, were not oboists who applied their work-a-day skills at IBM nine-to-five Monday through Friday; they were IBMers who happened to play the oboe in the local symphony. Your "outside interests" just didn't count for much in the traditional workplace. Benjamin Hunnicutt, professor of leisure studies at the University of Iowa, goes so far as to suggest that Americans came to see work as a kind of religion. It is in work, he argues, rather than in traditional religion, that "we look for the answers to the cosmic questions such as 'Who am I? Where am I going?'"

But fealty to the job has changed. And the "dutiful employee/paternalistic employer" mindset that permeated the workplace for so long is unraveling. Not only do "traditional permanent jobs" become more and more the exception rather than the rule in advanced economies around the world, they are not what they used to be. "Holding onto a job now takes precedence over upward mobility or a decent raise," noted a recent *New York Times* article. "Longer hours on the job have displaced the . . . goal of more leisure time. And job insecurity—'cowed labor' as economist Paul Samuelson calls it—has become an accepted means of prolonging economic prosperity by holding down wage increases and inflation."

What today is a real job is an evolutionary turn of the wheel where the only reliable permanency comes from the ability and willingness to take one's skills and labor "where the jobs are"; where the only security lies in

7

employer demand for the skills one possesses; where career management and upward mobility are left to the employee; and typical employee benefits come not from the organization where you work but from the "agent" who works for you. This is an unnerving and frightening workplace for generations accustomed to the predictable and for a younger generation that wants what its parents had—job security and prepackaged careers. But, as Generation X is wont to say, "Get used to it." The old workplace is gone, and the new one has a lot to offer. Former U.S. Secretary of Labor Robert Riech explained it this way in a recent *Context* magazine interview: "This New Economy provides extraordinary upside opportunities, an exciting, buoyant, vibrant world in which bright people have more opportunities thrust in their direction than ever before. This is a much better environment if you are young and well-educated and creative, a much better environment than the old bureaucratic mass-production system of 40 years ago. But, by the same token, it is an extraordinarily unstable environment."

> What one proclaims to be today is not solely defined by a job. Rather, it's the life people live that defines them, including the skills and competencies they bring to their work—wherever and whatever that work may be.

Unstable, yes. Rickety, no. The New Economy/Workplace is just a whole new ballgame.

Employment today has little to do with *where* you work or *who* you work for, and nearly everything to do with *what you do* and *the skills you possess*. Ask a young person in the workplace today what he or she does, and you may well get answers like this: "I'm a cyclist and race coordinator. At the office, I develop computer software for insurance companies. . . . I raise two frenetic little children and telecommute from home. With a Ph.D. in economics, I assist with a project in Indonesia. . . . I'm a piano player on an Allegheny Riverboat. During the day, I'm a mortgage broker. . . . I'm a blacksmith. The rest of the time I handle lighting for a rock-and-roll band."

What one proclaims to be today is not solely defined by a job. Rather, it's the life people live that defines them, including the skills and competencies they bring to their work—wherever and whatever that work may be. "I'm an accountant, a freight handler, an insurance adjuster, a bricklayer, a financial analyst, a cowboy, an engineer"—that's what you do;

it's not always who you are. In this sense, you are your own job. Leaving one assignment for another does not mean that you leave your skills behind; you take them with you. When it's what you do that counts and not who you do it for or where, you cannot be "right-sized" any longer. You just take your competencies elsewhere. And when you show up at the next employer's place of work, you often arrive with more experience and sharper skills than in-house personnel. And productivity suffers little as you adjust to the next job assignment. Marketable employee skills are the key. So long as there is

The business world where the big eat the small has evolved to where it's the fast that eat the slow.

employer demand for those skills, and the ability to match the one with the other (via one's own efforts or an agent's), employees will always have a job. And employers will always have the personnel needed when needed.

Essentially, *FlexLife®* marks that point where job security and stability are more properly associated with occupational flexibility, nimbleness and adaptability than with traditional full-time employment. The business world where the big eat the small has evolved to where it's the fast that eat the slow. Employees and employers who adapt best to this new reality remain in the hunt, while those who don't are consumed. The mere existence of work to be done no longer means a full-time job for someone. Tasks can be accomplished by free agents hired "just in time," especially for the situation, then released to move on to the next assignment. Permanent applicants need not apply.

In today's competitive economic environment, permanent employees beyond the essential core staff are a luxury few employers can afford. Consider: If an employer could operate with a minimal core staff of full-time employees and hire on a "need-only" basis the talent, skills and other human resources needed for intermittent or unplanned situations, that would be construed as a good thing in most hiring circles. If employees could work when they wanted and for whom they wanted and be assured of that, if they got paid the equivalent of a full-time wage for the skills and experience and education they brought to the job, if traditional employee benefits were theirs for the taking and they could "fire their employer" if things didn't work out and start a new assignment the next day, if these things were possible, most employees would find that a good thing.

9

Organizing Your Workforce

A – Core Staff

These are the "process owners," those employees who define the organization's uniqueness. They provide organizational continuity and embody and impart the organization's corporate culture. In a flexible workplace, the core staff is usually the organization's permanent workforce.

B – Specialists

Employees with specialized skills who are called in or consulted to support the organization's operations. Typically, specialists work on a just-in-time basis which may range in length of service from several years to several months or weeks. HR, marketing, IT, finance and legal services are representative of the range of frequently employed specialist skills.

C – Generalists

*This category of employee fills in around the **core staff** and the **specialists** to round out a fully operational workforce. A great many generalist jobs are ideal for just-in-time employees. It is in the generalist realm that the traditional "temporary help" concept used to flourish.*

To a degree not yet appreciated, *this is the shape and context of employment in developed economies far into the 21st century.* This is not mere supposition on my part. In certain fields, *FlexLife®* is a *fait accompli*. It is conspicuous in the entertainment business and professional sports, for example. But *FlexLife®* doesn't end with the rich and famous. A good computer expert would be short-sighted in today's marketplace to work long for a single employer. He or she might not be exposed to enough new and different situations to keep skills up-to-date. For this very reason, employers might be ill-advised to retain in-house computer specialists full-time. With a good employment service—perhaps a specialized staffing agency like CDI Corporation of Philadelphia or Modis, Inc., of Jacksonville, Florida—computer expertise can find ready employment at top dollar for as many hours of as many days a year as a person wants to work. Computer experts capable of installing sophisticated commercial software, for example, can earn as much as $2,000 a day. The average annual salary of Microsoft Certified Systems Engineers (MCSE) is in the six-figure range. Inticing "sign-on" bonuses are routinely paid for the skills of senior programmers, database analysts and other hot Information Technology (IT) expertise. Employment security? These people have it. Control over their lives? You bet. Employee benefits? Increasingly, the staffing agent's organization provides it. And employers have the luxury of drawing upon a depth of experience and skill that they could hardly justify 52 weeks a year, year after year.

Britain's Spring Group PLC, a specialized staffing agency, supplies school systems with interim teachers. Another British firm, Executive Interim Management, places chief executive, chief financial and chief operating officers in short-term job assignments at the very top of organizations, large and small. These are high-priced temps to be sure—$1,000 to $5,000 a day—but temps nevertheless. "Overall, it's going to continue to be more acceptable," said Alice Snell, senior analyst for Kennedy Information, which publishes newsletters, directories and research reports on the executive search and management consulting industries. "It really is consistent with a lot of employment trends, including the lifestyle that more executives are looking to establish." On Assignment, Inc., of Calabasas, California, delivers brains to the workplace—chemists, biologists, physicists and other scientists. Commercial labs, research operations and high-tech firms across the country employed the company's highly educated workers to the tune of $132 million in 1998. With branch offices from Seattle to Miami, On Assignment places thousands of scientists in job assignments that last between two weeks and four months. In true *FlexLife®* form, chief executive H. Tom Buelter likes long resumes from people who constantly hone their skills in different working environments. Buelter explained why to *Forbes* magazine recently: "What you . . . sell is your skills, not your authority."

> *What you . . . sell is your skills, not your authority.*
>
> – H. Tom Buelter

The Glidden Partners law firm in Houston, Texas, successfully tackles complex corporate litigation with a flexible staff of temporary attorneys. Pushed by corporate clients clamoring for lighter legal bills, law firms across the U.S. now make use of just-in-time lawyers. But Glidden Partners has gone further than the rest. "The fact is that clients don't want associates reviewing documents with the meter going at

$150 an hour when a temp can do it for less than a third of that amount," says founder Graig Glidden. Scores of staffing agencies now serve this important niche market.

Keeping track of documents and records in Washington, D.C., has made librarians a hot commodity. Agencies like Telesec Staffing Services match this demand for skills with those who need them. Clients get the skills they need when they need them and avoid undue labor costs when they don't. The librarians enjoy employment security, good pay, the same benefits package available to full-time employees . . . and none of the anxiety of downsizing or the stultifying wear and tear that comes with the same workplace routine over and over again.

Interested in a career in politics or government? PoliTemps of Washington, D.C., might be able to put you to work in a political campaign, as a congressional aide, with a public relations firm or in some other job that exposes you to the myriad workings of the political process. Need an environmental accountant or a speech pathologist or an on-line sales manager? An engineer or technical writer or truck driver? Web site developers, security guards or musicians? Increasingly, labor exchange services put these and other skills to work in a ready, willing and able marketplace.

So, yes, *FlexLife®* is real. It's new yet, but already a large slice of the overall workforce. Governments, particularly in Europe, have not always been friendly to the spread of flexible employment. Labor unions generally are suspicious of *FlexLife®*, though some now see opportunity where before they saw only threat. And the public confuses *FlexLife®* with part-time work and low wages. But, despite it all, *FlexLife®* has forced a toe in the door of the modern workplace. And every foreseeable trend points to substantial increases in this form of work.

Workplace Trends

- Corporate boundaries blur, confusing traditional work arrangements in the process.

- Talent exchange services spread into the general workplace.

- People want more freedom and flexibility in their lives, jobs included.

- Non-traditional jobs have become more acceptable.

- People adopt simpler lifestyles and find much to like about them.

- Demographics and "generational attitudes" work against long-term career commitments and corporate dependency.

- The global marketplace leaves nowhere for the noncompetitive to hide.

- The very concept of "office" has changed.

Corporate boundaries blur, confusing traditional work arrangements in the process. Which came first, *FlexLife*® and its ilk or the redesign of the corporation? There is no chicken or egg mystery here—major employers reconfigured operations, and flexible forms of employment emerged to match the new paradigm. Again, Robert Reich, former Secretary of Labor, shed light on the development.

"We're seeing traditional [corporate] boundaries vanish. Companies are becoming networks of partnerships and units, sometimes spanning vast arrays of industries and subgroups. Sometimes, contracts are formal. Sometimes, they're informal. Sometimes, they're within large master contracts. Sometimes, they're spot-market contracts."

On-line, business-to-business auctions add to the muddle of where a given company ends and suppliers begin. These exchanges, Reich said, are "replacing the innards of big companies. Big companies are ripping out their fixed costs, and they're ripping out their bureaucracies, and they're increasingly substituting B2B [business-to-business] auction models that are based on the Internet." In this environment, where does one company end and another one begin? "It's impossible to tell . . . a meaningless question," he said.

Cisco Systems, for example, reportedly ships more than 50 percent of its products without ever being touched by a Cisco employee. How can that be? Only in business arrangements where the production and delivery of goods and services are fluid, cash flows are properly allocated and property rights are clearly identified. With these basics in place, little else that is traditional in the corporate world is necessary nowadays.

In this environment, traditional work arrangements take a beating. Who works for "the company" and who works for a supplier? How long and secure is the contract, if the latter? Where does one's allegiance lie? Who's taking care of the workforce? Which jobs are "in the loop" and which are not? Which way is up in the corporate hierarchy?

Reich suggests that the answers to these kinds of questions don't really matter in the New Economy as long as the company performs well. Of course, that may be so for the corporation, but it isn't for those employees seeking old-fashioned job security.

With this blurring of conventional corporate boundaries, it inevitably follows that an overtone of insecurity settles over the workforce. *FlexLife®* and "talent exchange services" that embody it have stepped forward in response to this general insecurity.

"Talent exchange services" spread into the general workplace. Whether it's the Internet, staffing agencies or any of a number of other labor exchange devices (see Chapter Six), the modern workplace is rapidly developing the infrastructure necessary to efficiently match employee competencies with employer needs whatever the skill level or duration of employment. The Internet with its "e-cruiting" capabilities spreads into the general workplace from the "techie" enclaves of Information Technology while "employment agents" gravitate to the mainstream from their origins in "temping" and the entertainment field. Very quickly the two concepts are merging to give rise to a dynamic new kind of "talent agent"—not the hustling, bustling, streetwise variety that makes stars of actors, musicians and literary figures but a different breed of hustling, bustling, streetwise professional that builds careers for skilled and talented employees in the general workplace. Essentially, this person is an "employment agent" or, perhaps, a "free-agent agent." You might call him or her a "staffing agent," as we do at Randstad. For purposes of this book, let's just refer to this emerging purveyor of skills

14

and talent as a "FlexLife agent"—he or she who helps skilled and talented people get a job and get a life.

FlexLife agents, in a generic sense, are not limited to Randstad North America, nor do they exist in numbers large enough to service the general workplace. But their forerunners are very much in evidence today, and all the trends point to a growing need for this higher grade of staffing professional.

Agents for stars on one end of the employment scale, agents for temporary workers on the other end, but agents for the vast middle of the workplace that powers developed economies throughout the world? It's hard to imagine for older workers who grew up on a steady diet of traditional permanent jobs (TPJ), but for younger workers, it's as likely a development as a telephone/computer device on every wrist.

Look where the Internet is headed as a pure employee/employer matching device. Web sites offer "talent markets" where job seekers can tout their skills and put themselves up for auction to the highest bidder in a needy workplace. Whittling the nub even further, employers can now post projects and solicit bids from teams to perform the task. These Internet-based matching services give skilled, flexible workers the one thing they never had before—a vehicle to market their competencies to a broad, attentive audience of employers. "This puts them in the driver's seat," says Jeff Taylor, founder of Monster.com. And, for employers, e-cruiting is the quickest, cheapest and, some say, the most effective device for searching the workplace for recruits with just the skills needed. E-cruiting is the beginning of a process that will literally "change the way employers buy labor," reported *Time* magazine in August 1999.

For all the promise of the Internet as a matching service, however, it is limited in what it can do for the growing ranks of independent contractors, freelancers and other flexible workers. There is no warm and fuzzy face attached to the Internet, no third-party provider of employee benefits, no one stringing together a succession of job assignments to assure "steady work," no one whose job is to know the employee and his or her goals and aspirations, no one to assist with career growth

Far from replacing the middleman as so much of the advanced technology has done, Internet search-and-recruiting services make the flexible agent role more important than ever.

15

and development, no partner in the daunting task of forging a meaningful career in a workplace increasingly reliant on flexible (and insecure) forms of employment.

Far from replacing the middleman as so much of advanced technology has done, Internet search-and-recruiting services make the flexible agent role more important than ever. The greater the ability to find skills, talent and labor over the Internet, the greater the likelihood employers will adopt flexible, just-in-time employment strategies. The more flexible employment becomes, the less traditional permanent jobs (TPJ) are required and the greater the need for the kind of services relegated to the staffing industry. Add e-cruiting to the staffing agent's portfolio of services, and *FlexLife*® careers begin to make a great deal more sense for workers far removed from either the old-fashioned temp or the movie star.

How widespread is the FlexLife agent in the general workplace? It's a hard question to answer in purely quantitative terms. Keeping track of the growth in job titles that connote "employment agent" is not an exercise anyone engages in at present. Nor are there any statistics that indicate how much of the general workforce now relies on staffing experts for some degree of its employment. But like a tornado in the night, there is plenty of evidence to mark where the staffing agent has been. Remember this about the staffing business: from inception, it has been distinguished by the use of point men or women to deliver its services. "Agency representatives" called on employers with labor and skills to sell—labor and skills the representatives often developed themselves. Right from the beginning, these people were matchmakers and facilitators. Find a human resource need, match the need with the proper competencies, and try to keep both employee and employer happy. Much has changed in the staffing business since the early days but not the central role of those ever-present agency representatives. Where goeth the staffing industry, there goes first the staffing agent or his or her equivalent. With that in mind, consider the path carved by the staffing industry's front men and women.

Based on surveys from 1995 to 1997, employer use of agency-provided assignment personnel increased more than three times faster than the employment of permanent workers.

Employers turned to staffing organizations of one sort or another for talent and labor to the tune of $104 billion in 1998, and the reliance grows every year. Staffing organizations created nearly 300,000 new jobs in 1998 alone, nearly two million since 1994. Approximately three million people work in some form of short-term job assignment every day of the year. Based on surveys from 1995 to 1997, employer use of agency-provided assignment personnel increases more than three times faster than the employment of permanent workers. Four out of five employers use some sort of non-traditional employment arrangement to meet labor needs. Wages paid to assignment personnel in the industrial sector of the U.S. economy approached $15 billion in 1998, a four-fold increase since 1991. In the office/clerical segment, the figure was $18 billion, double 1990's level. Wages paid assignment personnel in the technical field also doubled between 1990 and 1998. How deeply has the staffing agent penetrated the general workplace? A fair deduction can be drawn from this excerpt from the National Association of Temporary and Staffing Services' Quarterly Staffing Survey, 1999: "The rise of the portfolio worker [another name for assignment personnel] is exemplified by the increasing prominence of independent professional experts employed within the staffing services sector. Payroll for professionals—including accountants, attorneys and paralegals, sales and marketing professionals and managers—has increased more than eight-fold since 1991. In 1998, wages paid to professional employees of staffing firms reached $2.8 billion."

Meaningful work and a balanced life are deep-rooted human needs.

– Barbara Ehrenreich

Clearly, staffing agents are among us, top to bottom in the workplace. And it is a much more manageable affair as a result.

People today want more freedom and flexibility in their lives, jobs included. And they're getting it. Employers are buying into the sentiment for two good reasons: They don't want to lose key personnel unnecessarily, and they find that "flexibility" pays off for the organization just as much as for employees. "Meaningful work and a balanced life are deep-rooted human needs," says author Barbara Ehrenreich. "[Those needs] can be repressed or ignored, but sooner or later they are going to assert themselves." Asked in an interview what workplace trends he sees as society moves into the 21st century, consultant and author (*A Great Place to Work, The 100 Best Companies to Work for in America*) Robert Levering replied: "I think the cutting-edge issues right now are related to flexible scheduling, accommodating people's families and other personal concerns. That has a lot to do with the young work-force and also the increasing number of women in the workplace—espe-cially the percentage of women working in higher levels. Those two fac-tors, coupled with a basic labor shortage, are putting pressure on com-panies to be very responsive to workers' needs."

Women have paved the way for more freedom and flexibility in their workday lives. But it's not just a gender thing. In a 1995 poll com-missioned by the Merck Family Fund, men were almost as likely as women to say they want a "more balanced life." Seventy-two percent of men, compared with 87 percent of women, said they wanted to spend more time caring for their children. Balancing work and family was a leading source of workplace pressure for 74 percent of men and 78 percent of women sur-veyed in 1997 by the American Society of Chartered Life Underwriters and Chartered Financial Consultants. A 1997 survey by the Council on Family Health found that 35 percent of working fathers interviewed said they routinely stay home to care for their sick children. Sixty-nine percent said they take their children to the doctor, and 81 percent said they administered medicines. In a survey of over 1,200 university business students in 10 nations, Coopers & Lybrand (now PricewaterhouseCoopers) reported in 1997 that 45 percent named a "rewarding life outside work" as their chief goal. In the same survey two years later, this time with 2,500 respondents, little had changed. "Tomorrow's business leaders share a desire to attain balance between their personal lives and careers," the executive summary concluded.

> *Tomorrow's business leaders share a desire to attain balance between their personal lives and careers.*
>
> – PricewaterhouseCoopers

Obviously, all these people are not acting out their feelings en masse or the flexibly employed would number much more than the labor statistics indicate. But the collective public mentality is clearly in favor of a better way to work and live. The statistics and the trend they reflect take face and substance in the personal employment decisions of an unprecedented array of people in today's workplace, top to bottom. Former U.S. Labor Secretary Robert Reich declined the offer of a second four-year term in the Clinton Administration, citing the desire to spend more time with his family. In a *New York Times* editorial, he explained that if you love your job and your family, "there's no way of getting work and family into better balance. You're inevitably short-changing one or the other, or both."

There's Bonnie Fuller, editor in chief of *Cosmopolitan* magazine. On a beautiful May day in 1997, she paced about, talking with her staff on a small telephone headset while nursing 19-day-old daughter Leilah. Fuller was at home, the staff was far away in New York City, and child, magazine and mother were all managing quite well. How did she do it? a reporter asked. With an unsentimental shrug, she answered with the confidence of one who understands that "what she does" doesn't require an office, an ever-present staff or any special dispensation for child-rearing. "I mean, I can edit copy while I'm nursing, or I can read, or I can talk on the phone," she said cheerily. "If I'm at work, I'm juggling 50 different things anyway. Here, instead of juggling those things, I'm juggling this." While some can success-fully bend their jobs to fit their personal lives, Pulitzer Prize-winning writer and columnist Anna

. . . happiness and satisfaction cannot be spared or wasted, and . . . whenever possible, dreams must be pursued, not deferred.

– Anna Quindlen

Quindlen couldn't manage it. So the most visible woman to *New York Times* readers (and probable heir-apparent to the executive suite) up and quit her job. It was a shock throughout the media world. All kinds of rumors spread as to what prompted her actions. So in a *Working Woman* magazine article, Quindlen explained her decision. In essence, she could-n't reconcile the demands of a high-profile job with her passion for fic-tion writing and her family. Something had to go, and it was the job. She would stay at home, care for her family and write novels. It was a deci-sion made easier, no doubt, by the "portability" of the skills and talent she possessed. You can write from just about anywhere. And plugging the family into the equation made the difference. As explanation for her decision, she wrote, "I once found in the keen sense of mortality I took from my mother's early death a belief that there was no time to stop an upward trajectory for even an instant. Today it means for me that the time we are afforded to find happiness and satisfaction cannot be spared or wasted, and that, whenever possible, dreams must be pursued, not deferred." An elegant rationale for "getting a life," I'd say.

Non-traditional jobs are becoming the norm. The point was driven home firmly for those of us at Randstad North America with the 1999 survey of 6,000 employees in the North American workplace by Roper Starch Worldwide, Inc. Fifty-one percent of respondents stated that they preferred non-traditional jobs "where they can work at home, work part-time or can drop in and out of the workplace." Only 34 percent stated a preference for traditional full-time jobs. These and other findings prompted Roper Starch Worldwide to note, "It is no surprise that the workplace today is vastly different from the workplace of 1950. But the workplace of 2000 is also vastly different from even 1990."

The old mystique of working for the great names in the world's corporate pantheon has faded. The reality is taking hold that "a job is a function of one's skills and flexibility, not where or for whom one works." Witness the remarkable growth in telecommuting. Born of downsizing and communications technology, 30 million Americans earn their livelihoods working from home all or part of the time, according to the New York Regional Planning Association. That's more than one-fifth of the U.S. workforce. Downsizing and outsourcing of work once done "in-house" has spawned millions of new home-based businesses and moved many full-time employees from the employer's premises to the employee's parlor.

> *Thirty million Americans earn their livelihoods working from home all or part of the time.*
>
> – New York Regional Planning Association

Employees like it because they have more time with family. Drive time, and the loss of productivity associated with it, are substantially reduced. Life is not so hectic, and work is more enjoyable. Employers like it because substantial savings are realized and productivity is improved.

To get a sense of the telecommuting phenomenon, consider Linda Stern's neighborhood in Tokoma Park, Maryland. "Some people join support groups or attend conventions to combat the isolation of working

Top 10 Industries for Telecommuting in 1997	
Healthcare	13.6%
Education	9.0%
Arch/Engineering/Construction	8.8%
Communications	8.3%
Manufacturing	7.4%
Business Services	6.5%
Agriculture/Mining	5.2%
Wholesale	5.0%
Retail	4.9%
Transportation/Utilities	4.3%

Source: 1997 IDC/Link Consumer Survey

at home, but I don't have to go that far," she wrote in *Home Office Computing* magazine. "A walk around the block does it for me. I can start upstairs where my husband runs his own advertising copywriting business. Or walk down two doors to Lorrie's. She works at home as a technical editor. Across the street is Andrea, a children's clothier. Within that block's walk are Chip and Leah, whose home-based publishing company prints teacher's guides and supplies school book fairs. Bruce has actually made a living these past 25 years as a folk musician. Paul's an architect. . . . Eric publishes the community newspaper. Jim, an attorney, had so many employees working in his home office at one point that he had to set up temporary space in a trailer parked in his driveway. Ed multi-level-markets herbs. Diana teaches stress reduction. . . . Fifteen years ago, my neighborhood was all but abandoned during the day as we all— except for the retirees—did the downtown scurry. But I live in a town full of people who want it all. We want small-town ambiance. . . . and big city aura (we're steps from the Washington, D.C., line). We want important careers, but we don't want to miss after-school soccer. We want to work with big companies, we just don't want to work for them. So, one at a time, we've found our solution: Work at home, at least part of the time."

If you think telecommuting is a departure from the staid old workplace of traditional permanent jobs, give some thought to what Finland's young Linus Torvalds has wrought. He's the guy who got on the Internet way back in 1991 and asked others to help him perfect some computer software that he felt was a better version of the industry standard UNIX operating system. Linus called his system Linux and programmers throughout cyberspace began contributing their own ideas for improving the product. Soon a "Linux community" evolved encompassing thousands of people around the world, all sharing their work freely with one another via the Internet. In this loose, unmanaged, informal way, Linux, within three years, became one of the best versions of UNIX ever created. But much more than that, the Linux experience showed the way to a workplace much different from anything ever known. Here's how the *Harvard Business Review* explained it in 1998: "What the Linux story really shows us is the power of a new technology—in this case, electronic networks—to fundamentally change the way work is done. The Linux community, a temporary, self-managed gathering of diverse individuals engaged in a common task, is a model for a new kind of business organization that could form the basis for a new kind of economy. The fundamental unit of such an economy is not the corporation but the individual. Tasks aren't assigned and controlled through a stable chain of management but rather are carried out autonomously by independent contractors. These electronically connected freelancers—e-lancers—join together into fluid and temporary networks to produce and sell goods and services. When the job is done—after a day, a month, a year—the network dissolves, and its members become independent agents again, circulating through the economy, seeking the next assignment."

Employee willingness to accept new, non-traditional modes of employment doesn't end with telecommuting, electronic networks and the vigorous U.S. economy. In the eastern part of Germany, where the 1997 unemployment rate exceeded 18 percent and unions fight to protect the "social contract" forged with employers over decades, employees, desperate for work, have begun to display a new attitude about jobs. And it's paying off all around. Case in point: CED Informationstechnik GmbH of Dresden. This small computer maker responds to market demand for its product by adding employees when orders are strong and reducing personnel when times are slack. With 1998 sales in excess of $15 million, the company is not insignificent. Its competitive advantage is speed. The company promises delivery of a computer, complete with extras demanded by the retail customer, in 48 hours. An inventory of standard machines makes no sense in this business. So the company's workload is completely dependent on orders received. And that varies substantially by season. The traditional "German way" is to keep employees on the payroll (at the highest wages on earth) for every contingency—whether there is a lot of business or just a little. CED management wasn't willing to take those risks. The pay rate wasn't the problem, it was the lack of flexibility. The company threatened to take its production facility out of the country. The unions said, "hold on there." Together, the two parties worked out a unique arrangement. CED would retain on employment contract 200 full-time "core" employees. Another 40 workers were promised at least 1,000 hours of work a year (an average of about 19 hours per week). And a third group of 300 or so employees would get periodic employment contracts for a month or so. So, when business boomed, the company could swell to 540 employees or more; when activity slackened, only 200 full-time workers had to be paid. In the German workplace, it represented unusual flexibility. Employees in all three groups were thankful for the work. Machine operator Heiko Foerster spoke for his fellow workers: "I don't have a problem with it. You have to be flexible nowadays." Acknowledging the reality of the modern workplace, the head of CED's worker council, Detlef Gubsch, remarked, "You can only keep your job when the company does well." The CED situation is more than an aberration. It's the way of the world, and German workers are too wise not to see and to adjust.

People today are adopting simpler lifestyles and finding much to like about them. It can be seen in the sale of push lawnmowers (up 150 percent for 1993-97 for the top American producer); the battered old pickup truck the CFO drives to work; more casual clothing in the workplace; the outpouring of books like *The Millionaire Next Door* (William Danker and Thomas Stanley), *Voluntary Simplicity* (Duane Elgin), *Your Money or Your Life* (Vicki Robin and Joe Dominguez), and *The*

Overworked American (Juliet Schor); seminars and workshops on how to work less, earn less, spend less and enjoy it more; the rise of second-hand clothing stores; the popularity of publications like *Simple Living Journal* (Seattle), *Living Cheap News* (Kansas City, Missouri) and *The Tightwad Gazette* (Leeds, Maine).

What's behind this off-and-on attraction to simplicity? Answers abound, all with some validity. But the principal motivation can be found in the workplace and people's paychecks. With the uncertainty of the job market, people are less sure of their finances. With all the economic growth experienced in the U.S. since 1993, for example, it wasn't until the beginning of 1998 that the nation's median income finally surpassed the figure for 1989. Between 1989 and 1997, in fact, wages for the majority of the great American middle class went down, not up; and the median wage actually fell 5 percent, according to Alan B. Kruger, professor of economics and public affairs at Princeton University. So, despite the general prosperity and wealth of jobs, the average American family has only enjoyed a few short years of truly unprecedented take-home pay. This is generally true elsewhere in the booming global economy. From 1994-97, the standard of living soared in many nations. Disposable income exceeded anything in recent memory. And it looked like there was no end to it. Simpler, more sustainable lifestyles seemed unnecessary. Then the flickering monetary crisis in Southeast Asia roared into an inferno and swept through the world's capital markets. And reality returned. Millions of people in advanced economies around the world resumed efforts to simplify their lives—because they had little choice, lots of Americans included.

Unfortunately, leading economists see no reason why personal income in the U.S. is going to improve dramatically any time soon. One reason is productivity. Though better at the turn of the new century, the growth of real gross domestic product (GDP) during the 1990s was only about half what it was during the 1960s and well below even that of the turbulent 1970s, according to James Gwartney, economics professor at Florida State University. Raising personal income across the board on this kind of productivity is an unlikely prospect. Factor in the drag of the global marketplace on

Jobs are not only moving away from the high cost of labor, but the facilities of production are too.

wages and it is easy to see why the growth of personal income fails to reflect the booming U.S. economy. Global competition holds down wages. Who's going to raise the income of high-paid Americans, Germans or Swiss when Malaysians, Mexicans and Chinese provide much the same talent and labor for a lot less cost? Unions continue to decline. Deregulation improves corporate flexibility and the ability to pare expenses, including personnel costs. Technology is ever at work replacing people and the costs they represent. And hanging over all economies at the start of the 21st century is the cloud of over-capacity.

Before the collapse of the Asian Tigers in 1998, there was so much capital loose in the global marketplace that investors didn't know what to do with it. Many just dumped it into additional plants, facilities and product capacity. For awhile, it seemed everyone was building cars, refrigerators, computer chips, office space and other hot commodities. Capacity pushed the limits of demand. A glut of product developed, even before the global marketplace contracted dramatically in the aftermath of the Asian monetary crisis. "Growing over-capacity, worldwide product gluts, price wars, shakeouts and consolidations" are the predictable results, *The Wall Street Journal* noted in August 1997. An excess of big-ticket consumer goods, semiconductors, commercial real estate, paper and basic raw material are still very much a concern at the end of 2000. None of this bodes well for job security or wage increases for employees in those industries affected.

Looking beyond the productivity issue, global competition and over-capacity, it's not hard to see other, more lasting reasons for a simplification of lifestyles in developed economies. Jobs are not only moving away from the high cost of labor, but the facilities of production are too. Downsizing becomes permanent job loss. The newest and the best of systems and technology are increasingly found where the labor is cheapest. That means the oldest and least efficient of facilities and apparatus house the most expensive workers. And when the economic crunch comes, whether the result of over-capacity, management-labor strife, lack of competitiveness or recession, it's the old and the inefficient that will fall silent. Consider what's happened at General Motors in recent years. The company has built more than 50 automotive parts factories in Mexico since 1978. As recently as 1996, Americans in Michigan earned $22 per hour making instrument panels and steering wheels for GM vehicles. In 1998, Mexican workers built those same components for $1 to $2 per hour. Delphi Automotive Services, GM's automotive parts subsidiary until a divestiture in 1998, held the distinction as Mexico's largest private employer at the time with 72,000 workers. With an investment of that magnitude, rest assured that GM put its very best automotive parts technology in Mexico, not in the U.S.

Having built so many plants in so many parts of the world, GM announced in 1997 that it would save money by constructing essentially the same facility in Argentina, Poland, China and Thailand all at the same time. They would be state-of-the art facilities, "the assembly plants of the future." Wages are low in these countries. Employees are eager to work. Downsizing to adjust to market conditions is not so difficult for employers. Sophisticated skills, when not available, can be brought in from outside. So when GM looks to cut costs by phasing out excess capacity or old, expensive production facilities, guess where the ax will fall? Certainly not in Argentina, Poland, China or Thailand, but in the U.S., Canada and other developed nations.

GM, of course, is not alone in its globalization strategy. Other auto makers hedge against the future in similar ways, if less extensively than GM. Same for the makers of chemicals, oil products, commercial aircraft, paper, semiconductors and more. People may not understand the economics behind all this, but they sense the unpredictability. And they strive, even in the midst of prosperity, to simplify their lives in the face of the perceived insecurity of the modern workplace.

Ironically, the tight U.S. labor market of the 1990s led some to believe that the good old days of reliable employment was back. In coverage of the giant UPS labor strike in August 1997, a leading newspaper reported, "These days, with the unemployment rate at a seasonally adjusted 4.8% of the work force, employers need their workers more than their workers need the employers, giving workers certain leverage. . . . The UPS strike, in fact, may mark the end of the 'job insecurity' phenomenon brought about by job restructuring in the early 1990s." In The Netherlands, similar sentiment was expressed by the government on the heels of strong employment, especially in the category of full-time positions. Employees anywhere in the global marketplace probably ought not to delude themselves with such notions. If the shock of the worldwide financial crisis of 1998 wasn't wake-up call enough, there is the subtle reminder expressed by professor Alan Kruger back in 1997 when everything looked rosy. You have to ask yourself, he said, "If real wages have not risen in the booming U.S. economy of the previous six years, what's going to happen when this economy inevitably turns down?"

Demographic and "generational attitudes" work against long-term career commitments and corporate dependency.

Demographers call them "Matures." Born between 1930 and 1945, they are the elders, the old guard of the modern workplace. As this once formidable force of 35 million dedicated employees passes into retirement, they take with them traditional attitudes about work that have characterized the workplace for over 50 years. Coming through the system behind them are 210 million prospective employees with much different attitudes about work, life, commitment, job loyalty, getting ahead and other matters near and dear to the hearts of employers everywhere. Instead of hanging onto the past, the workplace is having to remake itself—continually throughout the 1990s—to fit the expectations and, yes, demands, of not one but several dominating generations.

Baby Boomers, those people born between 1946 and 1964, never were of the same persuasion as their "Mature" parents when it comes to work. Boomers, as portrayed in the 1999 Roper Report, grew up free of the trauma of the Great Depression and World War II, and, by the sheer weight of numbers, began to remake the world more to their liking in the 1960s. More "laid back"—a Boomer term—and less fearful than their parents, they "used" the workplace to their advantage, not the other way around. No cradle-to-grave job commitment for them. It was "work on my own terms" or move on to something else, more casual dress, less formal work environment and flexible work schedules including the start of telecommuting. The workplace that emerged to accommodate the 76 million Baby Boomers was more unruly and unpredictable than the good old reliable standard set by the Matures, but it was manageable. Then came Generation X.

Born between 1965 and 1980, the 60 million Gen Xers were more like their grandparents than parents in surprising ways but unlike either generation for the most part. Gen X came of age during the 1980s, a time of great economic prosperity—and the tail end of the post-World War II workplace. They watched their parents, the Boomers, get downsized out of what seemed a birthright of job security and predictable futures in the early 1990s. The effect was profound. In their book, *Rocking the Ages,* Walker Smith and Ann Clurman of Yankelovich Partners, Inc., explained that the world inherited by Baby Boomers was one their parents built and filled with the seemingly certain promise of a better future. "But, say Xers, Boomers overindulged, heedless of the consequences, bequeathing a world in tatters, a world with difficult prospects for the future. So the first lesson Xers learned was never to take anything for granted. . . . You can never be sure of what to expect. The marketplace is unpredictable. Everything needs to be fixed. And because of this, you can't depend on any long-term plans. After all, Dad had planned on IBM—or AT&T or on GM—and look what happened to him. Even a college degree has ambiguous value for Xers—it's a guarantee of nothing."

Gen X came of age during the 1980s, a time of great economic prosperity —and the tail end of the post-World War II workplace. They watched their parents, the Boomers, get downsized out of what seemed a birthright of job security and predictable futures in the early 1990s. The effect was profound.

Cynical? Not really, say Smith and Clurman. Xers are just a product of their environment. "The uncertainties of life experienced by Xers have made them wary and cautious; but only in rare cases, apathetic, profligate or corrupt," they write. "Xers are determined to be involved, to be responsible, to be in control—and to stop being victimized by life's uncertainties." So when it comes to work, they have a different attitude than their Boomer parents. You could see it reflected in the hot job market for college graduates at the end of the 1990s. A *New York Times* article captured the Xer sentiment with comments from graduates, including 23-year-old John Warnecke, hired in 1997 as a sales person for IKON Office Solutions in Indianapolis, Indiana. Though much in demand—he received four firm job offers and took the IKON job at $30,000 per year—he remembered that when he was a high school junior his father was laid off as a plant manager and the family suffered. He couldn't forget that the workplace may not always be so sunny. "Fear drives you," Warnecke said. "I'm motivated by the idea that nothing is secure, that you'd better produce or you could be gone. In fact, when I was talking with companies, I was always keeping in mind where they might be five or ten years down the line. I think you've got to keep that fear, because it's when you get in a comfort zone, that you lose your competitive advantage."

According to the article, the overwhelming majority of college graduates don't see their jobs at graduation as the beginning of a straight line of advancement within a company but more a zigzag path from company to company, job to job and skill to skill. "Because these students were at least teenagers when all the downsizing happened, and saw, if not parents, friends, uncles, someone laid off, they begin with the understanding that there's no such thing as lifetime employment, and they're responsible for their own career," said Maury Hanigan, chief executive of the Hanigan Consulting Corporation, advisor to Fortune 500 companies on how to recruit college students. "You ask them how many know someone who was laid off and every hand in the room goes up. They believe its part of life, like getting a cold, so they know job tenure is a short-term thing, not a long-term commitment. It's an economic transaction that lasts only so long as it works for both sides, not a marriage."

We at Randstad North America found this thinking quite prevalent in the 1999 Roper Report. "For Gen Xers," the report states, "a career consists of an ongoing series of assignments or projects, sometimes within one company, but most likely with a variety of employers." The traditional "career ladder," in other words, has been replaced by the "career labyrinth," concludes Roper Starch Worldwide.

What loyalty no longer means is life-long commitment to one employer. Loyalty has become portable; like the skills and talents that employees take from job to job, loyalty is transferable.

This very sweeping change in employee attitude has given rise to an entirely new notion of loyalty. The Roper Report captured the essence of the development: "Employees have said loud and clear that while their sense of loyalty to their job is sincere, it is also something that moves with them when they go on to their next position. . . . What loyalty no longer means is lifelong commitment to one employer. Loyalty has become portable; like the skills and talents that employees take from job to job, loyalty is transferable. Employees are committed to achieving success for themselves, and for the enterprise they are part of—but they reserve their flexibility to dedicate their talents to the best opportunities available to them. In fact, in today's work environment, many feel it is foolish to commit to one employer."

What brought about this historic change? In many ways, it is a Gen X backlash to the downsizing activities of corporate America that began in the recessionary years of the 1990s. Commencing with the recovery period around 1993, a growing number of college graduates began to renege on job offers from major employers. A decade earlier, that was a rare occurrence. A 1994 study by Ohio State University's Director of Undergraduate Career Services found that two-thirds of students surveyed said it was all right to renege after accepting an offer. MBA graduates interviewed by *The Wall Street Journal* cited rumors of job-reneging *on the part of employers* during the early 1990s as the precedent emulated by students today; that, and the recent history of corporate downsizing. "If a company has the right during bad times to renege, students should have the very same right to renege in a competitive market," noted one University of Chicago graduate. An engineering graduate said, "My only responsibility is to myself, to cut the best deal I can. . . . Do you think the company wouldn't rescind its offer if it found someone better who'd work for the same amount of money? Please!" What goes around comes around, it's said. Nowhere does that old adage ring truer than with Generation X.

"Life is uncertain. Eat dessert first," says it well for many Xers. Of all the generations walking the streets today, the authors of *Rocking the Ages* report that Xers are most likely to agree that they'd be willing to "work at a boring job as long as the pay was good," and they are the least likely of all generations to describe work as a career. "It's not that they prefer boredom; rather, it's just that work is not an all-consuming passion for them. This is a distinctive balancing of priorities. Xers want a job *and* a life."

Hot on the heels of Generation X is their offspring, Generation Y— 74 million strong, born after 1980 and now elbowing their way in amongst the elders in the tumultuous workaday world of 2000 and beyond. What do they bring to the table? The Roper Report gives us a hint. The booming domestic economy ignited in the 1990s has "driven optimism among the nation's youngest generation to an all-time high," the report notes. Having experienced nothing but prosperity, they expect nothing less. And so they come into the workplace full of enthusiasm for the future. To their credit, Gen Y's optimism is built on a sound foundation of religion, family, a no-nonsense work ethic and a high degree of faith in technology.

This swirl of generational attitudes amidst a general U.S. labor shortage, intense global competition, the ever-quickening pace of business and a bona fide technological/telecommunications revolution means accommodations never before required of the workplace. And the target doesn't quit moving and won't for the foreseeable future. But there is a recurring mantra emanating from it all—flexibility, flexibility, flexibility. Baby Boomers have to be induced not to retire, or a tight labor market will become a crippled labor market. But don't expect Boomers to work like they used to. The jobs will have to be more flexible, the match of skills-to-needs more precise, the workplace more informal, clothing more comfortable, benefits better designed. This is the stuff of *FlexLife®* careers . . . make that "second careers" when it comes to Baby Boomers.

> *This swirl of generational attitudes amidst a general U.S. labor shortage, intense global competition, the ever-quickening pace of business and a bona fide technological/ telecommunications revolution means accommodations never before required of the workplace.*

Generation X has redefined company loyalty, work arrangements, career development and lifestyles generally, and they are not about to give these things up, nor is business interested in turning back the clock. This new approach to work is a winner for employees and employers alike.

Gen Y moves into the workplace on a model unlike anything that went before. Don't try to convince them that what's worked so well for most of their lives can't be sustained.

The workplace is left with making sense of all this, to create a stable, productive employment environment that benefits the most people for the longest period of time. One way or the other, the result will look like something very akin to *FlexLife®*.

The global marketplace leaves nowhere for the non-competitive to hide. The American public, among others, doesn't much care for globalization, judging from various polls. But people like the jobs, income and other benefits derived of "free trade." The reality of modern economics, unfortunately, is that you can't have the one (the

benefits) without the other (globalization). With trade in the global marketplace comes a steady dose of "tough love." The truth about the global marketplace is that it doesn't much care about grandiose values like social safety nets, guarantees of a reasonable quality of life, wage equities, health benefits or retirement; it just wants what it wants when it wants it. More and more in the real-world economy, if business can't get what it wants in one society, it will go to where it can get what it wants, social contracts be damned. Not to compete in the global marketplace is to run the very real risk of getting bypassed, sooner than later, with daunting consequences for the prosperity of a nation's people. Short of war or threat of war, no advanced economy can escape it, not with the capabilities that now exist to do business wherever it is most advantageous.

. . . the payback comes relatively quickly as profits rise on the back of increased productivity and corporate nimbleness. Employees have to become more skilled, flexible and marketable not to be left in the unemployment lines.

There is, of course, a downside to globalization for employers and employees, but, for both parties, it is generally short-lived. Business has to become more competitive (leaner, more efficient, cost-conscious) to succeed in the global marketplace. That can be expensive (new technology, improved quality, re-engineering) and disruptive (layoffs, mergers, divestitures). But the payback comes relatively quickly as profits rise on the back of increased productivity and corporate nimbleness. Employees have to become more skilled, flexible and marketable not to be left in the unemployment lines. That can be expensive and disruptive, too, especially after corporate "right-sizing" programs leave workers without jobs. But skills, flexibility and marketability can be acquired before layoff. And with that, employment security returns, if not in permanent jobs, in *FlexLife®* careers. That's the history of the U.S. workplace over the last decade, and those same skills, flexibility and marketability distinguish any nation that competes effectively in the global marketplace. India illustrates the point.

This huge hard-working democracy and quasi-socialist economy closed its market to outside products and services after gaining independence in 1947. And most of the time thereafter, India staggered along with minimal growth in gross national product and quality of life—until 1991. Then, a new government, faced with a critical balance of payment problem, moved to open the nation's economy to global competition. It has been difficult for a bloated, antiquated, bureaucratic workplace to get in the shape necessary to compete with the rest of the world. Employers and employees alike have suffered. Tata, the nation's largest industrial group, typified the adjustments made in the Indian economy. In 1997, Tata was a loose confederation of more than 80 firms and 272,000 employees that put the company name on everything from trucks, steel and electricity to telephones, information technology and tea bags. In an effort to reshape this far-flung, disparate empire into a focused powerhouse, Tata re-engineered, downsized, reduced the number of companies, shed unprofitable operations and otherwise re-invented itself. True to form, job security for most of the organization's workforce disappeared. A mandatory retirement age was set. Long-time employees faced early retirement. Jobs for employees' children were no longer assured. Company-school and company-town services were privatized. Security, cafeteria services and other functions were "outsourced" to cut costs. Non-performing subsidiaries could no longer count on a bailout by the once-paternal parent firm. Sound familiar?

As a result of this streamlining, however, Tata began to prosper and wages increased for the first time in decades. After wading into the global marketplace, Tata group profits rose fivefold to more than $750 million, and sales almost tripled to $8.7 billion. In a push to triple sales again by 2000, the organization made huge investments in steel, power, telecommunications, information technology, automobiles and a proposed airline. "What we'll probably end up being is about 30 companies instead of 80," said Ratan Tata, the company's chief executive officer.

The transition from insulated, sluggish behemoth to agile, competitive player in the global market is not over for Tata, but the start is impressive. The nation, too, made impressive gains. Just three years after taking its first steps to unshackle the business class, open the economy, lower tariffs and taxes and attract foreign investment, the Indian economy grew by 7 percent annually. Exports started growing 20 percent a year, foreign exchange reserves rose to $20 billion, inflation dropped to a tolerable 5 to 8 percent, and foreign investment went up 25-fold to $2.5 billion. A new nationalist government and the nuclear bomb test imbroglio of 1998 caused concern among India's trading partners and investors, but the economy remains more vibrant and promising than at any point in the nation's history. Gurcharan Das, chairman of Citibank India's Advisory Board and former CEO of Procter & Gamble India, had this to say about his homeland on the eve of its 50th year of independence in 1997: "India is in the midst of a social revolution rivaled, perhaps, only by the redefinition of Japan's merchant class during the 1868 Meiji Restoration, which helped transform Japan from an underdeveloped group of islands into a thriving, modern society and economy."

How is it that India was forced out of its economic cocoon? Why is it that Europe finally stirred from its rigid and expensive labor practices? What pushed America off its pedestal in the early 1990s? What made China such a mecca for western business interests? Why has Russia failed so miserably in its efforts to develop a functional free-market economy? In large part, the answer to each question lies in businesses' ability to go wherever in the world it can get the best value for the dollar. Let us count the ways business is able to go where it wants, when it wants.

1. Trade agreements
2. National and regional "marketing programs"
3. Mobility
4. Technology

Trade agreements that open markets and level the playing field for large economies and small. There are well-placed military men who dare suggest that warfare among nations could become passé. Given mankind's long history of military conflict, what would prompt such a notion? It's this: the more intertwined the commerce of nations, the greater the risk that belligerence will jeopardize the prosperity of all. If I'm doing well and you're doing well, and we are mutually dependent, the rationale goes, why fight? Let's negotiate.

If that school of thought has any merit, then the future looks very bright for the family of man. More than ever before, the commerce of nations is intertwined and interdependent. Edward Graham, author of *Global Corporations and National Governments*, calls it "the deepest integration of the world economy in history." In his highly informative book *Winning the Global Game: A Strategy for Linking People and Profits,* Emory University professor Jeffrey Rosensweig notes that the volume of money changing hands in the global marketplace in 1995 amounted to $1.2 trillion every day. Forty-three percent of Canada's 1996 gross domestic product (GDP) came from business dealings with foreign buyers, up from 29 percent in 1990. For Mexico, it was nearly 32 percent compared to just 2.2 percent in 1973. Exports of goods and services by the United States approached a trillion dollars in 1997, and imports exceeded $1.1

. . . the more intertwined the commerce of nations, the greater risk that belligerence will jeopardize the prosperity of all . . . why fight? Let's negotiate.

trillion. As recently as 1972, U.S. exports barely totaled $67 billion. There are a great many jobs and considerable wealth and prosperity tied up in current levels of international commerce. In this environment, Professor Rosensweig writes that "it is hard to imagine the Japanese dropping bombs anywhere near Hawaii now, given that they own so many hotels in that beach-laden state!"

Free-market economics has turned adversaries into trading partners, belligerents into entrepreneurs, crushing poverty into well-founded hope. Never has so much of the world taken its lead from the same page of economic theory and practice. Market-driven economics works. And not even the stumble in the booming global economy in 1998 detracted from that reality. Sure, there was a break in the action but not because the system is wrong or even flawed. The family of nations that constitutes the global marketplace just doesn't have enough experience with the system yet; the checks and balances haven't been tested over time. In an advertisement, Merrill Lynch explained the situation eloquently: "The world is 10 years old. It was born when the Wall fell in 1989. It's no surprise that the world's youngest economy—the global economy—is still finding its bearings. The intricate checks and balances that stabilize economies are only incorporated with time. Many world markets are only recently freed, governed for the first time by the emotions of the people rather than the fists of the state. From where we sit, none of this diminishes the promise offered a decade ago by the demise of the walled-off world. We're convinced as ever that the coming years will be a disappointing time

35

for pessimists. The spread of free markets and democracy around the world is permitting more people everywhere to turn their aspirations into achievements. And technology, properly harnessed and liberally distributed, has the power to erase not just geographical borders but also human ones. It seems to us that, for a 10-year-old, the world continues to hold great promise. In the meantime, no one ever said growing up is easy."

This action moved the EU a giant step closer to becoming the "United States of Europe"–a formidable presence in the global marketplace.

The common denominator in this first-ever global marketplace is free trade and the unrestricted flow of capital. Nations continually tinker with trade restrictions and protectionist policies, but the overall trend throughout the world is towards easier, more fluid commerce. The World Trade Organization (WTO) was launched on January 1, 1995, as a bigger and better facilitator of world trade. The U.S., Canada and Mexico entered into the North American Free Trade Agreement (NAFTA) in 1994 to eliminate barriers to trade in goods and services from the Yukon to the Yucatan. The European Union (EU) came onto the world stage in 1993—12 Western European nations trying to break down centuries of commercial, cultural and philosophical roadblocks that threaten the long-term prosperity of the whole. Since then, three other countries have joined the EU. And on January 1, 1999, 11 of the 15 began to employ a common currency, the euro. This action moved the EU a giant step closer to becoming the "United States of Europe"—a formidable presence in the global marketplace. Mercosur, a Brazilian-led South American trade group, provides exciting new opportunities for its members (Argentina, Paraguay, Uruguay and Brazil; Chile and Bolivia are associate members). The Andean Pact, a trade group of western South American nations, taps into markets never before available to member nations alone. The addition of Vietnam, Myanmar and Laos to the Association of Southeast Asian Nations (ASEAN) promises better returns on exports and imports for that corner of the world. Mexico and the European Union negotiate to create a free-trade zone. Switzerland smoothes trade relations with its neighbors. On and on it goes. Capital, the precious fertilizer of business growth, is spread far and wide by the International Monetary Fund, the World Bank, government treasuries, national banks and private investors of every persuasion. Advanced economies traditionally get most of this money, but developing nations have begun to get their share. Total capital flow to developing countries averaged more than $200 billion a year for the five-year period 1993-97. Countries that had never been considered for credit or equity received huge infusions of capital—about 80 percent from private sources. Everywhere, the trends are the same: nations and groups of nations moving inexorably to mesh and streamline a global marketplace from previously disparate parts and pieces.

The global marketplace that has emerged from the patchwork of national and regional trade agreements is far bigger and more lucrative than the sum of the parts that comprise it. In this marketplace, more nations than ever before have a legitimate chance to sell what they produce better and more cost-effectively than the competition. Maybe it's dirt-cheap computer chips turned out by former herders or hunter-gatherers in undeveloped corners of the world, or electrical power plants designed and marketed by engineers from the old Soviet Union, or mine-clearing expertise perfected in Cambodia by Cambodians. These kinds of things are new, unprecedented opportunities for a major portion of the world's populace. And the newcomers to the global market are learning, competing and growing—to the benefit of constituents and the entire global economy. The World Bank reported in September 1997 that economic growth in developing countries would accelerate at a rate of 5.4 percent annually for the next decade, well above the projected rate of 2.5 percent or so for the U.S. and the European Union. China, India, Indonesia, Brazil and Russia will become "economic powerhouses" in the next quarter-century, predict bank analysts in a report entitled *Global Economic Prospects and Developing Countries*. The rapid emergence of these nations is likely to "redraw the economic map of the world." By 2020, emerging nations will become a far bigger factor in world trade, creating huge economic opportunities for both industrial and developing nations. While all this is going on, the richest industrial

> *By 2020, emerging nations will become a far bigger factor in world trade, creating huge economic opportunities for both industrial and developing nations.*
>
> – Global Economic Prospects and Developing Countries

countries will see their share of the global economic pie shrink from 81.5 percent today to 66.7 percent. "Compared to long-term historical trends in the world economy over, say, the last 200 years, this change would be unprecedented in both its size and speed," said Milan Brahmbhatt, World Bank economist and principal author of the report on developing nations.

Professor Rosensweig puts these changes in perspective with an examination of telephone availability. Nations comprising over 85 percent of global population have only one-third of the world's telephones. Many of these nations are experiencing rapid growth, creating more and more consumers with the purchasing power to demand good, reliable telephone service. "What a tremendous opportunity for companies that have anything to do with telecommunications, information technology, etc.," Rosensweig writes. "[Here] are literally billions of people without telephones, in nations which, although relatively poor now, are demonstrating the potential to continue down the path of economic growth. . . . If economic growth proceeds to the point where the bulk of a nation's population just reaches a very lower-middle-class status, the demand for new telephony will be huge."

In this expanded business environment, the workplace is changing rapidly. Nations and companies gain, and nations and companies lose, and workers at every turn feel the impact, good and bad. Competitive pressures and the rapidity of change greatly reduce the margin for error in the global marketplace. When things move so fast, mistakes are accentuated—but so are good planning and wise management. In the turbulence of the global marketplace, political pressure builds to insulate workers. But wiser heads caution that there is little to fear so long as nations and businesses do the things necessary to compete. "Although there will be transition costs," said Joseph Stiglitz, the World Bank's chief economist, "there is little evidence to justify two of the most common fears, namely, downward pressure on unskilled wages in industrial and other developing countries and higher prices for food and

"Better education and training programs are likely to do more for helping American workers deal with a global marketplace than anything in a trade accord that describes labor standards." The same can be said for workers anywhere else in the world.

energy." Some will argue with that assessment, but the hard truth of the matter is that protecting wages and jobs in the modern workplace is just not very practical, given the magnitude of the global marketplace and the options it presents for business to "go wherever it can find the best deal." I. M. Deftler, a leading historian on trade accords and a professor at the University of Maryland, points to the only real guarantee of employment security in today's workplace. "Better education and training programs are likely to do more for helping American workers deal with a global marketplace than anything in a trade accord that describes labor standards." The same can be said for workers anywhere else in the world.

National and regional "marketing programs" that sell every competitive business advantage to attract business. Nations sell themselves in a variety of ways. Tax incentives, subsidies, grants, cheap labor, skilled labor, raw material accessibility, ready markets, transportation and energy advantages, port facilities, capital availability, cost of living indexes, entertainment offerings, educational levels, training facilities, climate, culture and on and on. Various marketing organizations from chambers of commerce, departments of industry and trade, trade associations and industry groups "package" a nation's features and benefits and target them to likely customers. Developed nations are old hands at promoting their competitive advantages with the rest of the world. But newcomers to the global marketplace are catching on.

In a battle against slow growth, rising trade deficits and waning foreign investment, nations of eastern Europe have started tossing out enticements to big business and investors to bring their money and jobs to the lands of the Danube, the Oder and the Volga. While some of these countries have long offered basic incentives, the government largesse has gotten richer as global competition heats up. In a break with tradition, for example, the Czech Republic recently dangled grants and incentives before Intel Corp. of Santa Clara, California, in hopes of attracting a planned European chip-assembly plant valued at several hundred million dollars. At the time, Intel was weighing similar offers from other traditional non-players like Portugal and Egypt.

Poland and Hungary "go to market" more aggressively, too. In 1996,

Nations sell themselves in a variety of ways. Tax incentives, subsidies, grants, cheap labor, skilled labor, raw material accessibility, ready markets, transportation and energy advantages, port facilities, capital availability, cost of living indexes, entertainment offerings, educational levels, training facilities, climate, culture and on and on.

Poland persuaded General Motors Corp.'s Opel AG to build a $300-million plant in the southern Kotowice region with a special economic-development zone that offered free infrastructure and a 10-year tax holiday. This broke the ice in Eastern Europe. Hungary, among others, began to loosen its rules and purse strings, explaining that it was necessary "to compete with the practices pursued in neighboring countries."

With big multinational firms scouring the globe for the most cost-efficient environment to produce their wares, no nation can afford not to compete for the business available. National prosperity is at stake. And it doesn't end at the national level. Regions and political subdivisions within national boundaries can't afford to leave jobs and local prosperity to the whims of federal officials. The 50 states of America, for example, field their own industry and trade operatives to lure jobs and capital from elsewhere in the country and from abroad. In many a large municipality, industry and trade groups are out beating the bushes of the world for business.

Then there are initiatives like those taken by the states of "Northeastern" Brazil, a huge pocket of poverty the size of South Africa wedged between the Amazon jungle and the Atlantic Ocean. The leadership in this impoverished backwater saw no prospects for a helping hand from the national government in Brasilia. So governors of the territory got together and began to tout what they had to sell— cheap labor, willing hands, tax incentives, raw material . . . and the global marketplace heard. Corporate investment flooded in. Tens of thousands of "Northeasterns" now earn wages making products from steel to JCPenny loafers. By 1998, northeastern Brazil became "one of the best investment stories in Latin America," said Robert Peon, chief of Latin American operations for BellSouth Corporation, which heads a group investing almost $1 billion in telecommunications there. Brazil's Northeast is far from prosperous yet, but a start has been made on a workplace with a real future for tens of millions of previously hopeless people—all of it spawned with some earnest marketing to an attentive marketplace.

Mobility. For the global marketplace to work effectively, employers must be able to set up shop where they want, capital must be able to flow to the best returns, goods have to be efficiently transportable, and the workforce allowed ready access to available jobs. Mobility for all components of commerce is vital to the new workplace. And it's happening. The global marketplace is a fact of life. Consider *The Wall Street Journal's* appraisal of the 1998 merger of Germany's Daimler-Benz AG and America's Chrysler Corporation. "[It] is stunning only in its size and scope, not because one player is based in Stuttgart and the other near Detroit. In the culture that leaders of global businesses inhabit, where shared values of open markets, hard money and standardized technology increasingly take precedence over old-fashioned nationalism, such transnational combinations are logical, and they are becoming more commonplace every day." Thomas Middelhoff, chairman of German publishing giant Bertelsmann AG, put it more succinctly: "There are no German and American companies. There are only successful and unsuccessful companies."

> *There are no German and American companies. There are only successful and unsuccessful companies.*
>
> – Bertelsmann AG
> German Publisher

The growing standardization and uniformity in global markets grease the machinery of commerce. In the context of this great economic machine, employee movement cannot be held back without disagreeable consequences (e.g., skill and labor shortages, unemployment, social unrest, capital flight and declining prosperity). Given the necessary prerequisites for economic growth, nations and regions enjoy important competitive advantages when language and culture and easy immigration policy converge. This is the case in much of South America where Spanish is the native or second language, where Catholicism is ubiquitous and unifying, and people are hungry for decent jobs. For employers looking for cheap and abundant labor, there is much to recommend this part of the world. Large swathes of Asia, and even the nations of the old Soviet Union, share similar advantages of easy communication, cultural familiarity and ease of mobility. These attractions are not lost on the global marketplace. Their absence is not missed, either. Most of Africa, south Asia, the Near East and—until recently—even Europe with its diverse cultures, languages, currencies and immigration/employment practices present barriers to the conduct of efficient, cost-conscious business. These countries are the losers, as business often takes its jobs and capital elsewhere in the global marketplace for what it wants.

As for transportation per se, it has never been easier for people or the goods and services workers produce to get to where they need to be. In the course of normal business, it's nothing anymore for company representatives to be in Kuala Lumpur on Monday, Sydney on Wednesday, Tokyo by Friday and back home for the weekend in San Francisco. With air carriers like UPS, DHL, Federal Express and Airborne, goods and services move just as fast as people. On the ground, a single 18-wheeler can deliver 15,000 television sets across 3,000 miles in three days. Coupled with the explosion in computer, Internet and telecommunications technology, this kind of delivery capability has been credited with taking much of the bust out of traditional economic cycles in the U.S. and elsewhere. "[The] strides made by corporate America in controlling inventories have gone a long way toward reducing volatility in the economy," reported *The Wall Street Journal* in August 1997. "Just-in-time" delivery of product can take much of the credit for this control of inventory. With the ability to deliver goods sold from manufacturer's stock instead of one's own warehouse, merchants avoid the expense and risk of large inventories, save on the cost of storage and find themselves in a position to respond quicker to consumer demand. Companies like Dell Computers, Wal-Mart and Procter & Gamble are conspicuous examples of organizations that have benefited immensely from just-in-time delivery capabilities. Dell, one of the world's hottest computer manufacturers, maintains a very low level of inventory because all PCs are produced after the sale is made and delivered in a few days. Procter & Gamble and its customer, Wal-Mart, have linked computer inventory systems to maximize efficiencies. Every time a tube of tooth-

Companies like Dell Computers, Wal-Mart and Procter & Gamble are conspicuous examples of organizations that have benefited immensely from just-in-time delivery capabilities.

paste or other Procter & Gamble product is "checked out" at a Wal-Mart cash register anywhere in the company's system, P&G knows and prepares its next shipment accordingly. No guessing over what's selling where, no long wait while the data is gathered and reported, no need for expensive inventory to cover every contingency. Procter & Gamble can accurately forecast demand and set production and delivery times. Wal-Mart, in turn, keeps well-stocked shelves and avoids the cost of distributors or middlemen. Because the company pays less, it can charge less— a decided competitive advantage that has helped catapult Wal-Mart to the top of the retail business. Other companies, including Toyota in 1999, watch Dell and follow suit with build-on-order production schemes of their own.

Technology. Volunteer rescue teams serving the last great American wilderness areas of Montana and Idaho are stretched to breaking by unprepared hikers who simply rely on their cell phones for help when they fall down, get lost, run out of food or weary of the wilds. From the tops of Himalayan peaks to New York City's teeming 42nd Street, the ability to communicate and "tend to business" is but a shirt-pocket cell phone away. Attached to a fax, computer, modem, printer and other technological marvels, the telephone-internet system provides a "virtual office" wherever and whenever one is needed.

That brings us to the Internet.

We touched on e-cruiting earlier. Suffice it to note here that the Internet has been a smash hit in the realm of human resources, even to the extent of using videoconferencing software to conduct preliminary interviews. Here's another view of online recruiting from Barb Ruess, director of marketing for Indianapolis-based E-Span: "The Web is an interactive medium that's perfectly suited for recruiting. And it's no longer limited to computer programmers and electrical engineers. Marketing, management and sales are now the three most common search items." For job-seekers without ready access to computers or free time during normal work hours to interview, there is the kind of service offered by Swiss-based staffing giant Adecco SA. With scores of interactive job-search kiosks strategically placed in shopping malls, college student centers and other public facilities throughout Germany, France, Spain and the U.S., the company has made job-hunting—and

Sampling of Web Sites for Job Hunters and Employers

The Monster Board	www.monster.com
Career City	www.careercity.com
Westech Virtual Job Fair	www.VJF.com
Career Mosaic	www.careermosaic.com
America's Job Bank	www.ajb.dni.us
CareerPath.com	www.careerpath.com
Online Career Center	www.ccc.com
Passport Access	www.passportaccess.com
CareerBuilder	www.careerbuilder.com
CareerMagazine	www.careermag.com
Headhunter.com	www.headhunter.com
Futurestep	www.careers.wsj.com
Hot Jobs	www.hotjobs.com
Collegegrad	www.collegegrad.com

recruiting—as easy as transacting banking business at an ATM. Through self-guiding instructions and touch-screen technology, kiosk software prompts users to specify the kind of work desired, experience, education, skills, salary requirements, availability and a schedule for possible interviews. From a central database, Adecco screens and matches the incoming information with available jobs. When a match is made, a staffing consultant contacts the applicant and completes the placement process.

Whether it's to reduce recruiting costs, speed up the selection and hiring process or to attract a higher caliber job applicant, companies turn to the Internet in one way or another for personnel needs in ever greater numbers. Citing a study it commissioned, iLogos Corporation of Ontario, Canada, reported in 1998 that 70 percent of computer software firms get their job applicants "on-line." For computer hardware firms, it was 60 percent, 35 percent for the aerospace industry and 30 percent for energy production operations. A sense of the speed with which Internet recruiting is progressing can be detected in the market's response to *The Wall Street Journal's* new job site Careers.wsj.com. In the first year of operation, reported *Staffing Industry Report,* the site attracted nearly three million visitors who searched more than four million job listings. Because it is so fast, effective and cheap, Internet recruiting can only grow, experts believe. Perry Boyle with Thomas Weisel Partners, predicts that e-cruiting could capture up to half the $30 billion search-and-recruiting market in just a few years.

There are several ways to use the Internet as an employee/employer matching service:

- **Job listings** - Virtually every major company now has a Web site, and most post job openings. Tens of thousands of small firms follow the same practice. A new development in this practice is the posting of projects to be done and a request for bids from interested service-providers. Then there are on-line recruiting services and massive job posting sites that compile employment opportunities from a variety of employers. Overall, the Internet is the world's largest single resource for job opportunities in all fields.
- **Post your resume** - There are a number of free sites on the Web and many where you pay to display your resume. Electronic "job search agents" can plow through the job postings for you. Around the clock, they seek matches between resumes and job postings by keywords. "Engineer. Software designer. Sales manager. Technical writer. . . ." When the electronic agent finds a match, it stores the information in the job seeker's own "mailbox" until it's retrieved.
- **Human resource auctions** - This is the virtual "talent market" described earlier. Internet talent markets provide an arena where independent contractors and freelancers can tout their skills and interested employers can bid for their services.
- **Research** - The Internet is the quickest, most efficient source of reliable information about employers and, increasingly, skilled employees. It is knowledge management at its best. The more employee, employer and labor exchange service know about one another, the

better the prospects for a quick and effective match.
- **Support services** - The Internet offers thousands of career-oriented Web sites and "chatrooms" that guide and assist people in job-searching. There are tips on resume preparation, interviewing and other particulars related to getting a job. You can connect with peers in your field of work to get advice or insight on industry openings.

In the Internet employment world, an engineer can display his or her credentials to prospective employers just as effectively as a puppeteer. Graphic artists or equipment designers can show samples of their work; writers their manuals, articles or books; instrument makers the sounds their equipment produces; traffic designers the models they developed; and so on. Where samples of one's work must be seen, they can be shown. Where an expression of one's capabilities must be heard, the Internet can convey it. Where the context or results of one's performance make a difference, the Internet is a truly awesome supplement to the previously mundane resume. In light of this high-tech job conduit, old-fashioned recruiting and selection processes followed forever by employers are increasingly outdated and inefficient. To lag behind in this important workplace trend is risky business—for employers and employees.

No question, recruiting is the first big human resources application for employers on the Internet. But there are others. The "outsourcing" of in-house jobs, including entire departments, makes a great deal of sense for many employers. Disciplines like payroll and benefits administration are routinely "farmed out" over the Internet to service providers that specialize in these back-room functions. The suppliers are experienced in the services offered, and they are usually more current, better equipped and deliver a superior product for less money than in-house personnel. Productivity improves, and the employer gains flexibility.

More and more, employee training takes place on the Internet. "Asynchronous" or distant learning allows trainees from various time zones and geographic locations to log on the Internet and participate in nearly any learning experience imaginable. If a participant can't make it at the appointed hour, he or she can pull up the instruction on the computer when time permits. Time and geography become superfluous. Travel and lost-time costs are reduced. More training can be achieved for the training dollar. Employee skills improve while in-house staff and training facilities shrink. Efficiency goes up and productivity too. Research and quality management monitoring are other jobs readily outsourced with positive results on the bottom line. The in-house jobs lost to this kind of innovation are eventually found at the service bureaus that land the outsourced work.

Globalization and telecommunications technology—like the chicken or the egg, it's hard to pin down which came first. But one thing's for sure: the workplace will never be the same because of the convergence of these two powerful forces. For one thing, business is apt to get smaller and more specialized, according to Esther Dyson, the most powerful woman in the "Net-erati," by one magazine's estimate. In her new book *Release 2.0, A Design for Living in the Digital Age,* she concludes,"... all this means a tendency toward smaller company size—even though most of what we hear about is mergers and industry consolidation as the media focus on giants. Little companies will find it easier to reach customers without massive marketing efforts even as they stay small, and they will be able to specialize in just one or two functions instead of facing constant pressure to grow to achieve economies of scale. Those economies of scale will diminish as even small companies get access to just the resources they need over the Net; the transaction costs of finding and negotiating work will drop for companies as well as for workers."

For all the above reasons, the concept of office itself has changed. The quest for profitability and efficiency has created new ways of operations unimaginable a few years ago. Laptop computers, modems, cell phones and fax machines have made the "virtual office" an absolute reality. Now workers can perform traditional office tasks from the front seat of a car, row 12C of the KLM flight from Frankfurt to New York City, the beach at Caracas, the local golf course, the waiting room at the dentist's office or nearly anywhere else people roam. Virtual organizations—where employees are stitched together via electronic networks and rarely, if ever, meet—grow routine.

Then there are new twists on the old office idea. IBM's sales operation in Cranford, New Jersey, for example, moved into a converted warehouse back in 1994. Spartan was the motif. No decorator's touch here. No fancy offices. No stirring views. Just 220 metal desks scattered throughout the cavernous, windowless space. And, for the most part, the desks didn't belong to anyone in particular. Nor were there ever more than 50 people or so in the office at any one time. The sales force was either out on the road or working from their home offices. Once a week or so, people dropped in at the office to pick up the mail, confer with colleagues and update laptop computers with new pricing, technical data and product information. They "borrowed" any desk available for the time they were there. There was a chair, a phone and a computer jack, and nothing else. Get in, tend to business, and get back out in the marketplace. That was the thinking and the message. The sales organization got the message loud and clear. With the move to the new quarters, the number of sales representatives was cut in half, and two levels of management were eliminated. With action like that, IBM began to regain the competitive edge it had lost in an earlier life. Don't look for a return of the bloated, out-of-date "Big Blue" of old any time soon. Management saw the future, and it was lean and flexible.

Where a traditional office environment is still the norm, employees find that their "space" has shrunk and the private office eliminated. From a national average of roughly 250 square feet of space per employee in the late 1980s, office space per employee in 1997 was more like 200 square feet. Telemarketing firms and customer service centers often shoehorn operators into 100 square feet or less. "It's all about lower occupancy costs for corporate America," explained David Tennery, vice president of the Atlanta office of developer Hogan Group. Even more than that, it's about competition. To compete in the global economy, lean and efficient is the requirement. And the fat trimmed from occupancy costs lightens the load on the bottom line just as effectively as a "downsized" workforce.

Fast on the heels of these changes in the traditional office environment has come a major new industry reflective of the times. It used to be the staid old office supply business. Today, it's big national retailers like Kinko's, Staples, Copy USA, Office Depot, OfficeMax, IKON Business Solutions, Mail Boxes Etc, AlphaGraphics and local competitors matching service for service, product for product with the big boys. They offer office supplies, services and/or equipment for the most modest home office to the most high-tech telecommuter to the most that is current in modern "officing." Videoconferencing, computer services, copy centers, fax and shipping stores and a host of other business services make it ever so attractive to cut back on "in-house" capabilities that add inefficiently to the cost of doing business. A Kinko's brochure explains: "Every day, people are reinventing the way they do business, and Kinko's is supporting this revolution by providing innovative ways to get the job done better." Kinko's motto: "Express yourself." That's what is going on in the modern workplace.

> A Kinko's brochure explains: "Every day, people are reinventing the way they do business, and Kinko's is supporting this revolution by providing innovative ways to get the job done better."

So the trends all point to further growth in the various forms of flexible employment, and *FlexLife®* more than most. For the new employment paradigm that rules advanced economies today is but half a loaf without a good and effective substitute for the components of job security provided until recently by employers. That substitute must be able to step in where employers leave off with benefits for "unattached" flexible workers, decent assurances of steady work within a person's skill-set, career guidance, training and a real, live human support system to provide continuity in a fluid, isolated job environment. The Internet can't do this. It's just an electronic conduit—an incredible market-making warren of a conduit, to be sure, but without the human touch. The one institution in place today that can provide the glue to hold together the flexible workforce is the staffing industry. Once a sleepy, marginal player in the workplace, the modern staffing industry finds itself in the right place at the right time. For employers to be flexible enough to contract and expand as competitive pressures dictate, they must have ready access to a reliable pool of employee skills and labor to meet every imaginable need but only for as long as the need exists. The staffing industry has always developed and managed flexible labor pools. With every passing year, the level of skills sophistication in those pools has grown, fueled by the demands of the marketplace. E-cruiting, e-lancing and other Internet search-and-recruiting services just make that part of the job that much easier. For employees to stay employed in a downsizing, unpredictable business environment, they must be able to manage their careers, "grow" their

For employees to stay employed in a down-sizing, unpredictable business environment, they must be able to manage their careers, "grow"their skills and successfully match them time and again with employer needs in an unbroken succession of assignments.

skills and successfully match them time and again with employer needs in an unbroken succession of assignments. This, too, is rudimentary to the staffing business. Human skills, talent and labor are what the industry has to sell. Pushed by the market, the industry continually improves and broadens its product.

The heart and face of the modern staffing industry are "staffing consultants or associates." They are the company representatives who employees and employers deal with at most staffing agencies. By whatever name, these positions constitute the critical interface in the local market between the needs of employers and the skills, talent and labor of assignment personnel. Staffing specialists make the matches that are the starting point of flexible employment. They assess employer needs, preferences, likes and dislikes; weigh the assessment against assignment personnel capabilities, preferences, likes and dislikes; then make the best match possible. Staffing specialists make it possible for many employers to trim down to a minimal core staff and, thus, to compete more successfully in the marketplace. It is this front-line position of staffing consultant or associate that constitutes the "agent-in-the-rough" in the modern workplace . . . agent-in-the-rough because not all staffing representatives are bona fide agents. Many—indeed the majority—are mere brokers of employee skills, talent and labor. The distinction between agent and broker is critical. Agents know the industry they serve. They know their business and add demonstrable value with their expertise. Above all, agents know their clients—assignment personnel and employers alike. They match employer needs with just the right employee competencies. They help develop employee skills, groom them in the trade, put them in situations that accentuate their strengths, shield them from assignments that expose their weaknesses, and stick with them in good times and bad. All in all, brokers don't take the time for this kind of commitment. They cover lots of ground, sell something here, something there, then move on. Agents are for the long run.

Making agents of staffing representatives is the challenge for the staffing industry. That the industry has accepted this challenge and moved in the right direction— some more than others—speaks well for the future of *FlexLife®*. Given the current state of affairs in the workplace, it's fair to say that if the staffing industry did not exist, it would have to be invented.

Employers hire what employees can do— their skills and talent and labor. And employers don't need all skills all the time.

– Dr. Frits Goldschmeding
Randstad's founder

Clearly, the staffing industry has come a long way since a few far-sighted entrepreneurs recognized the need for flexible employment and did something about it. One of those pioneers, I'm proud to report, is my colleague Frits Goldschmeding. Dr. Goldschmeding, a trained economist, is Randstad's founder and retired president and CEO. While earning a graduate degree at the University of Amsterdam in the early '60s, this son of Holland thought it curious that labor was construed as a "fixed" cost of business when other similar components of production were considered "variable" costs. Employers didn't hire employees just to be hiring employees, he reasoned. Employers hire what employees can do—their skills and talent and labor. And employers don't need all skills all the time. In this sense, Goldschmeding concluded, labor should be recognized as an economic resource similar to capital or inventory or raw material—all of it adjustable, flexible, employed when needed, curtailed when not.

Intrigued by the prospects of actually putting this thinking into practice, Goldschmeding wrote a master's thesis on the subject and, while still a student, launched the forerunner of what today is Randstad Holding nv. Right from the beginning, he meant for his company to be more than just a source of temporary help. If the skill and/or labor of a staffing employee was valuable enough to be hired the first time, it would be even more valuable the second time by virtue of the previous experience. Each successive "job assignment" made for an increasingly skilled staffing employee. Every customer served generated greater knowledge of employer needs and preferences. Through the years, Goldschmeding perfected the basics of *FlexLife®* and shaped his company in that mold. Immodestly, perhaps, I and others less biased believe that Frits Goldschmeding's approach to employment is taking hold in the staffing industry.

Certainly, many of the perceptions attached to temporary work in

51

the past are true, and the job market remains strong for just the kind of labor that spawned the industry stereotypes. At the low end of the flexible employment spectrum, traditional temps are readily "disposed of" by employers. It's a strength of the concept. Employers get "just-in-time" assistance at a low price, then let the people go until the next need arises. The temps typically earn a modest wage, working the way they want, with no obligations. Employers are thought to have total control in a traditional temp-employer relationship, but the temps have a fair share too. Their lives and careers are not tied up in a single job, and they can "walk" with impunity. Unfortunately, the stereotypes associated with traditional "temping" persist as the stereotypes for all forms of flexible employment, *FlexLife®* included. Nothing could be further from the truth. *FlexLife®* breaks all the stereotypes. At the high end of the flexible employment scale, power and control shift measurably to the "assignment" careerist. It's a bona fide career. Employment security is very high. Health and retirement benefits are provided. Good pay and the respect conferred on any "independent" business person come with the *FlexLife®* territory. And there's the one enviable benefit enjoyed almost exclusively by the *FlexLife®* careerist—flexibility, a balance of work and personal life that is much more befitting the human condition. Please excuse me while I proclaim the stereotypes associated with flexible employment dead and buried. A new era reigns in which flexible employment leads the way.

Chapter Two

Is that a dinosaur hidden in those statistics?

The relic of traditional employment

All is not what it appears to be in those neat little rows of labor statistics. A lot of distortion and misinterpretation are harbored there. That's an important point to remember when trying to quantify the size and vitality of the flexible workforce compared to "traditional employment."

For starters, it's important to understand that modern labor statistics grew out of a narrow focus on manufacturing jobs. Measures of other segments of the workforce were subsequently cobbled onto the original model—except for that marginal realm loosely referred to as "flexible or temporary" forms of work. As recently as 1997, one of the few numbers available that purported to reflect the scope of the flexible workforce came from the U.S. Bureau of Labor Statistics' report on "Contingent workers"—those who worked in jobs structured to last only a limited period of time. Just 4.9 percent of total employment qualified as "contingent workers"— nothing there to indicate a major change in the composition of the workplace.

The Traditional Permanent Job (TPJ) Often referred to as a "real job"; permanent employment with job security where the employer "manages" one's career and retains his or her services with paid or partially paid health insurance, retirement provisions, good pay, regular raises, advancement, paid vacations, sick leave, training and other wage and non-wage benefits.

For 1999, the American Staffing Association (ASA) reported that 2.2 percent of the U.S. workforce was comprised of temporary workers, double the 1990 level. In the United Kingdom and The Netherlands, which deploy the highest percentage of temporary workers in the world, the figures were higher but, still, only about 4 percent of the workforce. While these numbers reflect tremendous growth in just a few years, they appear modest enough vis-a-vis "traditional employment."

Elusive Target

The growth in nontraditional jobs can be seen in the *decline* of *traditional permanent jobs* (TPJ) reported by the U.S. Bureau of Labor Statistics in February 1998. In a study of job tenure, the BLS found that, overall, people were changing jobs more frequently. On average, young American workers between the ages of 18 and 32 changed employment nearly nine times. Wage and salary workers of all types had been with their employers for an average of 3.6 years, down from 3.8 years two years earlier. The job tenure for manufacturing employees declined to 4.9 years from 5.4 years in February 1996, a figure that had remained constant for 10 years. Tenure for automotive workers shrunk to 6.4 years in 1998 from 13 years in 1983. Younger workers, older workers, men, college graduates—they all showed declines in the length of stay with any one employer. Only women held to traditional tenure figures. In February 1998, Federal Reserve Chairman Alan Greenspan reminded the Senate Budget Committee that 300,000 jobs were lost each week in the U.S. even as more were created—a "very major set of churning forces," he called it. Downsizing in bad times, downsizing in good times; either way, it spells more insecurity for jobholders in the once predictable world of U.S. employment.

Downsizing in bad times, downsizing in good times; either way, it spells more insecurity for jobholders in the once predictable world of U.S. employment

Writer Daniel Pink started getting closer to the mark in a *Fast Company* magazine article later in 1998. Counting the self-employed, independent contractors and staffing employees, he estimated that there were at least 25 million "free-agents" (nontraditional employees) at work in the U.S., or 16 percent of the total workforce. To emphasize the conservative tenor of the estimate, Pink noted that the Internal Revenue Service (IRS) mailed more than 74 million copies of Form 1099-MISC to taxpayers in 1998. "The pay stub for free-agents," he called the form.

Finally, in the 1999 Roper Report described in Chapter One, Randstad determined that fully 51 percent of the North American workforce earned their livelihoods in nontraditional work arrangements. Still, that doesn't get to the bottom of the reservoir of flexible work hidden in traditional employment statistics.

Upon close examination, it turns out that 23 million of those officially listed as "employed" in the U.S. in 1998 were actually part-time workers—flexible work arrangements, not traditional permanent jobs. That's 19 percent of employed Americans. Part-timers make up large slices of the employment pie in Europe as well. Fully 38 percent of employed Dutch workers were part-timers as recently as 1996. That same year part-time jobs accounted for 25 percent of those classified as "employed" in the United Kingdom and 16 percent in Germany.

Independent contractors comprised about 7 percent of the U.S. workforce in 1998. Self-employed persons represent another 5-6 percent. There are many good jobs in these categories. Lots of high incomes. Entrepreneurs aplenty. But, like the previous jobs, this kind of work falls more in the realm of flexible employment. No job security of the permanent kind here. And so it is with on-call workers and day-labor who made up 1.7 percent of the workforce. Contract workers, representing 1.2 percent of the workforce, and agency-provided staffing employees, another 2 percent, are in a similar situation. These segments of the workforce do not fit the historical parameters laid down for traditional permanent jobs.

Upon close examination, it turns out that 23 million of those officially listed as "employed" in the U.S. in 1998 were actually part-time workers—flexible work arrangements, not traditional permanent jobs.

Then there is a big contingent in every nation who simply don't get counted when it comes to measuring the workforce. No *traditional permanent jobs* in this segment of society. These people include the chronically unemployed, retirees, students 16 years old and older, mothers with young children and older women who have never or rarely worked outside the home. In some nations, this "uncounted" segment exceeds the official unemployment rate. First instincts might be to discount these people, just as the statisticians do. But that would be to overlook a valuable resource, some serious problems and a whole lot of people. Take a look at the total number of potentially employable people in the U.S. at the beginning of 1997, for example.

Employed Americans	129.4 million (95 percent employment rate)
Unemployed Americans	6.8 million (5 percent unemployment Rate)
Unaccounted	67.0 million
	203.2 million

Ever wonder how the U.S. kept its economy running during the booming last half of the 1990s when statistics showed essentially full employment during most of that time? Full employment means "no more employees available," yet American industry added 7.7 million new workers to the payroll from 1994 through 1997. Where did these people come from? About 1.5 million came from youngsters reaching employment age, while the rest came right out of those "unaccounted" millions of working age people who never show up as part of the workforce.

Look at The Netherlands, one of the economic bright spots in Europe. Unemployment in April 1996 was reported to be 5.3 percent. Only Luxembourg and Austria had lower rates in the 15-nation European Union (EU). German unemployment at the same time was 9 percent. In France it was 12-plus percent and nearly 9 percent in the United Kingdom (UK). But dig into the numbers further, and you see that the Dutch didn't include a large share of the population that found unemployment benefits so attractive they simply stayed home or took early retirement. The government just didn't consider these people part of the workforce. The effect was sobering. The Organization for Economic Cooperation and Development estimated that Dutch *labor force participation* in 1996 was only 62.5 percent. That compared with 73.7 percent in the United Kingdom (UK) and 77.3 percent in the U.S.

The most striking characteristic of this category of unemployed people, noted the *Financial Times* (London), was the number listed as officially ill and drawing disability benefits or on sick leave. "There are more people in these categories than officially unemployed," reported the *Times*. "This constitutes the single largest form of hidden unemployment in the Dutch economy." A reduction of unemployment benefits since 1996 and tighter standards for getting them helped alleviate this problem somewhat. The fact remains, however, that not working still has its appeal in The Netherlands. The *OECD Economic Survey* 1998 grouped those uncounted, working-age Dutch adults in a statistical category called "broad unemployment" (i.e., unemployed and inactive persons of working age receiving social security benefits and persons enrolled in special job creation programs). The category represented more than 25 percent of the total labor force. "Uncounted workers" are neither traditional jobholders nor part of the flexible workforce, they are but some of the distortion and misinterpretation hidden in modern labor statistics.

> *"Uncounted workers" are neither traditional jobholders nor part of the flexible workforce, they are but some of the distortion and misinterpretation hidden in modern labor statistics.*

The point is clear: the traditional career-long, secure job has become a bit of a dinosaur, and flexible forms of employment have taken on a whole new dimension.

The Increase in Flexible Forms of Employment

Contrast the shrinkage in traditional permanent jobs (TPJ) to new job growth in the five-year period beginning in 1993. While one form of employment declines, another rises, and signs of a major transition become more and more compelling. From 1993 through 1997, employment in the U.S. grew by 13.9 million people. What's telling about this remarkable growth is how much of it occurred in industries generally known for flexible employment practices. Let's look at some industry figures.

Wholesale-Retail Trade – The old-line world of department stores, restaurants, malls, warehouses, shops and other purveyors of merchandise and service added 3.8 million workers during the five-year period. Twenty-one million people worked in the food and restaurant business alone. With a growth rate of 2 percent a year, the industry accounted for 27.7 percent of the total new jobs added to the U.S. economy from 1993 to 1998. What kind of work did these 3.8 million new jobs represent? About what they have always been—heavily part-time with relatively low wages. Not your typical traditional permanent job.

This is a major challenge for the flexible workforce and its supporters. For the new workplace to be all that it can be, restaurant workers, retail clerks and others so familiar in traditional consumer societies need employment security and career ladders to climb that raise them to respectable levels of employment. Things did improve for these workers during the period 1993-98, especially in the U.S. Wages grew as record-low unemployment levels forced retailers to pay more for help. Even bonuses were paid to lure and keep workers in many large markets. And the staffing industry began to step up and take the lead in developing a better system for matching the skills and interests of retail workers with the personnel needs of employers. Olsten Staffing Services and Simon, the world's largest mall operator, for example, entered into an agreement in 1998 that called for the establishment of six "in-mall employment service centers" in Florida, New Jersey, Ohio and Texas. Olsten, since acquired by staffing giant Adecco, provides a broad range of employment services for mall tenants including the placement of temporary and full-time employees, free job postings, candidate screening and interviewing, background checks and investigation, reliability and integrity testing and point-of-sale training. Seventy-two hours a week, mall employees and job applicants off-premises have ready access to a labor exchange system designed specifically for those seeking retail employment, not only locally but throughout the extensive Simon operation. This kind of thinking is just what's needed throughout the retail industry to convert temps into FlexLifers.

Another key to upgrading the quality and appeal of wholesale-retail work is to add value to the skills of the workforce. These people simply must create greater demand for their competencies in good times and bad. For, when the economy slackens and demand for workers subsides, it's those with the best skills that will work, not those who failed to keep up with the times. Employers have an important role to play in upgrading the skills and value of their workers, especially the lower-paying end of the scale. Because technology can only go so far in replacing personnel in restaurants and other retail operations, and because corporate earnings are directly related to the quality and efficiency of service rendered "where lower-paid workers meet the market-place," employers owe it to themselves to maximize the return on "floor-level" employees. That means training and other forms of skills development. But leaving training and career development to employers in today's workplace is a mistake. It is in their best interest to have access to qualified workers when they are needed, but not necessarily to be in the training and career development business all the time. The more businesses adapt to competitive pressures, the more they dispense with operations not directly related to their core business. That's the motivation behind the tremendous growth in "outsourcing" since the recession years of the early 1990s. With employers trying to get out of the training and employee development business, and lower-paid workers needing it more than ever, what's the conclusion? The flexible workforce is going to fail to measure up unless two things happen:

Because technology can only go so far in replacing personnel in restaurants and other retail operations, and because corporate earnings are related to the quality and efficiency of service rendered "where lower-paid workers meet the market-place," employers owe it to themselves to maximize the return on "floor-level" employees.

- *Employees* take on more and more of the responsibility for their own skills development and career advancement; and
- *Third-party personnel providers* (i.e., the staffing industry and other labor exchange services) fill the employee training and development shortfall created by cost-conscious employers.

The New Employment Paradigm

The Newly Old Workplace of Traditional Permanent Jobs (TPJ)		
EMPLOYEE	**AGENT**	**EMPLOYER**
• Relinquishes career management to employer • Loyalty expected and given in return for cradle-to-grave job security	• A non-factor in the general workplace	• Responsible for career management • Responsible for training, value-added skills enhancement and career development • Responsible for employee job security • Responsible for health care and retirement provisions
The New Workplace of Flexible Employment		
EMPLOYEE	**AGENT**	**EMPLOYER**
• Responsible for own career management • Responsible for own training, value-added skills enhancement and career development • Loyalty withdrawn from employer and bestowed upon agent • Agent loyalty gained for employer loyalty lost	• A growing factor in the general workplace • Major contributor to employee's career management, skills enhancement and marketplace preparation • Helps provide "employment security" for employees in lieu of "job security" • Client (employee and employer) loyalty gained for agent loyalty given • Provides access to health insurance and retirement provisions	• No longer responsible for employee career management • No longer responsible for value-added skills enhancement except where it's in the employer's best interest • Employee loyalty lost • Agent loyalty gained • Responsibility for employee job security relinquished • Responsibility for employee health care and retirement relinquished

These kinds of dynamics, coupled with labor shortages in many markets, breed innovative solutions that just may take the slack times out of retailing for employees. When business is slow in one sector, staffing agencies and industry groups have begun to swing personnel to other employers with swelling seasonal demand. When the season wanes, the employees come back to the first employer's place of business. It has been done successfully in Dodgeville, Wisconsin, where Lands' End, the big direct-mail merchandiser, partners with local cheese factories to help cover seasonal personnel needs. Starting in October of each year, Lands' End goes into a Christmas-season frenzy to pack and ship mail-ordered merchandise to customers around the world. As many as 2,600 just-in-time workers are needed during the period and, in a state with nearly 3 percent unemployment, they are hard to find. Part of the problem, of course, is the inevitable lay-off once Christmas is over. People who need full-time employment aren't easily attracted to seasonal jobs, no matter how attractive. It turns out that

Lands' End and the local cheese industry got together and agreed to share some of the same workforce. All parties to the agreement come out ahead.

the cheese business, for which Wisconsin is so famous, has much the same seasonal personnel problems as Lands' End—but the seasons are reversed. By October of each year, cheese manufacturing and distribution slows down, forcing layoffs no one wants and a constant struggle to rehire when production starts anew. Lands' End and the local cheese industry got together and agreed to share some of the same workforce. All parties to the agreement come out ahead. The employers are better able to control labor costs while gaining some assurance of critically needed labor supply. Employees come closer to year-round employment by switching back and forth between the two employers. Benefits are retained because each employer simply lends its employees to the other. Additionally, employees who participate in this arrangement acquire new skills that enhance their employment value generally. Look for more of these kinds of arrangements in the future. Until such work arrangements are perfected on a wide scale, however, wholesale and retail jobs will continue to provide low levels of personal income and little job security.

Business Services Industry – In 1993, the business services industry employed just over a third as many personnel as did the wholesale-retail sector and accounted for 8.3 percent of new job growth in the U.S. economy. Five years later, the business services industry employed nearly half as many people as wholesale-retail, added almost as many jobs (3.2 million) and accounted for 23.3 percent of new U.S. job growth. With a five-year growth rate of 7 percent, business services can

Business Services Industry	
BUSINESS SERVICES • Advertising, Marketing, PR • Credit Reporting and Collection • Mailing, Reproduction • Building Services • Equipment Rental • Personnel Supply • Computer and Data Processing • Miscellaneous (detectives, security, etc.)	**LEGAL SERVICES** **ACCOUNTING SERVICES** **ENGINEERING SERVICES** **MANAGEMENT SERVICES** **RESEARCH AND TESTING**

be expected to overtake the huge wholesale-retail sector in the near future. What kinds of jobs drive this incredible growth? They are predominantly flexible forms of employment of a higher kind.

It's the experience of the business services industry that best answers some of the sobering questions raised by the "new workplace." Will it fill the needs of society at least as well as the old one? Can a well-managed flexible workforce perform at a high level in good times and bad? Can employees find job security, prosperity and a more balanced personal life in this kind of environment? Let's look at business services more closely, segment by segment.

Business Services – Employment in the business services segment of the industry has grown at an "astounding 6.9 percent annually since 1972 and by 5.8 percent per year since 1988," reported the *Monthly Labor Review* in August 1997. This growth was powered in large part by two of the eight professions that comprise the category—personnel supply services (11.4 percent) and computer services (10.7 percent). Both expanded at more than five times the pace of the total economy since 1972. Personnel supply services (the staffing industry) employed 2.6 million workers at the end of 1996 and is the largest employer in business services. Traditional permanent jobs (TPJ) are a small part of the personnel supply industry; flexible employment is the very essence of the business.

Computer Services – Computer services employed more than 1.2 million workers at the start of 1997. Ten years earlier, the numbers were marginal; five years before that, computer services jobs didn't exist. And, quite literally, the business is just starting to extend itself. In 1995, for example, computer services to access the Internet grew at an 18.5 percent clip from the year earlier, then another 20.2 percent in 1996. Jobs for systems analysts increased by 34 percent from 1983 to 1995. Programmer jobs in the same period expanded exponentially. Eye-popping, seemingly unsustainable growth figures–but they proved quite the norm for the rest of the 1990s.

As the heart of the Information Technology (IT) field, computer services and related industries are the trendsetters for *FlexLife*®. These are the people with the skills, history and inclination to work a succession of short-term job assignments, build upon their expertise, grow their value in the marketplace and enjoy the flexibility and, yes, security that comes with the lifestyle. Traditional permanent jobs (TPJ) are not what computer services or other IT employees are after. Not long ago, the CEO of a well-established IT staffing firm commented that, five years earlier, one in five of the company's placements took permanent jobs within 90 days. "Today, it's one in 36," he said. Why the change? "The staffing people don't want permanent jobs. They're doing quite well as staffing personnel," said Bill Gower of Matrix Resources.

Engineering and Management Services – These jobs have grown more than 3 percent annually since 1972, more than twice as fast as all other industries combined. By 1997, the category employed nearly 3 million people. Here too, the marketplace makes FlexLifers out of traditional permanent jobholders. More and more, people employed in engineering services work on fixed-term employment contracts, employee leasing agreements or other flexible employment arrangements. Like personnel in Information Technology (IT), engineers are natural FlexLifers. They have advanced skills that many employers need but not always all the time. Far better for most employers to call in engineering skills when and where needed—even at expensive rates—than to retain full-time expertise for intermittent needs. The same is true for management services like business consulting, auditing, accounting and bookkeeping. Increasingly, employers outsource these needs rather than build the capability in-house, or employ the skills through staffing agencies when, and only when, needed.

Legal Services – Here is another traditional business that moves towards the *FlexLife®* end of the employment scale. According to *Staffing Industry Report,* the legal staffing niche is one of the hottest growing specialties in the staffing industry.

> *In the new and flexible field of law, just-in-time skills, talent and labor hold down overhead, reduce bill rates and attract more clients more frequently with a wider range of needs.*

"Demand from law firms and corporate legal departments for temporary and permanent placement of legal secretaries and support staff, paralegals and attorneys continues to expand as these clients embrace the concept—and benefits—of flexible staffing," the 1998 report noted. From 1996 through 1998, the legal staffing market grew 25 percent annually, exceeding $2.2 billion in size. Forecasts were for more of the same. "Temporary legal is really becoming integrated in law firms and corporations as an economical and efficient way to do their business. They're planning for it now," said Laura Black, CEO of Special Counsel, the legal placement specialists at Modis Professional Services. Here, as in so much of the business services industry, we are seeing a shift in the historical paradigm for the delivery of services. In the old brass-nameplate law business, a lot of personnel and resources swirled about, earning no income directly. Overhead, thus, was high, and client bill rates too. The high cost of doing business with a typical law firm, in turn, reduced customer demand for legal services, which limited the firm's exposure to new and different types of work. In the new and flexible field of law, just-in-time skills, talent and labor hold down overhead, reduce bill rates and attract more clients more frequently with a wider range of needs. FlexLifers in the legal profession are exposed to a wider range of challenging work, which enhances their value in the marketplace. And better people are drawn to flexible legal careers.

Accounting Services – Following a period of severe competition and lower profit margins in the mid-1990s, major U.S. accounting firms shifted into a more flexible service mode that looks very much like the staffing business. Clients of the nation's Big Six accounting firms, for example, can now get services like staff loan programs, search and recruitment, project management and outsourcing administration. Three of the Big Six firms are involved in temporary staffing, one in permanent placement and two in HR outsourcing. The motivation behind the accounting profession's shift in thinking is the same motivation that prompted historical changes in the law business, engineering and telecommunications—the need to be competitive. Keep core staff to a minimum. Cut those unbilled hours everywhere practical.

The business services industry shows the way of the workplace. Skills don't have to be those of computer experts, lawyers or accountants; they just have to be in demand by employers. Truck drivers are just as hot a commodity in the late '90s job market as computer analysts. The common thread between the two is the demand for their respective skills. With a well-trained, "net"-savvy agent to match those skills with employers who need them, and employee willingness to go where the jobs are, truck drivers and/or computer analysts gain control over their lives and careers. They don't need traditional permanent jobs.

Health Services - Health services experienced heady growth in the 1993-97 period despite unprecedented merger and acquisition, cost-reduction and general re-engineering. These movements usually signal personnel reduction. So where did the job growth in health services come from? Look to the expansion of flexible forms of health services employment for the answer. Many nurses downsized out of secure hospital jobs or squeezed to perform more for less pay, moved to home-care firms where they could work the hours they wanted, with good pay and benefits. And staffing agencies grew in importance as a vehicle for placing into service the skills and talent of medical personnel. On a typical day in 1998, for example, Saber-Salisbury and Associates of Southfield, Michigan, placed 38 doctors, physician assistants, anesthetists and nurse practitioners in temporary work assignments. Some of the assignments were as far away as Florida and Alaska, but most were within a couple hours drive of the staffer's home. Pay: $500-750 a day for doctors, $400-450 for physician assistants.

Combined with the construction industry, the wholesale-retail, business services and health services industries accounted for 9.6 million of the 13.9 million new jobs added to the U.S. economy from 1993 through 1997—nearly 70 percent of the total. The other 30 percent growth was provided by the following:

INDUSTRY	% of Total Growth over 5 Years
Manufacturing	6.4
Government	6.1
Education Services	5.0
Finance, Insurance, Real Estate	3.9
Air Transportation	3.8
Amusement and Recreation	3.5
Social Services	3.3
Hotel and Other Lodgings	1.7
Auto Repair and Other Services	1.4
All Other	5.2

Except for manufacturing and government, none of these industries exceeded a 1-percent annual growth rate during the 1993-97 period. Furthermore, as a percentage of total U.S. employment, both manufacturing and government actually shrunk over the five-year period. In summary, job growth has surged where flexible forms of employment prevail, and little growth—even shrinkage—is the norm in the rest of the workplace.

What do the statistics *not* tell you?

In 1995, the national jobless rate in Japan was a thin 3.3 percent, appreciably better than comparable statistics in the U.S. But there was an unfolding story masked by that very impressive employment figure. For workers 60 to 64, prime earning years in Japan's seniority-conscious workplace, the unemployment rate was 5.7 percent. And therein lay an important development.

Forced by the competitive realities of the global marketplace and a stubborn, lingering financial crisis, Japan was beginning to deregulate its economy, downsize its workforce and scrap the social contract that has meant lifetime employment and seniority-based pay for workers since the nation emerged from the devastation of World War II. It was becoming painfully clear that cradle-to-grave job security was no longer a luxury Japan could afford. A 1997 report from the Japan Federation of Employers Association shed some light on the nation's new workplace rules. "As the principle of free competition becomes the basis of Japan's economy and society, Japanese companies will have to be managed in more efficient and creative ways. Restructuring will become the most important theme for Japanese corporations." Those most affected by the downsizing and deregulation fall in the late-40s-and-older age bracket. By custom, these people are entering the highest paid years of their careers. Unfortunately, they represent unsustainable fixed costs in the nation's top-heavy management structure. Employers are twisting and turning to lessen the load. Performance standards have been instituted by firms like Honda and Sony. Fail to perform, and be gone. Many companies have established voluntary early retirement programs. Others have introduced term limits for management posts. The cry is raised for more flexible forms of employment (i.e., fewer full-time workers). The end result of these developments is higher unemployment, especially among older workers.

Cradle-to-grave job security was no longer a luxury Japan could afford. . . . Now companies are saying, "You have to be loyal while you are employed, but we won't take care of you for life any more."

– Kiyotsugu Shitara
General Secretary of the
Tokyo Manager's Union

This is not how the vaunted Japanese system previously worked. Traditionally, employees sold their working lives to employers in exchange for job security. "Now, companies are saying, 'You have to be loyal while you are employed, but we won't take care of you for life any more,'" said Kiyotsugu Shitara, General Secretary of the Tokyo Manager's Union. So, low unemployment rates do not always tell the tale. Often they convey an impression of job stability when, in fact, things are not quite so warm and fuzzy.

What's to be read in employment statistics from Germany? In October 1997, there was optimism among economists and government officials that this erstwhile economic powerhouse was shaking off the doldrums and starting to grow, perhaps on a scale to rival the boom years of the 1980s. The value of the German mark vis-a-vis the U.S. dollar had declined appreciably, making domestically produced products cheaper in foreign markets. Factories were running full bore. Absenteeism, notoriously bad for years, had hit a 20-year low. On the crest of these developments, unemployment, at 11.7 percent in October 1997, was expected to decline. Things looked promising. And, in important ways, things did improve. By the spring of 2000, however, Germany was clearly bumping up against engrained economic and social problems that threaten its prosperity. What sets Germany apart is the imbedded cost of doing business in the country. German workers are the highest paid in the world. Non-wage labor costs in 1997, for example, exceeded their U.S. equivalents by 175 percent and those of Japan by 140 percent. Not only are German producers moving operations out of the country for cheaper, more flexible labor, but investors look to put their money elsewhere in the global marketplace where a better return can be realized.

On the basis of these problems, Germany was listed among the "newly declining countries" at a workshop in July 1997 hosted by the Kiel Institute of World Economies and the Massachusetts Institute of Technology. Forced to compete in the global marketplace with what newspaper columnist Peter Norman describes as "a complex and unfair tax system, unnecessary bureaucratic hurdles, an inflexible labor market and a generous social security system that tends to smother individual initiative," Germany finds itself at a marked disadvantage. The situation does not bode well for traditional permanent jobs in Germany for the foreseeable future.

Germany's problems are, of course, reflected in France and elsewhere in the European Union. France addresses its employment problems and declining competitiveness with more of what created the problems to begin with. Reduce productivity with more people working fewer hours, and industry passing the added costs on to customers—it's a sure formula for driving customers and investors away. Job security and general prosperity are the losers in this scenario, given business's options in the global marketplace. As my mentor Frits Goldschmeding has always said, "Working less has never created jobs or made anyone rich."

The important measure in a strong economy is the number of work hours generated by the nation's commerce. Growth in work hours generally relates to growth in jobs. If the work hours don't grow, no division of labor among employees will solve the problem. Ten people doing 400 hours of work per week that pays a total of $5,000 for the labor turns out to be a 40-hour workweek and a $500 paycheck per employee. Twelve people doing the same number of hours of work for the same remuneration translates into a 33-hour workweek and a $417 paycheck. Stick 15 people into the equation, and the workweek shrinks below 27 hours and the paycheck to $333. It is reasonable to expect that most people would find the shorter workweek quite acceptable. But it is highly unlikely that many would find the reduced paycheck quite so palatable. Thirty-five-hour work weeks in France will put more people to work partially. Paying 40 hours of wages for 35 hours of work when productivity and customer demand doesn't grow simply increases the cost of business, and lessens competitiveness. Where's the job security, advancement and prosperity in that?

Sweden, quintessential welfare state, found key employers moving operations out of the country in 1997-98 in order to lower their cost of business. Electrolux, the nation's largest employer, announced an 11-percent reduction in its workforce of 105,000. SKF, the world's largest producer of ball bearings, set to work trimming 2,000 high-paying jobs from its payroll. These moves not only cost jobs but tax revenue as well. So Sweden had no recourse but to alter its social contract with the populace. The social contract in Switzerland, too, began to show cracks. AAB Asea Brown, a major employer, said it would trim 10,000 jobs from its operations in Europe and the U.S. and move more production to factories and plants in nations like Malaysia and Thailand. The gains to be realized in lower production and exporting costs far outweigh the negatives, the company reported. Far from a one-shot deal, AAB, which employs over 200,000 workers worldwide, planned to speed up the relocation of production operations from higher-cost industrialized countries to Asia. A company spokesman pointed out that this is probably bad news for some workers in the West, but it will mean thousands of new jobs for Asians.

Jobs fleeing the high cost and inflexibility of labor—same old story, over and over again. It all has to do with productivity, getting more for the same or lesser cost.

Jobs fleeing the high cost and inflexibility of labor—same old story, over and over again. It all has to do with productivity: getting more for the same or lesser cost. I recently saw a clipping from *Bank Technology News* that clearly illustrates just why productivity is so important to employers. The clipping was a simple chart showing the cost of bank transactions in the U.S. A customer transaction at a full-service branch bank cost the industry an average of $1.07. Banking by phone cost an average of 54 cents per transaction. A full-service ATM brought the cost down to 27 cents per transaction. Personal computer banking with third-party software cost one and a half cents, and banking via the World Wide Web (www) put the number at one cent per transaction. From $1.07 to one cent—that's productivity. That's why the traditional corner-lot banking house has declined and ATM machines have become ubiquitous. That's why the banking industry spent more than $60 billion between 1992 and 1998 getting into PC/Internet banking. Small yet, Internet banking was expected to be used in more than 16 percent of U.S. households by year-end 2000. Thirty percent of retail bank profits could flow from this end of the business, analysts predict. In light of this kind of productivity, don't look for the return of the friendly local bank on every commercial corner in suburban America. It's not going to happen. But neither will those bank teller jobs return that went with the branch office. They go the way of the telephone operator, service station attendant, assembly-line worker and other traditional permanent jobs.

That brings us to the China factor.

Consider these statistics and the impact they are likely to have on the Western workplace:

- The Chinese workforce, at roughly 740 million people, is larger than that of the 15-nation European Union, the United States, Russia, Brazil, Indonesia, Canada and Australia combined.
- With a median per capita monthly income of about $250 U.S. dollars, the Chinese workforce willingly works for approximately $10 per day.
- Non-wage labor costs (i.e., benefits) in China are pennies on the dollar of U.S., European and Japanese equivalents.
- The nation's "youth literacy rate" is 95 percent, and the figures for working-age adults are not too shabby either.
- Counting Hong Kong, China's cash reserves equaled nearly a quarter of a trillion dollars at the end of 1997.
- Forty percent of all direct investment in the developing world in 1996—$42 billion—flowed into China. Only the U.S. received more foreign investment. In 1997, the numbers were even higher. The Asian financial crisis chilled investor ardor for much of 1998, but by the end of the year the money began to flow again.

Except for the education, these things have happened nearly overnight. The ramifications of China's emergence will reach into every corner of the global marketplace, changing the traditional workplace in nation after nation. And the world is not ready for what's coming. That is the view of many respected observers, including Jeffrey Garten, dean of the Yale School of Management and author of *The Big Ten: The Big Emerging Markets and How They Will Change Our Lives* (Basic Books, 1997). Writing in the *Financial Times* (London), Garten responded to suggestions that western economic policy and practice would help reform China with this sobering assessment: "China is likely to change the global capitalist system as much as it will be disciplined by it. And the West is not remotely ready for the tumultuous dislocations ahead. China is not Argentina or Poland. Its birth as an economic force will not be plain sailing for the rest of the world. . . . China's emergence as a full participant in the global marketplace will be as disruptive as the rise to power of the U.S. at the turn of the century, or Germany and Japan in subsequent decades." The issue isn't just how to integrate China into the global marketplace, explains Kenneth Courtis, a Tokyo global economic strategist at Deutsche-Bank, "It's how to make room at the top."

China's impact on the traditional workplace throughout the global marketplace will be felt in deep and abiding ways, contends Garten.

- *First,* China is sure to become a "phenomenal export machine. The pace of its exports has been growing at three times the world average. China is set to displace much of the sales of low-cost manufactured goods from Thailand, Malaysia, Indonesia and the Philippines, worsening their economic problems. Moreover, it is fast moving upmarket, selling more sophisticated manufactured products, such as computer parts." In keeping with Garten's assessment, the World Bank projects that China will be the second-largest exporter in the world within 25 years—behind the U.S. and dwarfing Japan.

- *Second,* China will become a "bottomless pit for foreign capital, creating problems for countries that desperately need foreign investment." In the 1990s alone, capital flowed into the country at a rate five times previous investment levels. And this is only the beginning. "So far, nearly all this capital inflow has gone only to the coastal

71

provinces, and most has come from Hong Kong companies. As China's investment policies become more open, as other parts of the country begin to stir, as a $600-billion program of physical infrastructure takes shape, a flood of new foreign money can be expected."

- **Third,** China will continue to play by different rules, much like Japan has done for decades. Pushing exports while holding down imports is typical. In the first seven months of 1997, Chinese exports were up 26 percent, imports only 1.9 percent. In the fashion of Japan and South Korea, Beijing is creating giant state-assisted and directed conglomerates in key industries like electronics, petrochemicals and automobiles. "To the extent that these maverick policies succeed, they will provide an alternative to the American model of capitalism," Garten writes.

In light of these developments, the question arises, "Will China represent just another very large addition to the global marketplace, or will it force its Asian neighbors and the West into unwanted change?" Given the powerful capitalist currents loose in the global economy, Garten expects a lot of both.

These kinds of things are not reflected in government employment statistics, but jobholders everywhere are inevitably impacted by them, perhaps none more than employees in the West.

Faced with the looming prospects of the likes of China as both customer and competitor, is there any wonder why western employers scramble to "right-size" so as to match up better in the hardball game of global commerce? Not to do so is to become superfluous in a hurry. There's a saying, reckoned to be an old African proverb, that describes the situation well. It goes something like this:

> *Every morning in Africa, a lion awakes and knows*
> *that it must outrun the slowest of gazelles or it will starve.*
>
> *Every morning, a gazelle rises and understands*
> *that it must run faster than the fastest lion*
> *or it will die.*
>
> *It makes no difference if you are a lion or a gazelle.*
> *When the sun comes up, you'd better be running.*

Employers are not going to find workers in the West who are willing to work for $10 a day as they do in China. So, in running to stay alive in the global marketplace, western employers downsize to reduce labor costs as much as possible; employ "just-in-time" personnel to fill in when and where needed and only when and where needed; adopt labor-saving technology at every opportunity; move "transportable" jobs away from high-priced labor to low-cost labor; and otherwise maneuver to compensate for the human resource and productivity advantages held by the competition in developing nations.

It makes no difference if you are a lion or a gazelle. When the sun comes up, you'd better be running.

– Old African proverb

The clear losers in all this are those who aspire to the elusive, career-long, well-paying traditional permanent job "like Dad had, back in the old days." It just doesn't seem fair. Fairness—it's a valid theme and central to age-old tensions between labor and management. How can it be fair, for example, to move soccer ball manufacturing from the American rust belt where the going wage might be $15 per hour, to Pakistan where 12-year-old children do the job for as little as 50 cents a day. "It's not fair," proclaim U.S. workers. "Americans can't compete with 'slave wages.' "

Lost in this legitimate argument is the economic reality that the soccer ball manufacturer can't sell product that has a cost basis of $12 per ball when the competition, with third-world labor, sells the same item for $10. "It's not fair to work a child long, hard hours for 50 cents a day," proclaim child-labor critics. Missed in the debate is the reality of life in Pakistan and other developing countries. There, the 50-cent daily wage doesn't have anything to do with what's fair; it has to do with survival. Steady cash jobs in local economies are few and far between in the Pakistans of the world. That 50-cent-a-day job may well mean the difference between eating from a small sack of rice or eating out of the local dump. To make judgments in the prosperous West about the fairness of working a Pakistani child for 50 cents a day is to miss the point. What's at stake here is not what's fair, or even what's right or wrong; it's how to make the system work for all parties, including employees, regardless of the country in which they labor.

Pushing the soccer ball maker to give the Pakistani jobs to someone else isn't fair to the Pakistani children, not if they are doing the job well for the agreed price. Pushing the manufacturer to pay a non-competitive wage is not fair either, not without additional value in return. It's a proven formula for closing down businesses and losing jobs altogether. What probably is fair is for the international community to develop some type of mechanism to force business and investors to pay into a fund specifically targeted to raising the education and skills level of third-world workers so that the value of their work increases and, with that, their pay. The idea is not as wild as it seems. Nobel prize-winning economist James Tobin of Yale University has long advocated a tax on foreign exchange transactions to slow the movement of capital across national borders and help prevent the kind of wild currency gyrations that brought much of the global marketplace to its knees in 1998. In light of that experience, Tobin's proposal is being reexamined by governments everywhere. Tobin's tax would create some financial disincentive for traders to move large blocks of money into one economy when prospects are good, then snatch it out at the first sign of a better deal. A small tax of one- or two-tenths of a percent on every currency or securities exchange between nations could accumulate hundreds of billions a year, estimates Tobin. One reason the idea never achieved wide acceptance is the issue of what to do with the huge pool of accumulated cash. Some have suggested that it be used to fund the United Nations. Environmental remediation and other uses have been proposed. I suggest that revenue generated by the likes of a "Tobin tax" could not be better used than upgrading the skills and education of those Pakistani soccer ball makers and their ilk throughout the poor nations of the world. Without improved skills and better bargaining positions, third-world workers will continue to compete against themselves to the detriment of all. For, given the opportunities available in the global marketplace, business is going to go where it can get the best value for the dollar. That's just the way it is. It's up to the labor force, and their representatives, to learn how to play by the new rules of the game. The truth of this is not

> To make judgments in the prosperous West about the fairness of working a Pakistani child for 50 cents a day is to miss the point. What's at stake here is not what's fair, or even what's right or wrong; it's how to make the system work for all parties, including employees, regardless of the country in which they labor.

confined to manufacturing or third-world wages. Think back to the UPS strike in the summer of 1997.

On the essential issue of fairness, the International Brotherhood of Teamsters shut down the largest parcel delivery service in the world. The avowed point of contention was the company's use of part-time workers. Sixty percent of the UPS workforce worked part-time—20 hours a week for an average of about $9.00 per hour and full employee benefits. Altogether, the compensation package amounted to an hourly expenditure of $11.00 or more for each part-timer. But the union argued that so much reliance on part-time labor was unfair. The company, of course, thought it quite fair. And the public joined in the debate—who's right and who's wrong, the union or management? Both sides had their positions, each one vigorously defended. But what's fair, and who's right and who's wrong are the wrong questions to ask in today's workplace. As crass as it may seem, the proper question is "How do I get mine? How do I make the system work for me?" ("Me" being employee and employer; the "system" being the free-enterprise system.) UPS has clearly discovered how to make the system work to its benefit: operate lean and efficiently, computerize, bring in technology where possible to reduce labor costs, and fill part-time jobs with part-time personnel to further control costs and improve competitiveness. It works well for the company and has since 1907. The approach generates lots of jobs (185,000 drivers, loaders and sorters alone—before the strike); it creates wealth, pays taxes and mortgages and college tuitions, and suits a great many students and others desiring part-time work just fine. But the union didn't focus on the right question and, so, came up with the wrong answer. Make full-time work of part-time work, reduce productivity, increase costs and open the door for competition to take away business. The upshot of the labor action was the loss of 15,000 part-timers who couldn't wait around with no income while the issue was resolved, a reduction in pre-strike business volume that took 18 months to recoup and the forfeiture of $750 million in corporate revenue. It's hard to see how organized labor wins by reducing an employer's market share and competitiveness.

Had the Teamster's Union asked the question, "How do I make the system work for my membership?" the answer would ultimately have come around to something like this:

75

- Train my people, increase their skills so that they bring additional value to their work for UPS or anyone else.
- Create competition for the skills and value the part-timers bring to their work. (Nothing like losing good, skilled people to the competition to improve respect and earnings.)
- Find additional employment for the part-timers to flesh out a full 40-hour week.
- Sell the membership on the virtues and job security in *FlexLife®* careers.

"How do I make today's workplace work for me?" That's the crux of this book. Me, meaning those most affected by the changes examined thus far: employees, those who work for a living; employers, those who employ the skills and labor of others; public policymakers, those who regulate or would regulate the workplace; labor unions, those who represent the working man or woman; and labor exchange services, those who would be "everyman's agent." Each party has a critical role to play in the new workplace. I would like to turn now to an analysis of those roles and how each party can best serve its own best interests. The intent, in every case, is to make sense of the tumultuous workplace before us and to advance each party's prospects in the years ahead. Let us start first with employees.

Chapter Three

You don't have to be Michael Jordan to get an agent.

Making the new workplace work for employees

"If you find yourself in a work milieu demanding that you sell your soul for the company, then the solution is simple. Get out." That's the sentiment of a fine author of a well-regarded new book on balancing work with life. While I don't necessarily disagree with the thinking, I recognize that the advice is easier given than taken, especially when the job at stake is not your own. The great majority of people need their jobs or they wouldn't have them in the first place. And to simply "get out" begs the question "and into what?" Are other employers going to demand less of your time? Are they somehow immune to the competitive pressures that pare payrolls throughout the workplace, dumping more and more work on fewer and fewer employees? Is there another job out there with the same pay, benefits, convenience and prospects for the future as the one you are advised to get out of? Is that job yours for the taking, when you want it? Given the demands of the distasteful all-consuming job, is there time left in the business day to adequately explore new career pursuits?

Getting out of a stifling, barely tolerable job is certainly an attractive notion, but it is not always practical. Of course, more and more, the decision to "get out or not" is often made for you. Downsizing, outsourcing, re-engineering—these actions remove the decision-making from the employee's hands. And if there's anything worse than the anxiety of an all-consuming job, it's the anxiety of no job at all. As traditional permanent jobs (TPJ) shift out from under large sectors of the workforce, and the pace of global events forces workplace changes at astounding speed, employees can no longer just stand still, hoping that they will be the exception and not the rule. But, what to do? How do you prepare for the "flexible workplace" encroaching from every direction? There are but two ways:

- Fight 'em
- Join 'em

Fight 'em

Fight the trend by positioning yourself to keep the traditional permanent job you already have. The surest way to do that is to become "indispensable." Egos aside, that is more achievable than one might expect. Employee retention, after all, is a function of scarcity. The less there are of the special skills, talent and/or labor absolutely necessary to the conduct of a business, the more valuable those attributes are, and the more likely they are to be retained. Indeed, employers will tolerate a lot of aggravation from an employee critical to the success of the business. Another way to "stick" with one employer is to be flexible enough to move elsewhere in the organization to fill needs or when your current job loses its "indispensability." Lateral moves within an organization are not exactly the job security of old, but they can keep you in the mix and lead to new career opportunities, especially when re-training is part of the package. Walk through a little mental exercise, for a moment. If your employer were forced into drastic downsizing measures, who would be retained to maintain the productivity, corporate culture and operational continuity necessary to perform as needed? Identify those critical positions and functions—high-tech to the most menial—and you put your finger on the "core staff" that lies at the very heart of the organization. These people constitute the organization's "process owners." They possess the philosophies that distinguish the firm from others. They define the corporate culture and take care that it is preserved. Process owners determine the identity of the company and its products and services. And they establish the basic processes, procedures, systems and methods to run the show. Scattered throughout the organization in high places and low, process owners are scarce, very important people. Does your job fall within the purview of the core staff, do you add glue to the organization in just the right places? If there is some question in your mind about the answers to either of those questions, and you want to be one of those left standing when the smoke of downsizing clears, you are advised to push your skills and performance comfortably inside the circle drawn around the core staff.

Increasingly, core-staff positions are the last bastion of traditional permanent jobs. Nearly everyone who doesn't fit the core-staff profile lacks the job security normally associated with traditional permanent jobs. What criteria do employers use to decide who constitutes the core staff? One way or the other, employers make core-staff decisions based on the scarcity of critical skills, including a fair share of intangibles— qualities like:

Loyalty – While loyalty has morphed into a less constraining version of the original, it is vital in core-staff jobs. Loyalty remains a necessity for any organization. It doesn't have to come from everyone who draws a paycheck, but loyalty does need to be present in sufficient depth to provide operational integrity and continuity. With so many people coming and going in the modern workplace, loyalty must abide in the core staff.

Keeper of Tradition – Holders of core-staff positions must know the organization's history and persona, its philosophy, aspirations and special niche in the big picture, then convey that knowledge to all comers, especially the flexible workforce. New employees, full-time or just-in-time, need to know the organization's traditions to perform effectively. And the organization needs the continuity to maintain its identity in the marketplace.

Guardian of the Way – If not core staff, who would new employees turn to for how things are done, where the bones are buried, who the chief players are inside and outside the organization, why certain procedures and processes are followed, how systems work, what the customs are? And who else would see that processes and methods, systems and procedures do not drift into ineffectiveness and obsolescence?

Flexibility – Core-staff personnel hold traditional permanent jobs, but these people must be flexible nevertheless. From an operational point of view, core staff must be flexible enough to accommodate and facilitate the coming and going of the flexible workforce. It will fail without sufficient core staff in all the right places, ready and willing to assist, to bind the workplace together. Furthermore, employers recognize that the best management talent is flexible, adaptable and cross-trained. Rarely anymore do managers rise through an organization steeped solely in finance, marketing, operations or any other single set of skills. Atlanta-based BellSouth, for one, does not consider executives for senior management positions who do not have experience in international operations. The MIS vice president who studies for an MBA degree, the director of corporate communications with a background in foreign languages—these are skill combinations that ensure employability in today's workplace.

Knowledge Management – As the glue that holds an organization together, all core staff must be willing and capable of teaching corporate tradition, past experience, history, processes, methods, procedures and systems when and where necessary. It's vital that this body of knowledge not be lost. The teaching process, however, is hardly ever a formal classroom exercise, but more a function of the ever present helping hand, tips, impromptu instruction, patience, sensitivity to the insecurities of flexible employees and a hundred and one other small acts that make up a normal workday in a typical organization.

Ambassador - There must be those who will speak up in support of the organization, internally and in the marketplace. If it is true that an organization is defined by how it is perceived, then who is to advance and maintain that perception? Certainly, the responsibility falls to those who remain a fixture in the organization year after year, whether they be senior manager, executive secretary or forklift operator on the warehouse loading dock.

These intangible assets are implicit requirements of every core-staff position, whether specified in the job description or not.

Employers may not use the terminology noted here; they may not even be aware of the selection process that results in the creation of a "core staff." But, one way or the other, sooner than later, every successful employer will build its organization on a tight, well-defined core staff and fill in around it "as needed" with flexible employees of one kind or another.

The benefits of core-staff jobs are obvious: job security, health insurance, retirement plans, paid vacations, regular pay raises, steady advancement and so on. These are jobs still highly coveted in the modern workplace. Yet, the principal drawback to such positions is the requirement to "sell your soul to the company" in return for the security provided. If that is an acceptable price, go to work to position yourself among the core staff. Or if you want to get a traditional permanent job, the same strategy applies. But keep in mind that core-staff jobs, by definition, are tough to obtain. Competition, technology and experience with flexible forms of employment converge to reduce the core staff to smaller and smaller percentages of a given organization's workforce. That means all other positions come without the job security of traditional permanent jobs. You may find this intolerable and opt to "get out" of the situation by searching for a core-staff position elsewhere. Or you might find the security you want in a *FlexLife®* career. If you can't fight 'em, join 'em.

> *The benefits of core staff jobs are obvious: job security, health insurance, retirement plans, paid vacations, regular pay raises, steady advances and so on. . . . Yet, the principal drawback to such positions is the requirement to "sell your soul to the company". . . .*

Join 'em

If the trend is to flexible forms of employment, perhaps you shouldn't fight it. Job security is not confined to traditional permanent jobs. Become a FlexLifer. Leave the long hours and constant pressure to the core staff; take control of your own life and career. Despite all that's happened to create instability in the workplace, employers cannot perform without the skills, talent and/or labor employees possess. The workplace has changed, and there's no end to the changes in sight. But that doesn't mean you don't have options. Quite the contrary. Job security and career management are no longer stipulations in the implied social contract employers have with employees. But in the absence of job security there is employment security that is just as good, if not better. The loss of traditional career paths laid out by employers is replaced by self-guided careers where you set the course and control the process, where you get a job and a life, and your identity becomes what you do and not who you work for. True, you may be looking at a "career labyrinth," as the Roper Report calls it, but it's more attuned to the times than conventional career management. "In today's evolving workplace," reports Roper Starch Worldwide in the Randstad North America *Employee Review*, "belief in climbing the [career] ladder may be an ideal, but it may no longer be a reality. Instead, many employees seek further development and training through programs that can result in a career labyrinth, where advancement can be horizontal, diagonal, vertical, or all of these." Why is this important? The report lists some very compelling reasons:

- Companies today are more inclined to build a leaner, flatter corporate structure, which itself collapses the ladder.
- Baby Boomers, some of whom are still 20-plus years away from retirement, now occupy many mid- and upper-level positions, which limits opportunities for promotion that characterize the career ladder.
- Team-based approaches to projects emphasize problem solving by individuals contributing to the team's effort, instead of focusing on individual task-oriented efforts.

Many employers, therefore, have turned from traditional career management to a variety of training and development strategies that add to an employee's portfolio of skills. Increased "employment security" is the result.

For these workplace changes to accrue to your benefit, however, you must get comfortable with the new rules and understand that there can be security and permanency in what used to be insecure and temporary. And you must have skills employers demand with sufficient regularity to keep you busy and well-compensated. *FlexLife®* is a function of the specialization of the workplace. Period. It makes no difference whether the skills are those of a good crane operator, concrete worker, travel consultant or nuclear physicist. The key is that what you do (i.e., your workplace competence) is needed by employers. The very process of applying your skills in a variety of job assignments makes for a more experienced and valuable employee. Smart employers will advance your career with challenging responsibility and in-house training and support. The better labor exchange services will help train and prepare you for the workplace. But it's left to you, the employee, to look after your own future by developing and honing skills that make you a valuable commodity in the marketplace. Rita Carey, author of *Work in the 21st Century*, makes the point: "Staying current in one's field will become an individual responsibility. Reading professional journals and business magazines; joining professional and community associations; and participating in education/training programs will become increasingly important to all workers, but will require greater individual initiative from those not on the employer's regular payroll. . . . What does all this mean to those of us who want and need to work? It means that we have to compete for our jobs. Job security will reside with the individual—through acquisition of the required knowledge and skills for today's marketplace. Our package of capabilities must be current in order to remain valuable to the organization in which we want to make our contributions. The graduate degree of the '70s will not cut the mustard. Employers today are asking questions such as 'What book have you read recently about this field? What training programs have you completed recently? What do you think the greatest challenge is to this industry? How proficient are you in the XYZ computer software?' Lifelong learning will be a prerequisite to meaningful employment in the 21st century."

There's nothing to fear for those who seize on the opportunities afforded by *FlexLife*®. About the only people who will suffer in the new workplace are the die-hard generalists, the "well-rounded, jack-of-all-trades, master-of-none" dinosaurs so typical of early Baby Boomers. Back in the 1960s and '70s, people could get by on personality, chutzpa, connections, family ties and a little aptitude for a variety of things. But not so in the workplace before us. Marketable skills are a necessity. To be a generalist within a given skill set is to increase your value in the job market; to be cross-trained in two or more skill sets is to ensure your employability. But to move into the workplace as an untrained, inexperienced worker is to put yourself in a precarious situation.

IT'S OK

Downsizing in all its many forms has become a fact of life in the modern workplace in both good times and bad. Traditional Permanent Jobs (TPJ) are no longer looked upon with favor by employers in developed economies. Job security is a relic of another era. But, all in all, it's OK. The new workplace develops solutions to meet the demand of the times.

EMPLOYERS	EMPLOYEES
• Beginning to treat human resources (HR) as an economic resource.	• When treated as an economic resource, workers may begin to lose their sense of loyalty. Giving their all for the team suffers.
• Beginning to employ workers on an "as-need" basis more and more.	• Job security disappears, worker anxiety increases.
• Jobs become more specialized.	• Education and training requirements increase; generalists find it harder to get a job.
• Continuity of labor supply becomes a critical issue.	• Continuity of employment security improves for those with skills and capabilities demanded by the workplace.
• The need for professional staffing agents or some other effective "labor exchange" device to fill employer needs grows rapidly. And the needs of employers are reconciled with the skills, talent and/or labor available in the workplace.	• The need for professional staffing agents or some other effective "labor exchange" device to keep skilled employees gainfully employed grows rapidly. And the employment needs of employees are reconciled with the demands of the job market.

How do employees make the new workplace work for them? What does it take to dig job security and the good life out of a succession of job assignments? How does "job-hopping" translate into stability, employability and fulfilling career? It all begins with a reality check and some serious self-evaluation.

Reality Check

1. Job security is increasingly difficult to find, and you'd better start looking for it in non-traditional places. (But that's OK. There are

attractive alternative careers aplenty outside the old familiar workplace).

2.   Flexible employment arrangements are proven cost-cutting tactics, and employers everywhere embrace the concept.

3.   The traditional employee/employer relationship has changed. Employers can no longer afford the paternal cradle-to-grave protection of the workforce as in the past. Survival is the first responsibility of business, not job security for workers. But that's OK. There is a new employment paradigm to take the place of the old—the three-party relationship of employee/agent/employer. And it works just fine. The change is the result of plain old free-market economics, working on a global scale. In this setting, you have to learn how to make the system work for you.

4.   Loyalty is not dead, it's reallocated. One is loyal to a faithful partner, someone or some thing that stands by you through thick and thin, that looks out for your best interests, that advances your cause at every opportunity. While that may no longer be your employer, it certainly fits the definition of a good FlexLife agent.

5.   Career management no longer consists of a ladder placed before you by the employer with tacit instructions to "climb here." You, the employee, must take on the responsibility of guiding your own career. Training, seminars, education, skill enhancement of every other stripe—it all falls to you and/or your agent. And that's OK. The two of you are sufficient for the task. This is a scary proposition for many people accustomed to doing things the "company way." But to those who have a sense of where they want to go in life, managing one's own career is the best of all worlds. Who else is going to give it more attention? Who else can be counted on to put your interests ahead of all others?

6.   A succession of short-term job assignments can be a very attractive career path, especially with an agent preparing the way, apprised beforehand of your tastes and desires, strengths and weaknesses, expectations and career goals.

7.   A succession of short-term job assignments can pay better than a traditional permanent job if managed well.

8.   The parochial view of work is dying the same slow death as the traditional permanent job. Nine-to-five, Monday through Friday.

Carpooling with the gang from the office. Relocation every three to five years. Growing old and senior on the job, the years measured by increased pay, more responsibility, a bigger desk, fatter retirement benefits. But it's OK. New routines are being established, and opportunities abound.

9.   Prepare yourself in advance for the irrevocable forces churning the workplace, or wait for downsizing to push you from the nest where it's fly or crash, ready or not.

Self-Evaluation

Now, self-evaluation time. How would you rate your present lifestyle, job included? If you are happy with it, and confident that things will continue in the same vein, no sweat. Skip this chapter. But if you are searching for a better way, then give some thought to the benefits of *FlexLife*®

1.   Full-time employment arranged by a professional staffing specialist whose livelihood is tied to keeping you as busy as you wish to be.

2.   Flexibility and control over who you work for, when you work for them and how long you work. Time off becomes your election, and need not fit some department head's posted vacation schedule. If an assignment becomes unbearable, fire the employer and move on to the next assignment. There is no intent here to suggest a lack of commitment to an employer or to the job, once on the job. FlexLifers must be reliable above all. But they can arrange job assignments around their schedules, their interests, their preferences. And they don't have to put up with a bad situation for fear of losing their jobs. The next assignment awaits.

3.   Skills refinement and growth by virtue of multiple assignments in a variety of job situations, all utilizing your skill set.

4.   Employment security derived of market demand for advanced skills acquired of wide experience.

5.   Increasing pay for proven expertise and added value.

6.   Health insurance, retirement benefits, paid holidays and vacations, training and the other perquisites of traditional permanent jobs.

7.   The prestige and status afforded the successful entrepreneur or independent contractor.

8.   Career management of your own design, supported and assisted by

a personal FlexLife agent.

9. Then there's that full-time job offer you can't refuse. What better way to resolve all doubt than a short-term job assignment to test the waters? Temp-to-hire. According to the National Association of Temporary and Staffing Services (NATSS), 40 percent of just-in-time employees are offered full-time positions at an office where they worked.

How do these benefits stack up with your present job situation? Looks interesting, you say? If so, let's go further.

There are three requirements for a successful *FlexLife®* career:

1. Competencies that employers are willing to pay for (i.e., skills, talent, labor, experience).
2. Employers that need the competencies you possess.
3. An intermediary to match "1" and "2."

A person's competencies are what he or she has to sell in the job market. They are what create employment security. Enthusiasm, dedication, integrity, hard work, personality and perseverance are important "soft skills" that enhance a person's employment appeal. But without marketable competencies, well-matched to employer needs, those soft skills alone will not move one far up the flexible employment scale—towards *FlexLife®*. From pretty and glamorous as fashion design to ugly and plain as plumbing repair, employee skills run the gamut of human imagination and enterprise. And a great many of these competencies are in demand throughout the workplace. Purchasing, for example, is a universal requirement in every organization of any size. Do it well for one employer, upgrade the skill with training, seminars and conferences, and many other employers could make good use of the competency at least part of the time. Risk management skills are a constant need in today's litigious societies, and they are quite transportable. And the more the competency is stretched and tempered in different job settings, the more skillful and valuable the employee becomes. Equipment handling, systems operations, scheduling, legal services, architectural know-how, media production, bookkeeping, inventory control, accounting expertise, data entry and retrieval, marketing and sales—on and on it goes, universal competencies that could be done for a succession of employers rather than just one.

Think about it. Are your skills of a kind that employers would employ them as need arises, if only for the duration of the need? If not, you should give serious thought to upgrading your competencies or acquiring new ones so as not to be left among the poorly employed if the workplace spits you out on the street for some reason or another.

How do your competencies add up? Tally your skills, know-how, experience, education, training and other assets to determine what competencies you and/or an agent might sell in the workplace. Jot them down in a format reflective of a proper *FlexLife®* resume, a personal skills marketing tool that stresses what you do rather than how long and dutifully you have served any single employer.

Human resource (HR) departments everywhere are still prone to evaluate personnel on "job stability," though the practice is at odds with how competency-based credentials should be presented or analyzed. New times call for new recruiting and selecting processes, starting with the traditional employee resume. But like so much of what's going on in the workplace today, the art and science of selling one's skills in the flexible job market have not kept pace with the churn of business. While there are many good resume services available to job seekers, I venture some suggestions on how best to craft a competency-based *FlexLife®* resume.

First, state right up front "what you do."

I am a clay artist, presently working in high-fire stoneware with cone 10 reduction glazes, as well as earthenware pieces that are low-fired in an electric kiln.

That's how Layna Portugal recently positioned herself in the ceramics trade.

Padgett Brown is a professional business writer and author with 20 years of major-market experience to his credit. He is a skilled and honored communicator in the areas of motivation and performance in the workplace, environmental enterprise, the emergence of the flexible workforce.

There you have one writer's description of what he does.

Make note of your Web site. If you don't have one, get one. In the modern workplace, he or she who steps forward the quickest, with the best credentials and most compelling story to tell, usually gets hired, over and over again. Today, there is no faster way to convey your competencies than the Internet. Use it, or fall behind those who do.

Somewhere, state that you are a *FlexLife*® careerist and define the term.

FlexLife® *is a self-managed, full-time career of short-term job assignments strung together by a professional staffing agent. The agent provides employee benefits, assists with the FlexLifer's professional growth and development and represents him or her in the workplace.*

This disclosure distinguishes you from a mere "temp" or conventional job seeker. It also puts you on a different plane with employers. You come to work as an acknowledged short-timer, and will leave at assignment's end. You have other work to go to. You are covered by employee benefits, so there's less of a risk of employer liability on this matter later. You know what you're doing. And no one has to hold your hand. That provides a lot of security for employers, relieves them of some anxiety, and, ironically, increases your appeal as a prospective full-time employee. The confidence you exhibit by disclosing in the beginning "how you work," and the experience you bring to the job, will not work against full-time job offers from discriminating employers.

Next, highlight your skills and experience in enough detail to convey the depth and breadth of your competencies. Address the "learning curve" issue.

Professional media buyer skilled in negotiating and sustaining media buys with network, cable and syndicated channels. Experienced in prime time and sports programming, prescreen programs, Nielsen rating monitoring and reporting, inventory allocation, proposal analysis, post analyses of buys and negotiating additional units. Trained and accustomed to applying my competencies in a variety of challenging workplace settings, I am able to reach full productivity in a minimum of time.

What have you been able to accomplish with your skills? In a young person, the accomplishments may be relatively small and seemingly insignificant, but, carefully expressed, they always convey something of value to a prospective employer. Remember, results get employers' attention. Where possible, be specific about your accomplishments. Examples: cut shipping delays by 15 percent, improved market share by 10 percent, reduced development time by 10 weeks.

As a student teacher at Collins Montessori School, I was credited with an important role in reducing customer complaints by 17 percent.

Working with the chief labor negotiator for the Collins County School Board, I provided liaison that contributed to an amicable contract settlement with county teachers.

List your most recent/prominent job assignments, complete with starting and ending dates, direct supervisors and reference to letters of recommendation.

As a FlexLife® careerist, my competencies have been employed in the following job assignments:

- *xxxxxx*
- *xxxxxxx*
- *xxxxxx*

Letters of recommendation attached.

Letters of recommendation, for all their value as an indicator of a person's competencies, play a negligible role in the conventional job market. The reasons are simple: people who work five to ten years for one employer cannot be expected to produce many written endorsements of their work; and most severance situations are not conducive to glowing reports of a departing employee's competencies. But this is not the case for *FlexLife®* careerists. Job assignments in a normal year may be several in number. In just a few years, a dozen satisfied employers could experience a FlexLifer's competencies. By planning for this kind of endorsement at the beginning of job assignments—perhaps with a sample letter of recommendation—you will improve your employment security immeasurably. Of particular importance in a *FlexLife®* letter of recommendation is a reference to how much the person may have saved the employer in labor costs compared to a full-time employee, and a statement that the individual's services helped preserve the employer's flexibility in the marketplace. These things may be addressed as the conclusion of a sample letter of recommendation. Something like this:

> *The task Ms. Schippers performed so ably saved my organization _____ percent of the cost of a full-time employee capable of the work. By filling our needs "when needed, and only as needed," Ms. Schippers not only saved us money but helped the firm to maintain the flexibility we need to compete successfully in the challenging business of _____ .*

Introduce your "representation" or agent.

> *Represented in the workplace by Universal Staffing Services of SomeTown, Anyplace, XX. Staffing agent Lisa Fox; employee benefits provided by the agency.*

Post your availability.

> *I am currently working on assignment with _____ until April 30, 2001. Thereafter, I am available without break through December 2001. Contact my staffing agent for details.*

Specify educational credentials, including training courses, seminars, workshops, professional affiliations and other skill-enhancing activities.

BS Economics, Eastern Oregon University, LaGrande, OR, 1985.
Certificate, European Telephone Switch Repair course, Siemens,
Munich, Germany, 1987. Continuing Education, Information Systems,
Cochise College, Sierra Vista, Arizona, 1989.

Finally, indicate any special qualifications that reflect favorably on
your value as an employee, including sabbaticals.

Dual citizen of the U.S. and the United Kingdom.
Lived overseas in Vienna, London and Marrakech.
Six-month sabbatical as laborer with Habitat for Humanity, Bolivia.

Fleshed out fully, a typical *FlexLife*® resume might look like this:

Connor Foster

FlexLife® careerist skilled in international sales and marketing, advertising and promotion, customer service, negotiations and the management of same.

Represented in the workplace by Universal Staffing Services
of SomeTown, Anywhere, XX 00000
Staffing Agent Lisa Fox (657) 657-6576 / Fax (657) 567-5675
See Web site at CFoster@aol.com

SKILLS – *Trained and experienced in macroeconomics, international market research, market plan development and implementation, joint-venture and licensing negotiations, contract supervision and team management. Highly proficient in MS Word, Excel, Access, Lotus, Datastream, Reuters 2000 and various statistical packages. Proficient in spoken and written Spanish and French, and spoken Mandarin Chinese. Accustomed to applying my competencies in a variety of workplace settings, and am able to reach full productivity in short time.*

ACCOMPLISHMENTS –
- As an intern, analyzed over $70 billion in international trade activities for XYZ Corporation that targeted three new markets for the company's product.
- As one of a three-person advance team, helped Jean Pierre Fragrances of Luxembourg penetrate the Chinese cosmetics market. Through joint-venture and licensing agreements, the team's actions generated $17 million in sales in three years and achieved a 7-percent market share.
- Devised a marketing strategy for Cleveland-based Green Steel Products that cut delivery time by nine weeks and increased sales in 1966 by 11 percent.

CURRENT ASSIGNMENT –
- July 1998 to Present – Green Steel Products, Cleveland, OH. Wrapping up marketing plans for breaking into the Canadian specialty business. Direct Supervisor: Brent Randolph, 770-770-0770. Letter of recommendation attached.

PREVIOUS ASSIGNMENTS –
- October 1996 to March 1998 – Jean Pierre Fragrances, Luxembourg, Belgium. Direct Supervisor: Melissa Baerlein-Fath, 1-11-609-54678. Letter of recommendation attached.
- September 1993 to August 1996 – XYZ Corporation, Anywhere, XX. Direct Supervisor: James Wright, 809-445-8090. Letter of recommendation attached.

EDUCATION – American University, Beirut, Lebanon, BS International Marketing; Emory University, Atlanta, GA, Master of Business Administration.

PROFESSIONAL OBJECTIVES – To remain at the edge of international sales and marketing developments in the rapidly evolving global marketplace.

BACKGROUND – Born 3-17-65, Omaha, Nebraska; Dual citizen of the U.S. and United Kingdom. Divorced, one child, Dean, age 8.

FlexLife® is a self-managed full-time career of short-term job assignments strung together by a professional staffing agent. The agent provides employee benefits, assists with the FlexLifer's professional growth and development and represents him or her in the workplace

There's more to *FlexLife*® than marketable skills, a good resume and the willingness to forge a career from a succession of short-term job assignments. You really ought to get an agent. A good agent can put order and equity back into the old employee/employer relationship distorted by global competition and the downsizing phenomena that followed. The good news is that steady, reliable work is readily available, complete with the accouterments of traditional permanent jobs—if you don't mind a succession of short-term job assignments. This may read like a veiled promotion of the industry to which I am so closely tied. That's not my intent. It just works out that the staffing industry is the only institution available to the average working man and woman that can fill the role of "everyman's agent." As acknowledged earlier, the staffing business is not yet at a point where every staffing specialist is capable of being your personal representative in the workplace. Nor are there enough of these people to serve the general workplace. Nevertheless, the industry is evolving in this direction. And already there are plenty of good staffing consultants with an agent's predisposition and training. Explore the possibilities with prospective agents in your local market. The major players are listed in the Yellow Pages of the telephone directory under Employment Agencies—Temporary.

How do you find an agent, one suited to you and your skills? Try this:

1. Do some research on the staffing agencies represented in your local market. Go to the library and read their annual reports. Check out their Web pages. Invest in some general reading on the industry.
2. Place a few phone calls to likely agencies in the local market. Express your interest in a *FlexLife*® career, briefly state your competencies, and ask a few questions:
    *   Does the agency represent people with your skills?
    *   What employers does the agency serve?
    *   Is the agency plugged into the Internet search-and-recruiting pipeline and to what extent?
    *   Who in the agency might best represent a person with your competencies?
    *   Ask that person: "Do you consider yourself to be a staffing agent?" And get the person to explain what he or she means.

- Does the agency work for the staffing employee or the companies that hire or both?
- Determine how much affinity the prospective agent may have for your skills by asking if he or she has ever done your kind of work or represented those who have?
- If the answers to the previous questions prove acceptable, ask the prospective agent if it makes sense to meet and discuss the possibilities.

3. Go to the interview prepared with a resume (preferably in a *FlexLife*® format), samples of your work, if applicable, and your thinking and questions on a *FlexLife*® career.

4. With each prospective agent, describe your skills. Go over your career aspirations, objectives and plans. Relate your strengths and weaknesses, training needs and how you want to work (e.g., 40-hour weeks, 20-hour weeks, 8:00 a.m. to 3:00 p.m. only). Lay it all out on the table so that the prospective agent gets to know you.

5. Get a response from the prospective agent before going further. Be quiet. What you are looking for is a sense of whether the person is really interested in your career or just adding another body to the pool of available staffing personnel.

6. Ask what the prospective agent and his or her organization can do for you.
    - Can they offer challenging assignments in your field of expertise?
    - Can they keep you as busy as you wish to be?
    - Are they prepared to work with you on a career development plan, including necessary action plans to help get you to where you want to go?
    - Do they offer professional training in the basic skills of normal employment (e.g., computer software updates, communication skills, corporate culture)?
    - Do they offer professional training in how to be a successful FlexLifer?
    - How about your particular set of skills—any provisions for upgrading in that field?
    - Does the firm offer benefits? If so, what are the specifics and what costs do you incur?

7. Quiz the prospective agent about his or her background, education,

training and interests so that you come to know the person. An employee-agent relationship is a long-term affair, and you need to know the person who may be your partner.

8.   Weigh the positives and negatives of each prospective agent and agency, and make a choice.

9.   Monitor the agent's performance on an ongoing basis. If it fails to measure up to the standard promised, fire the agent and select another. Continue the process until you find one you can partner with for the long run.

Those who would pursue a *FlexLife®* career are obliged to put a lot of care in the selection of a staffing agent. It's through this medium that the successful match is made with employers, time after time, and career growth and continuity are achieved. A poor choice for staffing agent can result in intermittent income, underemployment and misadventure on the job. There are no winners in this situation. The good and diligent agent puts continuity in *FlexLife®* and quality in the career choice.

With an agent to push your competencies in the marketplace, what's left to launch you successfully on a *FlexLife®* career? Here are some other matters to consider:

Education – In the modern workplace, the requirement to expand your skills and competencies doesn't diminish for young or old. The gap between what you know and what the marketplace demands you know

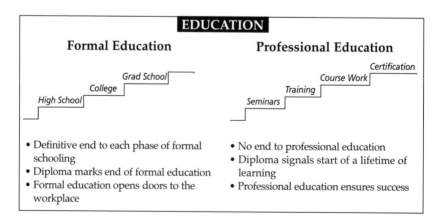

EDUCATION

Formal Education

Grad School
College
High School

- Definitive end to each phase of formal schooling
- Diploma marks end of formal education
- Formal education opens doors to the workplace

Professional Education

Certification
Course Work
Training
Seminars

- No end to professional education
- Diploma signals start of a lifetime of learning
- Professional education ensures success

changes rapidly. Closing that gap, and keeping it closed, is one of the real challenges for people in today's workplace, especially just-in-time workers. I have a young friend who is a promising disc jockey in a major U.S. market. He told me recently that he had learned about all he could at the station and thought it time to look for a new employer. I asked if he understood the technology behind the microphone, if he knew how to develop a "play list" of music to match the station's market niche, if he was doing anything to broaden his universe of knowledge so as to be more entertaining and relevant, if he was versed in the advertising end of the business? To these questions, he essentially answered "no." The point was made: my young friend had not learned all he could on the job and was relying primarily on a mellifluous voice. That blind spot and, more importantly, the mentality behind it, would ultimately inhibit this person's professional growth and development if he didn't wake up. This fellow's job description didn't call for him to become knowledgeable or proficient in other facets of the broadcast business. His manager, no doubt, is primarily interested in on-air performance, not his breadth of knowledge in the field. Nowhere, it seems, was anyone suggesting that this young man become a student of his profession, to learn it—on his own if necessary—top to bottom, left to right, front to back. Good career management calls for a student's proclivities about one's chosen occupation. Employment security depends on it. This sort of thing ought not to be left to employers or anyone else. Ultimately, it's the employee's responsibility to prepare himself or herself for a long and fruitful career.

Here are some suggestions for doing that:

1. Get serious about acquiring expertise in personal money management, financial planning and managing your time. In *FlexLife*® careers, paychecks can come at irregular intervals for varying amounts. You will have to learn how to budget and save. Unless you are established with a good staffing firm, there is no employer to take care of little things like payroll taxes, administering your retirement program, filing health insurance claims and a host of other services. You ought to know how to tend to these matters. Flexible job assignments normally have a starting and ending point. It's not the same as nine-to-five, five days a week, week after week after week. You may need some schooling in how to manage your time.

2. Check in with nearby colleges and universities. Much is going on in

the educational field to make curricula more relevant to the workplace. The University of California recently offered a special master's degree that updates the computer skills of engineering veterans. Multimedia techniques and digital networking theories are typical examples of the curriculum. The University System of Georgia studies ways to turn out better-prepared workers in a variety of fields, including information technology. Other states and educational systems are doing much the same thing, hoping to land quality job-creating industries by filling critical skill needs. Major corporations are partnering up with academia—all the way down to elementary school—to assist in the development of employable skills. In today's employment environment, you just may discover educational opportunities that did not exist a few years ago.

3.   When on the job, whether new hire or veteran, take advantage of the employer's training and development programs. And push the envelope for schooling and training outside the employer's traditional offerings. Sell management on the benefits the company will gain by improving your skills. Perhaps the firm will defray the costs of additional education or at least provide the flexibility necessary to attend classes. Get involved in cross-functional teams, if available, so as to expose yourself to career-broadening opportunities. Make suggestions for new and better ways to build staff competencies. Show a sincere interest in acquiring advanced skills, and doors may just open for you.

4.   When "between jobs," schedule some of your excess time to "go back to school" in your field of expertise—at least at the local library or the Internet, if not literally. Get up to speed on the marketplace, in general, and your business niche, in particular. Look for good cross-training opportunities to extrapolate your skill set as far as possible. The more you know in a given field, the less likely you will find yourself between jobs.

5.   Don't expect schools and colleges to turn you out into the workplace ready to hit the road running. If young, explore your field of interest in summer jobs. Get involved in intern programs early in your education. Look for work-study programs that give you on-the-job experiences not taught in academia. Ask for greater responsibility if the work is irrelevant. You may be pleasantly surprised. In the tight U.S.

labor market, many employers have recognized that dull, mindless internships are a good way to run off promising new workers. "If you want to be competitive, you really have to provide a meaningful experience," said Eileen Kohan, executive director for Career Services at New York City's Columbia University. Chase Manhattan Bank, for one, understands. "We want to have [interns] leave here with a good taste in their mouth about Chase, and you don't do that by having someone file all summer," acknowledged Gregg Knowles, vice president and manager of University Relations. Beyond challenging job assignments, seek out mentors who can show you the way. Volunteer to get as much exposure as possible to your chosen profession. Make yourself useful at every opportunity. Fix an eye on where you want to get to, and chart a course, with management if possible, without it if need be.

Loyalty – We covered the topic for core-staff personnel earlier in this chapter. But what about FlexLifers—free agents with no ties to a single workplace? To whom is loyalty dispensed—if at all—in the typical employment relationship in which they operate? Yes, we know from the Roper Report and empirical evidence that the definition of loyalty has changed, but that doesn't really address the question, "To whom is loyalty dispensed if you are a Flexlifer?" Some contend that loyalty ought to flow to the source of one's paycheck. Depending on the employment relationship, that could be either the employer or a labor exchange service of some sort. Others say loyalty is dead, particularly in the flexible employment realm. But loyalty is more complex and noble than that. It doesn't just die because the old employer/employee relationship changes. Certainly, loyalty is owed the employer for whom one labors, no matter the temporary nature of the assignment. Such loyalty cannot be expected to reach the depth of a core staff employee's, nor is it necessary. The requirement for assignment personnel is primarily to perform well, honor the "rules and style of the house," speak well of the employer or not at all, and hold confidential sensitive information to which the employee may have become privy. Besides the ethics involved, there are perfectly good business reasons for being loyal to any employer, regardless of the length of time spent on the job. Repeat business—using you over and over again—springs from performance and the loyalty you displayed.

Loyalty is also owed one's agent, the deep abiding kind of loyalty traditionally reserved for "the good employer." The agency pays the staffing employee's income, provides employee benefits including job training, places him or her on assignment, bills the customer and assists in the management of the person's career. The major difference, of course, is that the staffing agency is not the employee's place of work. At its best, the staffing or FlexLife agent is the just-in-time worker's partner, an alter-ego that makes the person whole in the workplace. For this, the worker's loyalty is warranted.

Finally, FlexLifers must be loyal to themselves and what they are doing. The job won't just be there Monday morning like traditional permanent jobs if the flexibly employed don't follow the plan and tend to business. "This above all, to thine own self be true," advised Polonius in Shakespeare's *Hamlet*. It's excellent management advice for the *FlexLife*® careerist.

Reputation Protection – An organization's greatest asset is its reputation. A good one masks a lot of shortcomings, a bad one can drag down the best of capabilities. The importance of reputation applies no less to FlexLifers. And since they manage their own careers, their reputations cannot be left to the public relations department. They are the keepers of their own public perception, and they must comport themselves accordingly. Some fairly logical do's and don'ts are in order for just-in-time specialists. Don't go into a job assignment without quizzing your staffing consultant on the employer's corporate culture, house style, dress code and idiosyncrasies. Use your head. Walking into a new job situation overdressed, underdressed or inappropriately dressed is a mistake. If you are into body piercing, tattoos and painted hair, save it for after-hours. Don't be party to sexual allusions or innuendoes. Save discussions of politics, religion and other personal ideologies for friends and family. Watch that you don't cut into the production of others with too much chatter. Show up at the appointed hour and stay as the job prescribes. Be diligent. Be a team player. Bring your best attitude to the job. Perform at your best. Give value-plus for value received. When in doubt, ask; don't just experiment. Leave a good impression. Your reputation in the job market either verifies your competencies or belies them. Guard well how you are perceived as a staffing employee. Your career depends on it.

Ambassador – By the sheer weight of their value, competence and comportment, assignment personnel convince employers of the wisdom of just-in-time labor. Again, some advice. Be an ambassador for the flexible workforce. If it's to be your livelihood, anything you can do to bolster its image and acceptability will come back to you in increased demand for your competencies. Make it happen for FlexLifers in general, and you make it happen for yourself. It's part of how you manage your own career. So build it into your business strategy.

What Staffing Employees Should Expect from Staffing Agents–
A good staffing agent is not your personal valet, whipping boy, guru or savior. But there are certain things you should legitimately expect from him or her.

1. He or she should be an employment expert. In-depth knowledge of the local job market and the workplace in general are the first qualifications of a legitimate staffing agent.
2. Your agent and his or her supporting organization should have excellent working rapport with local employers.
3. The agency should be well-connected on a regional, national and even an international basis. Certain jobs know no boundaries, and employees who fill them go where needed.
4. The agent should know well any workplace where he or she places just-in-time personnel. Here is the best source of insight into corporate culture, house style, dress code and so on.
5. Your agent should have the necessary "tools of the trade" to keep you as busy as you wish to be. These tools include full-blown e-cruiting capabilities, a comprehensive database of local employers and their staffing needs, computer power where needed, promotional and marketing clout sufficient to grow the business and expand job opportunities for staffing personnel, attractive quarters that build confidence with employers, and a reputation for performing well.
6. The staffing agent should be particularly effective in helping you to transition from one job assignment to another. No unscheduled breaks in employment. No confusion or loose ends at the end of one assignment and the start of the next. No surprises for employee or employer.
7. You should expect the staffing agent to be looking ahead for the skills

101

that will be necessary for ready employment a year from now, then help prepare you in advance for the coming changes.

8. On a more personal level, you should expect that your staffing agent understands the depth and breadth of your competencies, knows your career preferences and objectives, keeps you as busy as you want to be, raises the quality of the assignments you fill, increases the pay scale for the services you render, counsels you over rough spots, defends you with employers where appropriate, exposes you to training that enhances your value in the workplace and serves as your eyes and ears in the marketplace so that the unexpected doesn't catch you by surprise.

9. It's reasonable to expect the staffing organization to offer training programs that improve your skills, advance your career and retain your services. The industry is moving rapidly in these areas (see Chapter Six). The more FlexLifers and would-be FlexLifers demand meaningful training assistance, the more quickly the industry will deliver.

What Staffing Employees Should Expect from Employers –
Since you come to the employer's place of work as a newcomer for a relatively short stay, it is not unreasonable to expect to be treated with the simple courtesies afforded any visitor. Cordiality. Respect. Proper introductions and indoctrination. Patience. Ready response to questions. But, because you come with competencies in the field for which you are hired, those courtesies do not extend to a lengthy tolerance of poor or unacceptable performance. Any employer has every right to expect you to perform to high standards. You should expect that. The employer should not expect you to perform well, however, without the necessary prerequisites to do the job assigned. This means a good many things:

1. While you bring skills and competencies to the job, you probably lack familiarity with the employer and its processes and procedures. It's the employer's responsibility to fill in these deficiencies to the extent necessary to perform well.

2. The task you are expected to do must be clearly explained, not only in the beginning, but as you encounter obstacles along the way. Don't be afraid to ask questions. Clear up any misgivings or uncertainties related to your assignment.

3. The resources to do the job must be available, in working order, and you must be adequately trained, if need be, in their use.
4. There must be someone to turn to for assistance, at least in the learning phase of the assignment.
5. Supervision should be constant during the early stages of the assignment. Hours or days spent doing the wrong thing because the employer didn't monitor your work will inevitably be recorded as your fault. Ask for a quick review if uncertain.
6. The place of work should be tolerable, safe and as comfortable as possible.
7. You should not be exposed to indignities or any other personal affront. You are a professional flexible employee but, first and foremost, a human being. Decency and respect are due, especially when it's earned with hard work, quality performance and personal dignity.

If a job assignment is found wanting in any of these areas, you are perfectly justified in firing the employer and asking your agent for a new assignment.

Getting a Life – Wouldn't it be an unfortunate irony if you put yourself in a position to truly balance work and personal life and didn't do it? It will surely happen if you don't plan in the beginning where the one ends and the other begins. Using the flexibility acquired with a *FlexLife®* career to simply work more and more is to defeat the objective. Using the acquired flexibility to avoid the responsibilities of a wage earner would be just as bad. Balance is the key. "Don't just get a job, get a life too." That's the message in *FlexLife®*. The balance is yours to design. Take it seriously. Think it over carefully. Consult with your spouse and/or other loved ones. Talk it over with your agent. Weigh all the possibilities, including the seemingly far out. The stories are many of the computer whiz from Silicon Valley turned to moviemaking or the school teacher from Madrid becoming a bush pilot in Argentina or the fireman making a killing as a commodities broker in Amsterdam. Such stories

> *Wouldn't it be an unfortunate irony if you put yourself in a position to truly balance work and personal life and didn't do it? It will surely happen if you don't plan in the beginning where the one ends and the other begins.*

often have their origin in wild ideas or childhood fantasies. But the more people think and plan and follow through, the more obtainable their dreams become.

Perhaps you have a dream. *FlexLife®* can help you live it. Define how you would use the time freed up by *FlexLife®*, and stick to the plan. Maybe you could "get a life" far removed from the big city and earn a good living too. Maybe you could work 7:00 a.m. to 1:00 p.m. or 2:00 p.m. to 8:00 p.m. six days a week; or 8:00 a.m. to 6:00 p.m. four days a week; or a cycle of 20 days on, 10 days off; or nine months out of the year and vacation three months. Maybe you could use your competencies and *FlexLife®* status to travel the world, or live in Tahiti, or hobnob with the rich and famous, or assist the fragile and underprivileged. The possibilities are enormous when you have the flexibility inherent to *FlexLife®* and the imagination to use it well.

Chapter Four

You started this, now finish it.

The employer's role in shaping
the flexible workplace

Consider for a moment the evolution of employment. As the Industrial Revolution flamed into existence, the factory owners had to secure good, cheap labor to man operations. But the local workforce was already engaged in agriculture or husbandry of some sort. How were the new industrialists to induce these people to lay down their burdens and come to the city to work assembly lines? The farm and the pasture, after all, were familiar and proven—so long as the weather cooperated and the vermin were controlled. Why give up the security provided by the land, as modest as it may seem from afar, for the unknown? The answer, of course, is that the factorymen offered workers the bedrock of what would eventually become the social contract employers and employees work under today—regular work at a known wage. Factory jobs did not suffer from the seasonality and unpredictability of farm labor. The wages may have been poor, the working conditions deplorable and job security nonexistent, but week after week, month after month, there was income. With a relatively dependable cash flow, plans could be made, goods accumulated, credit acquired, savings set aside, leverage gained. More money went into circulation because more people were getting paid year-round. Business grew as a result, additional jobs were created, and the whole process built upon itself. The

The Evolution of Employment

Pre-Industrial Revolution	Post-Industrial Revolution to WWII	Post-WWII to 1991-92 Recession	Today
• Labor mostly a variable cost of production	• Labor evolves into a fixed cost of production	• Labor a fixed cost of production	• Labor a variable cost of production
• Job specialization confined to certain crafts	• Specialization grows, resulting in more workplace flexibility	• Specialization grows, resulting in more workplace flexibility	• Specialization soars, making workplace flexibility paramount
• Employment subject to local labor demand	• Employment subject to local and regional labor demand	• Employment subject to local, regional and national labor demand	• Employment subject to local, regional, national and global demand
• Social safety net nonexistent	• Social safety net a philosophical debate	• Social safety net becomes entrenched as a fixed cost of business	• Social safety net begins to unravel
• Employee benefits at the discretion of employer	• Employee benefits at the discretion of employer	• Employee benefits evolve and the formal relationship with employer becomes the only practical way to get them	• Third-party "agent" becomes a viable vehicle for employee benefits. No longer necessary to keep "traditional job" just for benefits
• Negligible job security	• Minimal job security	• Job security the norm and the expectation	• Job security evaporates
• Minimal mobility of labor	• Growing labor mobility as workers move far and wide for jobs	• Labor mobility constrained by the prevailing corporate culture of the time	• Mobility soars as the traditional workplace unravels
• Family culture the prevailing lifestyle	• Family culture the prevailing lifestyle	• Corporate culture the prevailing lifestyle	• *FlexLife®* lifestyle begins to emerge
• Individualism over collectivism the norm	• Individualism gives way to collectivism	• Collectivism over individualism the norm	• Individualism over collectivism the norm
• Global competition nonexistent	• Global competition negligible	• Global competition begins to rear its head	• Global competition becomes the norm, changing the workplace around the world dramatically
• Agent role in employment negligible	• Agent role in employment negligible	• Agent role grows, primarily in the entertainment and professional sports industries	• Agent role spreads into the realm of average working men and women

seed of consumer-driven economies began to sprout. Prospects for a better life grew brighter. And it happened. Over ensuing generations, industrial-sector wages improved. Working conditions became more tolerable. Job security gained a measure here and there. And the prosperity of industrialized nations grew. After World War II, the idea of a social safety net for employees took hold. Vacation time, sick pay, medical benefits, seniority, shorter work weeks, pensions, early retirement, scheduled pay raises, widespread organized labor intervention—the whole package. And it became institutionalized, creating what I refer to as traditional permanent jobs (TPJ). They became the standard for employment in advanced economies, the very essence of the implied social contract between employee and employer. Only the smallest and least substantial employers dared offer employees anything less than traditional permanent jobs; only the daring, or least skilled, workers worked for anything less. From that long-ago offer of regular work at a known wage, to the guarantees of the modern welfare state—that's the evolution of the workplace. But evolution doesn't stop. Things keep changing, like it or not. The workplace is no exception. That brings us to a historical turn of events of recent origins—the flexible workplace.

A good case can be made that FlexLife®, and the flexible workplace we know today, emerged from corporate America's reaction to the recession of the early 1990s.

A good case can be made that *FlexLife®*, and the flexible workplace we know today, emerged from corporate America's reaction to the recession of the early 1990s. Right up to the very beginning of the decade, the U.S. economy charged along fairly oblivious to forces at work in the global marketplace, despite clear warnings from such developments as the Arab Oil Embargo of the early 1970s and Chrysler Corporation's near collapse a decade later due in large part to competition from Japanese auto makers. Business in the U.S. boomed for most of the 1980s. Trade agreements still protected many industries from hungry competitors gathering strength around the world. The nation consumed 90 percent of what it produced and a disproportionate share of what the rest of the world had to sell. The labor movement had gone quiet on the strength of full employment and general prosperity. Profit margins were good, management was self-assured, and long-range plans called for more of the same. Employment was high, jobs secure, paychecks robust and the future looked bright for employees. Nothing seemed to be broken, and there was no rush to fix anything.

Then a number of historic developments converged in a short span of time as the U.S. economy slipped into recession in the early 1990s. Real estate values began to plummet. Banks started calling in loans. By the end of 1991, the entire industry, particularly the savings and loan sector, found itself mired in some of the poor banking practices that rocked Southeast Asia seven years later: reckless lending, insufficient reserves, inadequate government oversight, speculation, greed and corruption. By the close of 1993, $150-$200 billion of capital disappeared in the savings and loan debacle. Trade agreements, long in the works, began to clear the way for global commerce on an unprecedented scale. The Berlin Wall had fallen in 1989, bringing dozens of new, hungry nations to the marketplace searching for a buck. China was astir, following the lead of Hong Kong and the Tigers of Southeast Asia. Everywhere, foreign businesses looked to tap into the other guy's market, the U.S. in particular. The influx of imported goods accelerated, with prices American producers could not match. And consumers bought. Bloated with heavy payroll, inefficient and slow to respond, the U.S. economy found itself poorly prepared to compete in a fierce new ball game contested by lean and nimble players. It was not a case of simply riding out the storm until the good old times returned. What American business began to experience in the depths of the 1991-92 recession was what management strategist James Martin described several years later as the "imminent arrival of a global marketplace so highly automated, so fast-paced, so ruthless, and so inescapable, that Main Street norms like caution, continuity and conservatism will become only fading memories. As Martin put it in 1997, nothing less than "the total reinvention of employment" would do.

Long before these words were written, the U.S. business community got the message. As the recession groaned and creaked through 1990, 1991 and 1992, business cut costs feverishly, beginning with personnel; top managers, middle managers, supervisors, hourly workers, staff functions, research, old-timers, sacred cows—any position that didn't relate directly to the company's "core" business. (Thus emerged the terminology of today's flexible workplace). The blood-letting was awful. Entire departments and divisions in hundreds of major organizations were lopped off. Many operations were "outsourced" (more of the lexicon of today) to reduce personnel costs; many more were simply found to be superfluous, and the jobs disappeared altogether. Hundreds of thousands of well-paid, highly skilled, admirably educated employees found themselves out on the street—an unprecedented assault on the vaunted "American Dream." Finding a new job didn't necessarily help. Downsizing struck many employers over and over again as the phenomenon swept back and forth in a workplace undergoing deep, structural change. The U.S. unemployment rate went from 5.2 percent in the summer of 1989 to 7.8 percent at the depth of the recession in 1992. And for every person unemployed, several more were underemployed, earning less—often far less— than two years earlier.

Hundreds of thousands of well-paid, highly skilled, admirably educated employees found themselves out on the street—an unprecedented assault on the vaunted "American Dream."

And employers weren't through. Where jobs could be transferred to cheaper labor, they were, especially in the blue-collar sector. Mergers, consolidations and acquisitions brought clout and viability to industries and markets across the spectrum of American business. But more and more people lost their jobs. Capital equipment investment increased 70 percent from 1991 through 1996, all of it designed to upgrade capacity and productivity, most of it to replace people. More jobs lost, never to be available again. Technology that had lain around for years, in many cases, was adopted to replace personnel and/or expedite business. Voice mail, once confined to small businesses that couldn't afford a receptionist or secretary, became omnipresent throughout the workplace. The fax machine, commercially available since the early 1980s, exploded in popularity. Sales of personal computers (PCs), a novelty for much of the 1980s, skyrocketed as business began to dig itself out of the hole with leaner operations and better productivity. The Internet and e-mail took off as the nation climbed out of recession.

Attitudes about work started to change during this time. Given the ruthlessness of downsizing, the old employee/employer relationship eroded. Personal expectations declined. Trends to simpler lifestyles and more individual freedom emerged. Bummed out by giving their all to the company, people started looking for a better way—a job and a life. In important ways, the downsizing phenomenon that swept through the U.S. workforce during and after the 1991-92 recession freed hundreds of thousands of capable, talented people to take risks and innovate for the first time in the modern era. And that's just what happened. While big business retrenched, recouped and generally reinvented itself, that army of perfectly good downsized talent began to bubble and brew into hundreds and thousands of small businesses. Entrepreneurship exploded during and after the recession. Dun & Bradstreet reported a 21 percent increase in new business starts from the recession low in 1991 through 1994, and the pace quickened thereafter.

The workplace that emerged on the other side of the 1991-92 recession was very much different from what it had been for the 50 years prior to the close of the 1980s. The recession covered but a short time span to be sure, but the confluence of trends precipitated by this economic correction packed a wallop out of all proportion to its duration and depth. Five years after the official end of the 1991-92 recession, veteran employees still shook their heads and expressed a common refrain: "I know the economy's good, but it doesn't seem like we ever really recovered from the recession." There was good reason for that sentiment. In very real ways, the U.S. workforce had not recovered from the recession of 1991-92. That's because people expected a return to the norm—renewed wage levels and the warm and fuzzy old workplace of traditional permanent jobs. What they got instead were lower-paying jobs (it wasn't until 1998 that the median take-home pay, adjusted for inflation, reached 1989 levels) and a new attitude among employers. Labor, after all, was not a fixed cost of doing business, but a flexible cost. U.S. business had put the theory to the test during the recession and afterwards, and found that it was good. Downsizing, outsourcing and other practices developed as survival tactics in the early 1990s proved to be marvelous inventions for improving competitiveness and profitability.

A lasting effect of this new approach to employment is that the social contract known to the workplace for most of the post-World War II era has been irretrievably broken. Employers have lots of good work to be

. . . it wasn't until 1998 that the median take-home pay, adjusted for inflation, reached 1989 levels. . . .

done at good pay but don't want to be locked into expensive permanent payrolls if not absolutely necessary. Except for the critical core staff, why retain skills, talent and labor that can be acquired just-in-time, anytime, then released? Makes sense–for employers. But for employees, it's an appalling proposition unless something is done to compensate for the general loss of traditional permanent jobs (TPJ). There is no health and stability for anyone in a workplace divided into victors and victims. What's good for employers must be good for employees as well. That's the beauty of *FlexLife*® and other forms of enlightened flexible employment—both employers and employees win. The major problem at present is that the transition from the old workplace to the new isn't yet complete. Things happened so fast in the early 1990s–first the recession and the crisis management that ensued, then the recovery and frantic maneuvering to catch the wave of prosperity–that business had little time to mull the new workplace it created. Then the Asian-born financial crisis captured employers' attention in 1998, assuring that the problem would go unresolved for a time yet. What's left is for employers to finish the paradigm for the new flexible workplace so that more and more employees reap the benefits inherent in a *FlexLife*® way of life.

So, where to from here for those who employ the skill, talent and labor of others? Give some thought to the following:

- Do the right thing.
- Upgrade your HR practices.
- Recognize generational differences and "workstyles."
- Ensure your labor supply.
- Create a flexible workplace.
- Manage the flexible workforce.
- Know what to expect of staffing agents.
- Know what to expect of just-in-time personnel.

Do the Right Thing

Understand that the new workplace, with its growing emphasis on flexibility and cost-efficiency, does not negate the requirement for employers to be socially responsible to those they employ, whether they are full-time or just-in-time employees. Today's social contract no longer suggests a promise of traditional "job security" for the workforce. But it does demand fair play, responsible behavior, a certain loyalty and enlightened human resource (HR) management. Think about it. Whether you retain 100 percent of your workforce the old-fashioned way—52 weeks a year, benefits and all—or spread the work over a labor force comprised of 40 percent full-time core staff and 60 percent just-in-time employees, you still must have the skills and labor you need when you need them.

A deep, capable, local labor force is a function of training, experience, education and motivation. And it can't all be left to schools and colleges. In the aggregate, employers are the biggest educational institution anywhere. They have a social responsibility, rooted in vested self-interest, to upgrade the skills of employees while on the payroll, whatever the length of employment. The old adage about teaching a person to fish is very appropriate in the modern workplace. Employers that provide a day's work feed the employee for a day; employers that improve an employee's skills help feed that person for a lifetime, and earn his or her respect and loyalty as well. A better grade of employee is loosed into the general labor pool. When it's your turn to draw from the reservoir, you are more likely to catch a winner, a winner motivated to perform well for you. Improving the employment security of just-in-time workers can be accomplished in a variety of ways:

> *In the aggregate, employers are the biggest educational institution anywhere. They have a social responsibility, rooted in vested self-interest, to upgrade the skills of empolyees while on the payroll, whatever the length of employment.*

1. Develop a "flexible workforce management team" that gets the most out of the investment in just-in-time employees and enhances their employment security as well. With so much of the workforce comprised of free agents, employers are remiss for not creating the management framework necessary to meld these people seamlessly into the core organization.

2. Provide training especially tailored to the flexible workforce. From Randstad North America's survey of the North American workforce, it's clear that employees want to learn. Fully 77 percent of respondents to the Roper Report said that they would "prefer a job where they had to learn new skills all the time." Capitalize on this desire. It could be instruction in new computer software, career

management, the employer's business or any number of worthwhile disciplines. By so doing, you will improve the appeal of your organization as a place to work. The cross-training that the just-in-time employee acquires in this manner not only advances his or her career, it returns a more valuable worker the next time he or she is hired.

3.   Provide for a flexible workplace, right down to parking arrangements, building access, after-hours security, time-sheet control, a welcoming and departure routine, and a quick-start indoctrination program for just-in-time tasks.

4.   Place them in positions that add to their skill and confidence levels. Mix them in cross-functional teams, for example, so that they get a better perspective of your business, the possible career paths and development opportunities. Open the way for flexible workers to switch from one task or specialization to another. Who knows what talent or career objective lies in a just-in-time worker pressed into service for an employer who knows little of the person? That file clerk with "administrative experience" might be a perfectly competent replacement when the office manager goes on vacation—or leaves for another job.

5.   Develop awards and recognition programs, financial and otherwise, for top-performing, just-in-time employees. It will keep them coming back and bolster the image of the *FlexLife®* career choice. The better the universe of just-in-time skills, the better it is for employers.

6.   Look for ways to contribute on a merit/incentive basis to the benefit plans of assignment personnel—perhaps a bonus paid into a person's Medical Savings Account (MSA) or portable pension plan. With a little legislative help (see Chapter Five) such action would go far in taking the insecurity out of just-in-time careers.

Upgrade Your Human Resources Practices

The new paradigm for employer-employee relationships in tight labor markets like that of the U.S. is "strongly employee-needs driven," states the Roper Report. Human resource professionals cannot fail to grasp the impact of this development if they are to keep their organizations competitive and viable. If you view employee benefits as you did three to four years ago, the organization's recruiting and employee retention is suffering. If you believe that the "flexible workplace" means minimum wage vacation replacements and fill-in workers, then you don't understand what's going on in the workplace. If your organization hires and fires as it did in the mid-1990s, you are out of step with the times. If you evaluate employee credentials as you did then, you are obsolete. If the Internet is not part of your recruiting arsenal, you are undergunned. If you don't know how to design a flexible workforce and manage it once in place, you have a lot of catching up to do. If you are not releasing downsized/flexible employees better trained than when they came on board, you are ultimately hurting yourself. If you are carrying personnel 52 weeks a year when you need them only part of the time, you are spending money unnecessarily and negatively impacting productivity.

Too much has changed too rapidly not to take a good hard look at the organization's basic HR premises. What exactly is the organization's philosophy regarding human resources? Is it to build and maintain the best organization money can buy? Is it to get the best return on human resources for the money invested? Is it to operate the business with minimal personnel costs? Whatever the answer, another question is left hanging: Is the organization getting the most for its HR dollar? That raises the issue of workforce composition. Have core-staff positions been identified that require permanent employees, and has intermittent work been identified that can be handled with just-in-time personnel? Has anyone explored the possibilities of electronic networks and virtual organizations that draw on skills and service far removed from "headquarters"? If not, how can the organization know if it is getting the most for the HR dollar? If, in a 100-person workforce, for example, 60 positions are actually core-staff jobs, yet 85 people enjoy permanent status, then the organization's costs exceed those of the

> *If you evaluate employee credentials as you did before the recession, you are obsolete. If the Internet is not part of your recruiting arsenal, you are undergunned. If you don't know how to design a flexible workforce and manage it once in place, you have a lot of catching up to do.*

competitor who operates with a better mix of permanent and just-in-time workers. This is not just a juggling of numbers but real money. These days, competitive advantage swings primarily on cost-effectiveness.

Without a careful analysis of workforce composition, another basic HR function can get skewed—personnel evaluation. The newly old school of HR recruiting and selecting said you looked for a certain longevity in the work history. Any evidence of "jobhopping" or long breaks in the employment record was taboo. The prestige of previous employers was important. Job titles that smacked of apparent responsibility scored big. But, in today's workplace, what exactly is a "good hire"? Is it a full-timer when the need is intermittent? Is it a commuter when a telecommuter or e-lancer would suffice? Is it a special-skills need that requires constant training for the employee to stay current? Is the "good hire" the person who held a position for five years at a single place of employment or a just-in-time specialist who stayed busy the last five years serving 10 to 12 employers one short-term assignment after another? How about credentials? Who is likely to be more competent in his or her field: the full-timer who has known nothing but the needs of one employer, or the FlexLifer who filled the needs of a number of clients on an ongoing basis? The winner is obvious. Nevertheless, the traditional HR mindset judges the full-timer to be more stable and misses altogether the point about relative competencies. Such shortsightedness can be costly for employers.

Is the "good hire" the person who held a position for five years at a single place of employment or a just-in-time specialist who stayed busy the last five years serving 10 to 12 employers one short-term assignment after another?

So, in the same way that employees must present their skills and competencies in a different way (see "Writing a *FlexLife®* Resume," Chapter Three), the HR department must interface with the job market differently. Improving the employment security of just-in-time workers as previously noted is part of this requirement. Here are some other suggestions:

1. Fill jobs only after the workforce composition has been carefully determined.
2. Recognize that employees today are more mobile than ever and probably won't spend their entire careers with any one organization, including yours. This is not a sign of instability but an indication of employability and desirability. Applying a set of skills in a variety of job settings has the effect of refining competencies, not diminishing them.
3. Adapt HR policy to fit the mobile workplace. This means, among

other things, more transportable employee benefit plans to attract younger workers in particular. Portable retirement plans enable employees to begin a slow, steady accrual of benefits that can be taken with them whenever they depart for a new job.

4. Keep track of assignment personnel that have performed well for you, former employees that might make good independent contractors, talent you have considered hiring and those who turned down your offers of employment. This can be accomplished with an in-house database or the job can be outsourced to a labor exchange service. Either way, employers ought not to lose sight of the skills, talent and labor that best match their needs.

5. Develop a "personnel retention plan" that offers, among other things, the option to leave the organization without leaving. There are many gradations today between a traditional permanent employee and an outright, never-to-be-seen-again departure. As management consultant Bruce Tulgan tells employers, "build internal escape hatches. Give people the chance to reinvent themselves right within the company—move into new skill areas, work with new people, take on new tasks and responsibilities, work different hours or from a new location. . . . Offer them the chance to continue adding value on a part-time basis, or as flex-timers, telecommuters, periodic temps, or consultants; and offer sabbaticals. When they do leave, make sure to do some more career planning to make sure they stay in your talent pool."

6. Interviewing techniques must be revised. If it's skills, talent or labor that you are after, then that's what you want to get a sense for in the prospect's resume and evaluation sessions. The traditional HR mentality has to stop penalizing applicants who show multiple employers. In many fields, a long list of "client work" in the space allotted for employment history says to the recruiter that the person is experienced, used to new places and people and challenges, and knows the routine.

7. Does the applicant define himself or herself as a FlexLifer, free agent or some other derivation of the term? This indicates that the person understands what's going on in the workplace and is positioning himself or herself accordingly. Implied in the declaration is that you, the employer, recognize what's going on as well. Do you?

8. Does the just-in-time employee note that he or she is covered by third-party employee benefits? This can help establish the FlexLifer's status

as a temporary employee, not a member of the organization's permanent core staff. In the current regulatory environment, this distinction is very important. Companies of the stature of Microsoft, Xerox, Allstate and Time Warner have gone to court recently to clarify the distinction between temporary and permanent employees so that labor costs can be predicted and employment flexibility is maintained.

9. Be careful not to expose the organization to the potential liabilities inherent in vague or inconsistent distinctions between the various forms of temporary employment and permanent jobs. These steps can reduce the risks:

   - Don't confuse service agreements with employment contracts. The first is a stipulation of the agreement between company and service providers like staffing organizations; the second implies an employer/employee relationship that may not be in the company's best interest. Your staffing organization should know the difference and not let its client drift into potentially entangling contractual language.

   - Draw up service agreements with independent contractors and other just-in-time workers in strict compliance with the jurisdictional tax code. Chief among these in the U.S. is a multi-point test applied by the Internal Revenue Service.

   - In agreements with staffing providers be sure to specify that the party rendering the service is the "employer of record" and, therefore, responsible for employee benefits, if provided, and the submission of payroll taxes. Recognize that all labor exchange services, including staffing organizations, don't offer benefits for assignment personnel. Keep this in mind when choosing your staffing agency. Employee benefits are basic to retaining and securing good employees, whether they be short-timers or permanent.

   - Federal tax regulations in the U.S. enable employers to shield themselves from the cost of paying employee benefits to "leased employees" (i.e., assignment personnel). Upon election to do this, the employer should expressly exclude just-in-time workers from the organization's employee benefits plan. But, to help protect these valuable employees, make sure the organization that provides them offers a good benefit package in your stead.

   - If employers want added protection, they might include a written waiver in the service agreement that prohibits personnel hired on a just-in-time basis from claiming rights to benefits provided by the organization's group plan.

- To further emphasize the company's intent when it comes to long-running temporary assignments or "outside" contractors, some firms have resorted to a mandated break in the duration of employment of just-in-time personnel. (Termination for 90 days after 18-24 months of continuous employment, for example.) As you will see later, there are drawbacks in this development and justifiable fear of a creep toward the kind of workplace regulation that dogs Germany's handling of flexible workers.

10. Provide letters of recommendation where just-in-time employees have earned them. Develop policy and procedure for the practice so that it becomes routine. This will help the next employer and ultimately come back to aide you as well. Be specific about the tasks the FlexLifer performed and the quality of his or her work. Where estimates can be made, note any monetary savings the person represented for the organization compared to the cost of a full-time employee. Acknowledge his or her contribution to the organization's flexibility.

11. Stretch to use and help develop those traditionally categorized as "chronically unemployed." Skills, talent and labor can be hidden from view in the most unlikely places. Often it just takes a little consistent effort to sort nuggets from the dross. Desperate for willing hands, some U.S. companies reach into the prison system to sign up parolees. Welfare-to-work has made huge strides in the American workplace in recent years. Disabled workers have proven their mettle in the fast-paced U.S. workplace of the 1990s. But most of these breakthroughs are motivated by unprecedented low unemployment. Will it all dry up with an economic slowdown? If so, a lot of good groundbreaking practice will be lost to the detriment of the workplace.

12. Look closely at your organization for opportunities to outsource work, including HR functions.

13. Give careful thought to the management and direction of your business. Employees have a major stake in your success and your failures. Downsizing, it turns out, is not always a response to competitive pressures, improved technology or other market dynamics. All too frequently, it is merely the inevitable consequence of poor business

decisions and practices. One of those practices is to treat labor as a fixed cost of business when, in fact, it is as flexible as employers are willing to make it; another is to misinterpret the business your organization is actually engaged in. The Sarah Lee Corporation is a good example. This venerable institution made famous by pound cake took a hard look at itself in 1997. What management concluded was that Sarah Lee's core competencies were not in the production of baked goods, or the meat packing and textile manufacturing that comprised a large part of the business. First and foremost, the company was judged to be a marketing organization. There are lots of bakeries, meat packers and textile mills around that could provide products for the company to sell. And so Sarah Lee reorganized. It outsourced most of its production operations, sold off plants and capital equipment, downsized the workforce and reduced costs substantially. On the strength of these moves, the company's stock soared to 25 times trailing earnings. Some observers criticized the initiative as a selfish maneuver to improve stockholder equity. Others see it as a brilliant example of enlightened management. Wherever the truth may lie, Sarah Lee represents just how far an organization can go in redefining itself in the flexible workplace of today and tomorrow, and just how deeply employees are affected by management decisions.

Recognize Generational Differences and "Workstyles"

No thoughtful speaker would launch into a presentation without a fair understanding of his or her audience. Would, then, an employer attempt to achieve organizational objectives without a fair understanding of the personnel expected to do the jobs necessary to succeed? The answer, of course, is, "Yes, all too frequently."

In this time of pervasive workplace diversity, employers who fail to take into account the differences in age, sex, culture or race of those who work for the organization will surely fall short of attainable performance levels—sometimes far short. Conversely, those employers who come to an understanding of employee values and attitudes based upon real life circum-

In this time of pervasive workplace diversity, employers who fail to take into account the differences in age, sex, culture or race of those who work for the organization will surely fall short of attainable performance levels—sometimes far short.

stances gain insights that management can act on to the benefit of the organization and the workforce alike.

Strategically, it makes utmost sense to play to the strengths of the organization's workforce and to shelter or bolster it where weak. That's the winning formula in any competitive endeavor, business no less than sports. In the diverse, fast-paced workplace employers find themselves in today, the ability to "get a grip on what they have to work with" (i.e., the human resources at their disposal) is more difficult than ever. But there are ways.

In the course of its 1999 survey of the North American workforce, Roper Starch Worldwide found patterns in employee feelings and beliefs that shed a good deal of light on a key factor in workplace diversity—generational differences. With the knowledge gained from the survey, prospects for a competitive advantage in recruiting, retention and overall performance quickly emerged. Let me share those insights with you.

Six distinct "styles of working" emerged from the Roper Starch Worldwide survey, each one directly related to specific generations currently employed in the workplace. Let's look first at those "workstyles," then some suggestions on how employers might capitalize on the needs and desires of their employees, young to old.

Yearners – Most are younger employees just beginning their careers or starting a first job. Many, however, belong to the Baby Boomers and Matures generations. All share some degree of dissatisfaction with their jobs, a yearning to belong in the workplace and feelings of a lack of control over many areas of their work lives. Yet, they are highly motivated and committed employees if they find the right job and the right employer.

Seeker – Job hunters in an era of record employment, many are currently employed. They want to work, and have very positive attitudes about working. However, they are unsure of what they want to do or how to make all the pieces of their lives fit together and strike a balance with their careers.

Strivers – The new yuppies, they focus on money and career advancement. They are driven by ambition and always looking for a better opportunity. But because of their strong sense of loyalty, they also say they will stay with their current employer if they have satisfying, challenging work and good compensation. Loyalty to their employer is conditional and portable, and can be transferred to subsequent employers.

Autonomists – The new breed of employee for the new economy, they thrive on change, especially if it allows them greater professional fulfillment. Learning new skills and being in control of their own careers is very important to these people. They find long-term assignments or contract work highly appealing. They are committed and dedicated and have a greater sense of self-reliance and less of entitlement. Employers find them to be very adaptable to situations that may be specialized or project-oriented.

Loyalists – People who have found the right job with the right employer at the right time. They display a unique combination of loyalty, satisfaction and energy. The driving force behind their loyalty is the company's loyalty to them, recognition of their contributions, knowing that their work satisfies their customers and employer and the promise of career advancement.

Shifters – Content with this phase of their work lives, they are heading into the home stretch of their current careers. They are likely planning the next stage of their work life. More mature in both body and spirit, half of them are 50 and older. They now are shifting their center of attention to things they may have had no time for in the past. However, Shifters can be significant contributors, possessing a wealth of knowledge and experience that is worth its weight in gold. Their fundamental values, and the example they set, make them a tremendous asset to their employer.

Each Workstyle was asked the same questions:

1. **What do you personally find most rewarding about work?**
   Key themes that emerged across all generations (Generation X, Baby Boomers and Matures) included personal accomplishment, doing work that provides self-worth, the opportunity to learn new skills and helping both co-employees and customers. Responses to the question pointed directly to managerial actions likely to improve employee motivation and performance as well as employer competitiveness. Training programs could have a very positive impact on Gen X Seekers, for example, many of whom would welcome opportunities to

become better trained and more effective in their jobs. A successful tactic might be to give Loyalists a chance to manage a company-wide task force, giving them an opportunity to lead others and to feel they are making a solid contribution to the company's mission. Mature Shifters might relish the chance to work more independently on projects. They would probably react positively to an offer to increase their flexibility by choosing their work site. Both options fulfill their need to be independent while still making a meaningful contribution.

2. **What do you think is the single most important thing that employers should do today to hold on to good employees?**
    Key themes expressed were a desire for the company to "listen to them," to provide positive feedback about their jobs, to reward them for doing a good job, most often with little things or "soft" benefits; to be truthful about managerial decisions and even just to say "thank you" occasionally. Suggestions for management action that naturally followed the responses include employee recognition programs, a logical strategy for Baby Boomers, many of whom are Loyalists at heart still looking for the right employer. Such programs tend to nurture their need for constructive feedback and stimulates commitment to the company. Even Yearners might benefit from employee recognition programs. Perhaps periodic roundtable discussions could improve their feelings of belonging by giving them a chance to share their ideas on improving workflow. An effective tactic might be to design and implement an incentive program based on individual or group production. *Shifters* and *Autonomists* might respond very favorably to this opportunity.

3. **What do you personally find must frustrating about work?**
    Themes ranged from "no progress, no excitement" to "too much bureaucracy." Suggestions for avoiding the consequences of excessive turnover start with programs that foster flexible work schedules. They are a low-cost tactic that appeals to Gen X *Shifters* who often want added flexibility in work schedules for family reasons. A career planning program might be effective, one that uses the career labyrinth concept with its varied career options to allay the frustrations of both Baby Boomer *Seekers* and *Yearners* who feel stymied in their jobs. To measure their progress, the program could include modest goals and time-tables for achieving promotions or added responsibilities.

4. **What do you think is the single most important thing that employers do today that causes them to lose good employees?** "Perceived broken promises" by management and "unreasonable expectations" were the leading responses, pointing to a potential disconnect between what employees expect from their employers and what employers do to retain personnel. Forward-thinking companies increasingly recognize the retention value in programs to engage management and employees at all levels in constructive dialogue. Clearly, employees want consideration of their basic needs as people. Consider designing a schedule of regular meetings that offer opportunities for personnel to give direct feedback to management. Departmental forums, team building programs or a separate "intranet suggestion box" might be effective in nurturing and promoting cooperation in the workforce.

5. **What is the most important thing employers need to do to make working easier for employees with families?** Responses crystallized around the importance of family responsibilities and the demands of home life. Suggestions for turning these employee values into positive workplace experiences fall in the realm of flexibility and employee benefits. Perhaps employers could offer additions to their benefits package specifically targeted to family-related needs. One such benefit that grows in popularity is a day care or elder care provision offering employee counseling, funding for special care costs and flexible work hours to accommodate the needs of affected employees. Flexible work arrangements targeted to *Shifters* is an excellent way to increase both commitment and satisfaction among these valuable employees. Improved retention results.

On the issue of flexibility, it's important for employers to understand that restructuring time on the job doesn't mean fewer hours worked. Rather, it means restructuring the workday so that employees can meet both their professional and personal responsibilities. The wisest of employers will find ways to accomplish the necessary restructuring.

Ensure Your Labor Supply

The continuity of labor supply is critical. Employers must have the human resources needed to conduct business or business will decline.

In the new workplace where competition and the speed of market developments dictate an ever-watchful eye on personnel costs, labor supply continuity is trickier than ever. What do you do when there is a scarcity of needed skills for your business? Do you pay costly premiums to retain personnel full-time even when they are not needed full-time? Or trust that the skills will be available in the flexible labor pool when needed? It's a tough call. Will you be competitive with a heavier payroll in the first instance? Will those high-priced skills retain their edge employed exclusively in your operation? Can you navigate the flexible labor market skillfully enough to cover your personnel needs and hold down labor costs? Labor, skills and talent can be handled as flexible economic resources, but can you do it effectively? Do you have a system in place that moves critical skills in and out of your organization "just-in-time" and assures that the bearers of those skills will come back again? Do you know how to be socially responsible to those who work for you, short-term or long, and yet retain the advantages of flexibility? These questions cannot go unaddressed if you are to maintain the continuity and efficiency of a well-run business. Then there's the more immediate question of today's personnel needs and tomorrow's and the next day's. How do you keep the talent and skills you already have in a fiercely competitive employment market?

A nifty answer to the question was supplied by former U.S. Secretary of Labor Robert Reich in that *Context* magazine interview cited previously. Speaking to corporate management generally, he said, "You need to create an environment in which people can learn continuously and feel that they are on the cutting edge of learning. The company has to have a mission strong enough to make people proud of being associated with it. The company has to accord people enough responsibility and provide them enough just plain fun that they want to be there. The company also needs to take account of the practical demands that people have as they raise families and participate in their communities. . . . If you want to keep talented people, you have to respond to the needs of their whole lives."

Well put, and quite right. There's much more to employee retention these days than the old reliable "big two" employment incentives of salary and benefits. This is especially true with Generation X and their offspring, Generation Y. The Roper Report found ready confirmation that young people want to make more money and have an opportunity to advance, assume more responsibility and contribute more to the organization. No real surprises there. If they can't find it with their current employer, they have no qualms about searching elsewhere. But there turned out to be a third, rather surprising, reason for employee job-hopping: concern that they are falling behind the pace of rapid change. For the workforce, the revolution in technology and global competitiveness has driven home the need for new skills and knowledge. To get the exposure needed to stay abreast of developments, younger workers clearly will move from one employer to another. One obvious way to head this off is to give these workers what they are searching for: training in the skills they want. This is made all the more palatable when the training and skills enhancement come back to the organization in reduced turnover, improved efficiency and greater productivity. A word of caution: keeping up with benefit developments in your industry may be insufficient to retain your people. You are not competing for skills and talent just in your field anymore. The workplace in general beckons. Explore the possibilities throughout the job market for attracting and retaining good people. You may hit on a winner.

There are other tactics for retaining and attracting skilled personnel that cost employers little or nothing. Making employees feel appreciated is one of these. Flexible work arrangements, as previously explored, are a sure way to the heart of today's workforce. Rewards for good work pays off disproportionately to the cost of the program.

Contrary to what many employers assume, the Roper Report found a "strong willingness" among employees, including the younger generations, to commit to their jobs and employers. So why so much turnover? It is suggested that employers may be missing an opportunity to inspire and nurture a sense of commitment among employees. How? Survey responses point to an employee desire to be involved more in decision making processes within the organization. Empowering multi-functional teams to solve problems could also increase the level of commitment among employees.

Part of the requirement for ensuring your labor supply calls for speaking out against government action that directly or indirectly reduces business's flexibility in designing and managing its workforce. This includes support of legislative initiatives on at least three fronts:

1. Better legal, accounting and tax distinctions between just-in-time workers and full-time or core-staff employees.
2. Improvements in immigration law.
3. More creativity in the design of benefit packages for just-in-time personnel.

Just-in-Time vs. Full-Time

Microsoft Inc. raised a red flag for all employers in 1996 when a court ruled against the firm in a lawsuit brought by freelance workers employed as independent contractors. It seems that Microsoft failed to draw up its employment contracts and benefits plan with enough specificity to delineate independent contractors from regular permanent employees in the eyes of the Internal Revenue Service. It didn't matter that the IRS and other government agencies have been inconsistent in how they determine when a worker is an independent contractor and when a regular employee. The U.S. Court of Appeals for the 9th Circuit judged that no distinction existed between Microsoft's two classes of employees, opening the way for the freelancers to sue for the same lucrative stock options and 401(k) contributions granted to permanent employees. Similar situations later popped up at Xerox, Allstate Insurance and Time Warner. These cases shed light on gray areas of the law that have forced employers to protect themselves with steps that reduce the effectiveness of flexible work arrangements, promote turnover, hurt just-in-time workers and lessen productivity.

You can't just treat temps as temps anymore or you'll lose them.

*– Steven Orton
Xerox Site Manager*

As stated earlier, many employers now feel compelled to create an artificial break in the employment of just-in-time workers after a set length of time in order to show that they are not permanent workers. The worker may be performing brilliantly, the job could be at a critical stage, and the employer might be crying for the skills he or she is about to let go. But, to guard against the prospects of going to court over misinterpretation, employers are doing what they feel they have to do. It's an awkward development, as Xerox learned in 1998. The company was struggling to retain valued temporary telephone operators because newly instituted corporate policy required their dismissal for at least 90 days after 18 consecutive months on the job. The policy created severe turnover problems without any indication from federal authorities that it would serve the intended purpose. Good, trained, needed people were being shown the door. And good, trained, needed flexible workers don't have to wait around while employers figure out how to protect themselves from vague government regulation. To entice their temps not to take other assignments while "severed" from Xerox, the firm offered to pay them $100 per month for up to three months; and, upon their return, give them a bigger title, a better desk, and a sweatshirt that read, "I'm Back." As Xerox Site Manager Steven Orton told *Staffing Industry Report*, "You can't just treat temps as temps anymore or you'll lose them."

Continuity and flexibility clearly suffer when artificial barriers are interjected into the logical flow of work. Unexpected consequences inevitably follow. The barriers—and the consequences—could be eliminated in a couple of ways. One would be to designate qualified staffing organizations as the sole employer of the temporary workers they assign to customers for purposes of paying employment taxes and sponsoring benefit plans. This would pin responsibility for these two key provisions right where it belongs and eliminate confusion that can be turned against employers who use agency-placed temporary workers. The other way to reduce potential liability over the issue of perma-nent versus temporary workers is to draw a "clear, bright line" between the two categories of employment. It is easy enough to do, but legisla-tors balk at fears of a two-tiered workforce: one portrayed as the "haves" (permanent jobholders with traditional job security), the other as the "have-nots" (just-in-time workers with no bene-fits or job security). Neither image is accurate. Permanent jobs and job security are increasingly a last resort for many employers; a succession of short-term job assignments arranged by a profes-sional agent whose agency provides benefits is not the profile of "have-nots."

Government policymakers and organized labor fear that employers would use a two-tiered workforce to avoid the costs of benefits. Except

Competition for good assignment personnel within the staffing industry forces agencies to provide better bene-fit plans, and increas-ingly, to cover some or all of the costs of the plan. So there is little to fear in finally establish-ing a sensible legal/tax distinction between temporary and perma-nent employees.

for staffing firms, that would certainly be the case. Most organizations would be glad to reduce the cost of benefits wherever possible. Just as surely, they would love to operate with fewer labor costs. But competition dictates that business shall do what's necessary to attract and keep the skills, talent and labor required to run the operation. For core-staff personnel, that means competitive benefits and competitive pay. There's no escaping it. By using just-in-time workers, however, there is an escape— let the staffing companies provide the employment security employers don't want to provide. Competition for good assignment personnel within the staffing industry forces agencies to provide better benefit plans and, increasingly, to cover some or all of the costs of the plan.

So, there is little to fear in finally establishing a sensible legal/tax distinction between temporary and permanent employees. Free-enterprise economics provides. Employers are advised to recognize what's holding up progress in this area and to clarify for public consumption the compensating balances inherent in the new flexible workplace.

Immigration

Unavoidably, employers must take a stance on the sensitive issue of immigration. Especially in the West where decades of low birth rates have created a shortage of workers, "employee mobility" (immigrants, in many cases) may well dictate whether there are enough employees to man an operation or not. Business success or failure hangs in the balance. This subject is covered in some detail in Chapter Five, but it requires mention here as well. In the big picture, employers are well-advised to stand in support of actions like the following:

1. Minimal restrictions on work visas for qualified foreign workers where employers await with open arms. Since the last third of the 1990s, for example, American business has been faced with an acute shortage of Information Technology (IT) skills and has been restricted by federal law from bringing in ready, willing and able personnel from abroad to fill the breach. All the reasons advanced for barring such workers paled in comparison to the consequences of diminished growth in the hottest industry in the hottest economy ever known. Hot industries are job-creators and wealth-makers. That's what business is all about. That's what produces prosperity. Let the workers go where the jobs are—it's basic to the kind of flexible

workplace that holds so much promise for the whole of society.

2. Adequate accommodations and transportation for seasonal workers who return on a regular basis. Migrant farm workers are the classical example. To bring them in for vital work at low wages with no benefits is one thing, but to provide nowhere for poor people to live and no way but their own initiatives to get from one job to another is to do harm to the entire process. Growers alone cannot fund these basic costs and still provide their product to the marketplace at low prices. Somewhere, some way, others must ante up a fair share of the wherewithal necessary to put more honor and integrity in the employment of migrant workers.

3. "High-tech migrant and refugee clearing procedures" that lower the hurdles to moving across international borders. Italy, for example, should not have had to absorb hundreds of thousands of immigrants and refugees who flooded the country from Albania during the Kosovo conflict. They came not so much to reside in Italy but to pass through to other nations of Europe and the world where better opportunity awaited. For the lack of effective refugee processing procedures—and reciprocal arrangements with the community of nations—Italy got stuck with a huge human and economic burden. Given the advanced state of paperwork processing and background checks now possible, matching prospective foreign workers with employer needs nearly anywhere in the industrialized world is not unrealistic. The technology exists to smooth this process appreciably; what's missing is the political will. Pressure on elected officials from enough employers can correct that problem.

4. Simplify and speed up the naturalization process. Set reasonable standards, but don't use the bureaucracy to block the path to citizenship.

5. Pragmatic social services for legal immigrants. Government decree that takes away welfare benefits for legal immigrants (as the U.S. did in 1996, for example) simply shifts the burden of care, economic and otherwise, onto the private sector. When the options are to pay out of the right pocket (welfare contributions) or out of the left (emergency care, social unrest), why not tend to the problem with intelligent public policy that gets the job done correctly the first time?

6.   A workplace-friendly, overarching immigration policy. Deal with the illegal alien problem by first developing immigration policy that provides for the efficient movement, relocation and assimilation of foreigners who take the initiative to change their lives for the better. Once those policies are in place, tolerate no corruption of the system. But to deport, incarcerate or disenfranchise foreigners who have few alternatives but to operate as illegal aliens is an indictment of any nation that creates the situation. People are going to go where the opportunities are—that's a fact of life. To deny that is to create an intractable situation.

Better Benefits

Since the flexible workforce is of growing importance to employers, and since good affordable benefits are so basic an incentive to work as a FlexLifer, it follows that employers serve their own best interests by pushing for legislation that makes it possible for labor exchange services to tailor benefit programs to whatever requirements best suit just-in-time workers. Unfortunately, this is not the case in the general workplace, including the U.S. Here, current law blocks flexibility and innovation in the most flexible and innovative segment of the workplace—a major inconsistency in the general drift of employment. The subject is covered in more detail in Chapter Five, so, at this juncture, let me just encourage employers to become more familiar with the situation and use their collective influence to interject flexibility where flexibility is due.

Create a Flexible Workplace

An employer's need for skills, talent and other human resources may not vary from the traditional workplace to the *FlexLife®* workplace, but costs will certainly vary—even paying top dollar for assignment personnel. The difference lies in the costs associated with full-time, 52-week-a-year employees and all that they entail, as opposed to the outlay for a carefully managed "flexible workforce" where intermittent needs are tended to by intermittent labor. As stated previously, there is no escaping the requirement of a sound core staff of permanent employees. Beyond this essential core, however, there is a world of just-in-time talent, skills and labor that can ensure productivity, efficiency, competitiveness, growth, profitability and, yes, employee morale and motivation. With a well-

Organizing Your Workforce

A – Core Staff

These are the "process owners," those employees who define the organization's uniqueness. They provide organizational continuity and embody and impart the organization's corporate culture. In a flexible workplace, the core staff is usually the organization's permanent workforce.

B – Specialists

Employees with specialized skills who are called in or consulted to support the organization's operations. Typically, specialists work on a just-in-time basis which may range in length of service from several years to several months or weeks. HR, marketing, IT, finance and legal services are representative of the range of frequently employed specialist skills.

C – Generalists

This category of employee fills in around the core staff and the specialists to round out a fully operational workforce. A great many generalist jobs are ideal for just-in-time employees. It is in the generalist realm that the traditional "temporary help" concept used to flourish.

designed flexible workforce, core staff knows that the "flex" occurs with just-in-time personnel, not permanent employees. And FlexLifers are all about flexibility—they just move on to the next assignment. Here are some ways to ensure your organization's viability in the marketplace by putting some flex in personnel costs and innovation in the design of the workplace and workforce.

1.   Make flexibility a core value in your organization, complete with a menu of options that enables the workforce to give you their best while preserving a life for themselves as well.

 •   *Portable office* – Nowadays, assembling the workforce in one spot every working day may well be inefficient, counter-productive, costly and plain unnecessary. Develop programs for telecommuting. "Cyber" working arrangements are paying off big for some employers. Working out of customer facilities where interaction and efficiency warrant it is another effective tactic. Determine what works best for your organization, then provide the necessary resources to get the job done. Productivity gains quickly offset the cost of "stretching the concept of workplace."

- *Non-traditional schedules* – If the work gets done, productivity improves and important workers gain some precious time for themselves in the process, does it really make sense for employers to jam the workday into a nine-to-five, Monday through Friday time slot? The answer is a resounding "no." Every day is 24 hours long. There are seven days—168 hours—to the week, week after week. The possibilities are many for employers to get their 40 hours and more each week from those they employ. Experiment, loosen up, trust your people until they prove untrustworthy, be patient while the new schedule settles into the most effective mode. There is evidence aplenty that breaking from the rigidity of traditional working arrangements benefit employers and employees in a multitude of ways.

- *Team work* – Develop your own "skunk works," those in-house think tanks where talented, highly skilled people come together to develop solutions and strategies in team settings. Take advantage of the collaborative intelligence and imagination of your workforce. Give your people the flexibility to stretch to the fullest extent of their capabilities. It's good for them, it's good for the employer.

- *Job sharing* – Two or more employees splitting one job in ways that suit them is a way for some people to "get a job and get a life." It also helps retain valuable personnel and provides the employer with the best kind of backup for the job.

- *Non-traditional perks* – The modern workplace—certainly in the U.S.—is "employee-needs" driven. Not to recognize this is to find yourself short of the skills necessary to run a successful operation of any kind. Providing traditional employee benefits and a competitive salary or wage does not distinguish an employer in today's job market. But a little innovation and imagination can. Does your firm provide car washing and detailing services for employees? Some employers do. A growing number of businesses that keep personnel on the road a lot try to compensate with convenient dry cleaning services, pet care, even people to water their plants. Free or discounted tickets to choice events go far in building allegiance. Casual days, company-wide pizza lunches now and then—there are untold ways for employers to say to their workforce, "You are valued, respected and appreciated. Thanks."

- *Menu-based benefits* – One size doesn't fit all when it comes to employee benefits. Some employees are drawn solely to health insurance, others to 401(k) plans. Life insurance is a hot-button to many. Disability insurance means a great deal to certain employees. Innovative new benefits like an automobile lease subsidy are popular. Offering a wide-ranging menu of benefits allows employees to construct a package that best meets their individual circumstances. What does your menu of benefits consist of?

- *Vacation time* – Rolled into a single benefit, vacation time is at once a reward for services rendered, additional compensation and an attempt to avoid employee burnout that results in poor job performance. Maybe you could throw an occasional three-day weekend on top of the traditional two weeks off. Or break the two weeks into a succession of three-day weekends. There are some excellent opportunities to score big on the flexibility scale with vacation schedules. Give it a try.

- *Compensation flexibility* – Playing catch-up on the compensation front can be terribly costly for employers in a mercurial, competitive workplace where the unemployment rate is miniscule. Even being competitive today can leave you short of personnel tomorrow if you are not aware of where salaries/wages are headed on the short-run. Does your salary structure need revision? Are there provisions for variable compensation based on individual, team or company performance? Any reason incentives couldn't be paid quarterly or bi-annually instead of once a year? Give it some thought, your competitors certainly are.

- *Profit sharing and stock options* – Your organization may not be a high-flying, dot-com wunderkind that can toss around stock options, profit sharing and/or performance bonuses. But maybe you can do more of this than you first thought. Explore the possibilities. You may gain a real advantage vis a vis the competition in your field.

133

2.   Partner up with a full-service staffing organization. They deal exclusively in the flexible workplace and can help immeasurably with the development and management of a flexible workforce. They can explain the possibilities, research and prepare a flexible workforce plan tailored to your needs, implement the plan, run the operation on a contract basis, monitor performance and generally shorten the development time for employers seeking the benefits of a good flexible workforce. As it is with professional FlexLifers, it is important for employers to choose carefully the agency that serves them. Interview the candidates. Lay out your business plan, goals, objectives, skill requirements, target dates, contingencies requirements, performance expectations, management needs, budget—the whole schmear. See how far the labor exchange service will go in sharing the responsibility for developing and managing your flexible workforce. Demand that the prospective agency work with the competition, if necessary, to fill your order for human resources. Stress the importance you place on agency-provided staffing employee benefits. Make your decision on an agency, then monitor performance. If the organization does not perform as promised, discontinue the relationship and get another staffing partner. Help drive the local staffing industry to be all that it can be for your sake. It is not the place of employers to take what labor exchange services offer, but to get what employers need. Begin there, and you will serve your interests well and help push the staffing industry to new heights.

3.   Develop an assessment and evaluation routine to help managers target positions that lend themselves to just-in-time work. The practice results in better management of labor costs and higher productivity. Additional benefits accrue when the assessment and evaluation are tied to employee training and development. Well-conceived and delivered, these programs should improve employee skills, marketability, earning power and job satisfaction—key factors in personnel retention. Just as important, they should be targeted to skills the employer needs to succeed. The best time to identify these skills—

Seasonal work comes every season. There's no excuse not to be prepared with a good agent or other labor exchange resource during these periods.

and the training needed to develop them—is during the assessment and evaluation of just-in-time job slots. There's nothing wrong with advancing the careers of assignment personnel while also advancing the organization's best interests.

4. Develop and publish a "workforce plan" for your organization, complete with a list of core staff and just-in-time positions. Include job descriptions for both categories. Work from the "concentric circles model" exhibited earlier. What just-in-time specialists are needed to support the ongoing work of the core staff? When do the jobs begin? When might they end? What's the availability of the skills needed and what does it cost to acquire them? Intermittently, there will be just-in-time generalists needed to fill in for sick and vacationing core staff. Some of this can be anticipated and planned for, much of it cannot. That doesn't mean that plans can't be laid to meet these requirements when they arise. Seasonal work comes every season. There's no excuse not to be prepared with a good agent or other labor exchange resource during these periods. Spell out the need for core staff "intangibles" like loyalty, tradition, continuity, flexibility, knowledge management and goodwill (see Chapter Three).

5. Put pertinent systems and methods, processes and procedures to paper so that just-in-time employees have a reference to work from, and core staff doesn't vary from the "prescribed course" when it comes to training the short-timers. Make the material readily available. Update it regularly. Place good core-staff personnel in charge of maintaining the integrity of the program, including the conveyance of information to the flexible workforce. The best-laid plan for a flexible workforce will drift into chaos without careful monitoring and maintenance.

Develop training and counseling programs to assist personnel who may want to move from just-in-time status to core staff, and vice versa. Make it known to your workforce that it's OK to pursue the possibilities in either direction.

6. Develop training and counseling programs to assist personnel who may want to move from just-in-time status to core staff, and vice versa. Make it known to your workforce that it's OK to pursue the possibilities in either direction. Institute straight talk about the organization's current job situation and likely requirements

for the future. Give personnel an opportunity to plan and grow within the confines of your business plan. It's good for your personnel, and it's good for you. Get the workforce involved in the personnel adjustments made necessary by market conditions.

7.   Decide what business you are in, and staff the organization to do best what the organization does best. If the business is basically a printing operation with adjunct graphic arts capabilities, it's OK to promote yourself as a full-service graphic arts supplier. But, from a personnel perspective, you would likely build the core staff to support the printing operation and supplement the workforce with just-in-time graphic artists when business warrants. On second thought, however, company management may decide that profit margins are too low in the printing business due to the carrying costs of expensive presses. He or she might decide to switch heavily into the graphic services side of the business, sell off the printing presses and ancillary equipment, and outsource printing work to other vendors.

Help sell students on the need for skills development as a life-long educational activity. Stress the rapid pace of change in the workplace and the need to keep up.

The company's name and product line wouldn't change, but its core business would be altered substantially. From a basic printing operation, the firm would become a graphic arts and printing sales establishment. Personnel requirements would change. Press operators and printing-related managers would no longer be needed. More art directors and sales personnel might have to be added. The size of the core staff might shrink because there would be less capital equipment to operate, manage and maintain. The just-in-time segment of the workforce could grow as the graphic arts side of the business took on more importance. Through all this, however, much of the core staff would remain intact—if it was designed well to begin with. There are billings and receipts still to be processed. Marketing requirements change little. Products and services still have to be scheduled, produced and delivered. Management deals with essentially the same products and services. The point is, an organization's core business can change much more readily when management understands the possibilities inherent in a flexible workforce.

8.   Join in partnership arrangements with educational institutions from

middle school through college. Seventh or eighth grade is not too early to start a dialogue about jobs and the workplace, many companies feel. Help sell students on the need for skills development as a lifelong educational activity. Stress the rapid pace of change in the workplace and the need to keep up. Point to anticipated career opportunities in your organization and the workplace in general, five, ten years down the road. Set up work-study programs that introduce students to the real world of adult employment—and the virtues of your organization. Keep in mind the recent experience of the computer industry. When it really took off with the global economic boom of the 1990s, there were not enough computer science graduates available to fill the available jobs. What happened? For one thing, the "nerd factor" associated with computer geeks turned off many youngsters. The repetition and monotony of computer programming convinced many kids to go into other fields. There were other causes, but while the image of computer science was declining, the industry did next to nothing to bridge the gap between the perceptions of future workers and the realities of the profession. As previously expressed, computer expertise and other IT skills are some of the most attractive, secure niches in the workplace today. Yet the industry struggles for lack of competent personnel. Employers in every business ought to be thinking about these things and not just assume that the skills and talent needed five, ten years from now will be available. They just may not be.

9. Develop a quick and effective orientation program for just-in-time workers. It may be a film, short presentation, pamphlet or all of the above. Cover the basics from starting and quitting times to lunch hour details, protocol for scheduled breaks, pertinent house rules (e.g., smoking, confidentiality), parking, dress, pay arrangements, benefits and so on. Provide an overview of each staffing employee's job assignment. Introduce them to immediate supervisors and coworkers. Assign someone to answer questions for the newcomers. These simple steps shorten the learning curve for just-in-time employees and improve their performance. You, the employer, are better for the initiative.

10. With the help of your FlexLife agent, look for opportunities in the local marketplace to develop a pool of just-in-time employees that

you can use when needed, and other employers can use when you don't need them. With such an arrangement in place, the flexible employees will stay gainfully employed year-round and acquire important cross-training in a variety of skills. Two or three times through the circuit of participating workplaces, and employees develop into a reliable, flexible resource for participating employers. Employers who create and draw from the pool will have trained workers when they need them, with assurance that the skills will be available next time they are called for. There have been experiments with the concept, but employers need to force its development.

11. Increase the productivity and competitiveness of your organization by utilizing the skills and talent available via telecommuting and electronic networks. Creative, cost-conscious employers gain an edge on the competition by getting more done outside the traditional office/plant setting.

Manage the Flexible Workforce

The traditional nine-to-five workplace is a lot easier to manage and much more predictable. But it's also an anachronism. The well-designed and managed flexible workforce is cutting edge in every respect. It's just a little more frenetic and demanding to deal with.

A workplace designed to expand and contract to match market conditions has a dynamic to it quite unlike the staid old world of traditional permanent jobs. New people come and go on a regular basis, often at irregular hours and for undetermined lengths of time. They tackle old tasks with new skills and competencies, sometimes achieving remarkable results and always shedding new light on the subject. They bring new perspectives to old problems, a breath of fresh air to mundane corners of the operation, questions never before asked, approaches unimagined, and a certain tension and energy that inhibits complacency. Without intelligent management, it could all drift into chaos. But managed well, a flexible workplace can maximize productivity and ensure against creeping obsolescence. The traditional nine-to-five workplace is a lot easier to manage and much more predictable. But it's also an anachronism. The well-designed and managed flexible workforce is cutting edge in every respect. It's just a little more frenetic and demanding to deal with. The management required to maximize the effectiveness of a flexible workforce differs appreciably from that needed to extract top performance from the core staff. The latter is fixed, known and predictable. The former is fluid, less familiar and, consequently, more unpredictable. The relationship is not unlike the military equivalent of combining a regular army unit with a guerrilla band. Where and how they are joined is critical to the effectiveness of the total force. How effectively the guerrilla unit delivers its skills and competencies determines in large measure whether the combined force achieves its goals at reasonable costs. Just throwing the two units together is to invite problems. Joining them wisely and tending to the marriage as a matter of course is the way to go. Here are some management suggestions for employers in dealing with a flexible workforce:

1. Put people in management positions that understand and appreciate the strengths of a flexible workforce. It's getting to be important for a growing number of employers as indicated by a report from the Warton Business School Center for Leadership and Change Management. The document states that "Managers who issue orders are being replaced with those who negotiate results, and the skill for delegating work downward is being replaced with a talent for arranging work outward."

2. Develop a management team specifically for the flexible portion of the total workforce. This team should have two basic responsibilities:

    • To ensure maximum coordination with the core staff and create a seamless mesh of permanent and flexible personnel. The interface needs to be durable, flexible and efficient. The flexible side of the total workforce should be an extension of the core staff. When new assignment personnel step into the picture, productivity needs to surge, not decline.

    People work hard and perform well for a variety of reasons. Find out, one person at a time, what those reasons are.

    • To create and maintain the best environment possible for just-in-time personnel so that the organization realizes the highest return on the economic resource. A key feature is a monitoring system that measures commitment, performance and tenure of the flexible workforce. If the findings are less than positive, the fault may be management's. Are job descriptions reasonable, clear and well-communicated? Has personnel been chosen with the right skills for the job? When was the last time procedures, processes and methods were analyzed and updated? Have managers and supervisors been sufficiently trained to perform in a flexible work environment? Are the necessary tools, information and authority available to get the job done? If any of these problems exist, correct them. And try making just-in-time work more challenging and attractive. That doesn't always have to mean more pay or expense. People work hard and perform well for a variety of reasons. Find out, one person at a time, what those reasons are.

3. Don't lose sight of those previously described generational differences in your workforce and the "workstyles" most likely to increase employee performance, retention and recruiting. For attentive, leading-edge employers, a competitive edge is there for the taking.

4. Call upon a professional staffing organization to help manage your flexible workforce. You don't have to reinvent the wheel here. Draw on the expertise available to get the job done.

5. Once a workforce plan has been developed, make sure everyone in the organization understands it. Be frank about the need for labor flexibility and the ability to contract when necessary and expand quickly and effectively as need arises. It means improved efficiency, lower costs, better profit margins, increased competitiveness and greater job security for core staff personnel. Remove any assumption that core-staff jobs are more valuable or enjoy a higher status than just-in-time positions. The purpose of the workforce plan is to define the team and the players necessary to deliver a winning performance: the core staff at the center of things, bolstered by just-in-time specialists on one hand and generalists on the other. Together, the combined workforce slays the dragons and delivers the goods. On this team, the star is a hero and so is the ball boy. Everyone has value and status so long as they perform as prescribed. Allowing a sense of inferiority or second-class status to develop in the concentric

circles that support the core staff is self-defeating for the entirety of the workforce.

6. Recognize that loyalty is a two-way street. You want it from employees; employees want it from you. Ironically, employers become disloyal when they hire employees full-time, under-utilize their skills, fail to advance their careers, discover that idle human resources are too expensive, and downsize people unaccustomed to anything but full-time employment. Harm is done to the company's reputation and prospects. On the other hand, loyalty can emerge from short-term job assignments when employers add to the employment security of just-in-time personnel by putting them in the right situation, training them and acknowledging work well done.

7. Close the gap between corporate purchasing and the HR department. A great deal of credibility and productivity are lost in the split of the two functions. Just-in-time workers are not widgets, and, all too often, that's how purchasing treats them. It's OK to treat the skills, talent and labor of just-in-time employees as an economic resource, but it's not OK to lose sight of their humanity.

8. Advance the employment security of just-in-time employees with training and counseling whether you use them once for a few days or regularly for months at a time. In large part, employers pull out of the flexible labor pool what employers put in. Quality in, quality out. Don't leave the hard work of workforce training and grooming to others. Do your part. The training regimen can be quick and simple, formal and informal. Just design it with the intent to impart something of relevance and enduring value to a career. Be imaginative. Provide training on motivation and performance in just-in-time job situations. Like frequent flyer miles, give credit for hours worked as a just-in-time employee that can be applied to higher forms of education at local colleges or trade schools. Develop a presentation on the company's method of operation from core staff and flexible employee perspectives.

    Quality in, quality out. Don't leave the hard work of workforce training and grooming to others. Do your part.

9. Explore the possibilities of splitting the cost of employee benefits

among several employers for a pool of flexible employees. Employee benefits would add substantially to the appeal of this kind of work and make it easier to keep the pool well stocked with quality workers.

10. As much as practical, work through labor exchange organizations that offer benefits to assignment personnel so as to lessen the potential for claims later.

11. Announce retrenchment or expansion plans well in advance when possible. When employees know what's coming, they can make plans and adjust; when they don't, the negative impact is much more severe. And people don't forget. Trust is hard to restore in employees downsized or otherwise released on short notice. Watch your reputation as an employer. If you are heavy-handed and insensitive to those who work for you, don't reduce the core staff too much. You may not be able to attract just-in-time workers when you need them.

12. Recognize that polished FlexLife® skills and competencies may cost more than lesser capabilities—a premium made palatable by the short-term nature of the expense.

Know What to Expect of a Staffing Agent

The legal relationship between staffing agent and employer is service-provider and client. But the working relationship is much more a partnership. In any good and lasting partnership, "the partners" are compelled to bring something of value to the table. For the agent and his or her supporting organization, the value must of necessity include the following:

1. The ability and willingness to accurately assess employer labor needs.
2. The ability and willingness to learn the client's business and industry.
3. In-depth knowledge of the local job market and the workplace in general.
4. A comprehensive database of assignment personnel reflective of the local workplace. Where the employer's requirements diverge from the local profile, the agent must be capable of developing a suitable pool of skills in short order.
5. Effective e-cruiting and e-lancing capabilities.

6.   The know-how and experience to design, implement and manage a flexible workforce.

7.   Connections and capabilities on a regional, national and even an international level. Certain job skills are not always available locally. When necessary, the agency must have the ability to reach into the far corners of the job market to fill a client's needs. This may include the acquisition of skills and talent from remote service providers via the Internet.

8.   The necessary tools of the staffing trade must be at the agent's disposal if the employer is to be served fully.

9.   Staffing agent briefings and insights on changing conditions in the marketplace that may impact the employer.

10. A clearly written understanding about the possible permanent employment of agency-placed assignment personnel. There is no better way for employers to evaluate personnel than a temp-to-hire arrangement. The staffing industry understands this and offers a variety of appealing temp-to-hire programs that substantially improve the employer's recruiting and selection process.

11. The savvy to keep client employers out of trouble on the legal issues of temporary versus permanent employee status.

Know What to Expect of Just-in-Time Personnel

Those who pass through your door as just-in-time employees come from every walk of life and represent skills from the most rudimentary to the most technologically advanced. What should you expect of such a diverse, fluid workforce?

1.   In all cases, you should expect that these workers reflect what you requested of your labor exchange service. If you ordered an experienced general manager and received an introverted researcher instead, then you are not getting what you bargained for. If you expected ten fit people to clear out a warehouse, you shouldn't have to deal with anything less. If assignment personnel have presented themselves to be something that they are not, you are not obliged to go along with the ruse.

2.   You should expect compliance with the "rules and style of the house." Of course, it is incumbent upon the employer to adequately

convey the rules and style. The staffing agent should be provided this information at the outset of the client relationship so that he or she can help prepare staffing personnel accordingly. Then, as part of the on-site indoctrination, the employer should be sure to cover the rules and style of the workplace so that there is no misunderstanding on the part of the staffing employee.

3. Expect just-in-time personnel to be dutiful and responsive to instruction, but don't expect them to tolerate poor behavior from managers or coworkers. Assignment workers have options. They can fire their employers and get other job assignments in short order. That prospect should not be taken lightly. Word gets around, employers get a bad reputation, and just-in-time workers decline the call for assistance when it's needed.

4. Expect staffing employees to be interested in permanent employment, but don't be surprised if the really good ones decline your offer. Many FlexLifers are doing just what they want and wouldn't have it any other way. But use the just-in-time job assignment to the organization's advantage. This includes the assessment of potential permanent employees.

5. You should expect to be protected from co-employer liabilities, either by specific provisions in the employment contract or through agency-provided employee benefits.

6. You should expect just-in-time personnel to be receptive to training, especially that which improves their employment security. Consider offering this as an added incentive for just-in-time workers who perform for your organization. You may not always be able to pay the highest wages, but perhaps you can compensate with specialized training that improves the person's employability later. Make these programs meaningful and valuable. Use them as promotion devices for your firm. Provide verifiable documentation of the training received.

7. You should expect just-in-time employees to display a positive attitude and work ethic, to comport themselves professionally and to be open to instruction, to ask when questions arise and be loyal to you in the following ways:
   • By performing well.
   • By honoring the rules and style of the house.

- By speaking well of the employer or not at all.
- By holding confidential sensitive information learned on the job.

The prospects for lower personnel costs and heightened productivity have never been more exciting. By completing the transition launched in the first few years of the 1990s, employers in advanced economies can create a workplace that accentuates the positives and ameliorates the negatives like no other time in history. Sure, tough economic times will come again. Business will retrench and cut costs. And people will be laid off in distressing numbers. But by creating a truly flexible workplace, where employee skills can be matched with employer needs quickly and efficiently, then terminated, employers can ride out the storm more quickly and more nimbly. And the downsized will no longer be stymied by hiring freezes and unmarketable competencies. Indeed, it may be in periods of high unemployment that FlexLifers enjoy employment security above all other categories of employees.

Chapter Five

Don't lead. Follow.
Or get out of the way.

Government, labor unions and
regulation of the new workplace

The arrival of the global marketplace is a remarkable development. Every imaginable obstacle stood in its way. A babel of tongues—6,000 different languages and many more dialects—garble the conduct of business throughout the world. There are more than 200 different currencies and values to sort out. Mail and communications vary country to country. Transportation is as much a maze as a web. Accounting system differences assure confusion at the bottom line. Time zones leave half the world's buyers and sellers asleep while the other half clamors for business. There are special interests to protect, tariffs and other trade barriers to overcome, bureaucracies to deal with, mind-boggling cultural differences to wade through, gangsters, terrorists, coups and threats of coups, forest fires, monsoons, volcanic eruptions . . . you name it.

It's a wonder any business is ever conducted beyond local markets. But, through it all, despite it all, the global marketplace found its way and stands before us today strong and vigorous, an unprecedented catalyst of change and promise. And it is just getting started. With the global marketplace has come a new kind of workplace, new business practices, new technologies, new modes of transportation, new ways of doing things, a new reality. But not everything has changed to match the realities of worldwide competition. The public has been slow to grasp the ramifications. And government and labor unions are left spinning as the global marketplace roars right past them.

In the wake of the global marketplace, where competition is severe, flexibility paramount, and rapid response an absolute necessity, government and labor struggle to make sense of things–bound, it seems, to do something to restore equilibrium, even if it's wrong. The issues to be addressed reach to every nook and cranny of every advanced or developing nation. What's to be done about so much competition from so many quarters? How are jobs and stability and special interests to be protected? For fear of going forward, how is the status quo to be retained? For fear of falling behind, how do you capitalize on the opportunities presented? How is the "social contract" between business and the workforce to be revised to achieve fairness, harmony and global competitiveness? Do nations withdraw into a cocoon of isolation and "fight the competitors at the border," or run with the horses?

National economic policy matters more today than ever before because oceans and mountains and languages and cultures no longer shield countries from hungry foreign competitors or financial turmoil anywhere in the world. Standing still, doing the same old thing, is to slip backward on the international scale of competitiveness. Business suffers and jobs are lost as a result. As for organized labor, it must choose between fighting new trends with old tactics or adapting to the demands of the new workplace. Organized labor can work in concert with government on wise workplace strategies or work against them. It can do what's good for most of its membership

---

What's Winning and What's Not

- *Teamwork is winning; cross-purposes can't compete.*
- *Free-market economics are winning, and state-run business and welfare states are not.*
- *Deregulation surges to the front, and protective government policy falters.*
- *Labor flexibility is winning; fixed labor costs are not.*
- *Lean and nimble is winning; ponderous and slow bring up the rear.*
- *Employee mobility is winning; labor constraint flags.*
- *Education and skills-enhancement are winning; unprepared labor isn't.*
- *Competitive taxation is winning; confiscation of personal and corporate earnings to support expensive social contracts is losing.*
- *Hard money is winning; unsustainable fiscal practice staggers to finish.*

most of the time or follow a different agenda, leaving its constituents twisting in the wind. The possibilities are many. The stakes are high. And the winners and losers are beginning to separate heading into the back stretch of the race into the workplace of the future. Who's winning and who's losing? What's winning and what's not? Let's examine the field. . . .

Teamwork is winning; cross-purposes can't compete.

In the global marketplace, all nations are not created equal. Some are richer, bigger, more stable or blessed. Some are better positioned and / or managed, and others just do more with the resources they have. It's this last distinction that is most important. For success in the global marketplace depends on internal teamwork. While all nations are not equal in material wealth, each rises or falls on the backs of the very same team players: employers, the job creators; employees, the combined labor force; government policymakers, regulators of the workplace; organized labor, representatives of working men and women; and labor exchange services, matchmakers of jobs and skills. Winning economies are distinguished by how well the players are organized, how well they work together, and how well each plays its designated role. Greater size and wealth can't compete when the national team pulls at cross-purposes. One need look no further than Singapore, Hong Kong or The Netherlands for verification. No one of the three is as big or as populous as Pennsylvania, yet all are relative giants in the global marketplace. Singapore, with just three million people, is peerless when it comes to doing the most for its populace with the resources at hand. Hong Kong is rich despite the looming proximity of the biggest communist state on earth. The Dutch started pulling together back in 1982, and the results have made them the envy of all Europe. The story is interesting and instructive for nations anywhere that are serious about improving the standard of living of their people. It began at a time when the country suffered under what was known as the "Dutch Disease": too few people working. Too much cost wrapped up in the social contract with the workforce. Not enough flexibility in collective bargaining agreements. Declining productivity. A lack of competitiveness. Government, organized labor and employers were fighting over their differences and failing to capitalize on the common ground between them. All the while, the nation, like most of Europe, was slipping further into an economic malaise. Something needed to be done and, unlike the rest of Europe, the Dutch started doing it. In 1982, the parties to the problem got together at Wassenaar, a small village near The Hague, and essentially decided to work together for the common good. That was the master stroke. Everything else was basic goal-setting, cooperation on the easy stuff, give and take on the differences, and good old-fashioned teamwork. Government went to work trimming costs from the nation's generous welfare system without gutting it. Organized labor froze wage demands to bolster job creation. Employers agreed to cut working hours so that more people could be employed. These were not perfect or complete solutions, nor were they the end of the effort. The parties continued to meet, continued to keep the bigger picture before them and continued to make headway. Bureaucratic glitches were gradually reduced, streamlining the conduct of business. The labor market was significantly deregulated, creating better employment options for employers and employees alike. Social security obligations for employers were eased, lowering the cost of doing business. And constraints on the hiring, firing and movement of employees were slackened, making for a more competitive workplace. It took a few years, but from 1988 onward, the Dutch Disease began to metamorphose into the now famous Dutch or Polder Model. The country's unemployment rate of 5.5 percent was half that of Germany, France and Belgium, the Associated Press reported in November 1997. Among European Union nations, The Netherlands topped the list of lowest wage raises and the least number of hours lost to strikes. Since 1991, the Dutch economy has grown an average of 2.5 percent annually, faster than the rest of the EU and the U.S. as well. "The Netherlands today is the model country, the example for the continent," said Hans Tietmeyer, Germany's influential central bank governor. "While others gripe about the flood of economic challenges, the Dutch started early to get in shape."

Message for Government – Call together the principal players that comprise the nation's workplace. Try to forge a cooperative team to compete against the rest of the world. Look for the common ground where all are comfortable. Set national goals that directly benefit the most people. For the Dutch, it was employment, to do what was necessary to create good, growth-driven jobs. Develop a blueprint to achieve the goal. Proceed where there is consensus. Give and take on the differences—small steps at a time if need be, but keep moving toward the objective. Make adjustments as necessary. Stick to it, through changes in officials, governing parties, bad times and good times. As national policy, nothing will bring improvement in the standard of living of a body of people quite so reliably as concerted, consistent teamwork by the powers that be in the workplace.

Message for Labor – Abandon adversarial approaches to the creation of the "good life." The enemies of organized labor are unemployment, a declining standard of living and the inability to compete against suppliers of goods and services from abroad. The list does not include the nation's employers, the job-owners who are absolutely indispensable to a healthy economy. Team up with the capitalists and the entrepreneurs to put products and services on the market that attract more customers and grow the economy. The bigger the pie, the bigger the slice for organized labor. And your capitalist teammates in the workplace will serve it up gladly. But when the pie shrinks, so too do the slices. Refusing to take a lesser portion is, well . . . adversarial. And the team falls apart, to the detriment of all parties.

Free-market economics are winning, and state-run business and welfare states are not.

China and India, the world's two most populous nations—and largest markets—have recently emerged from long and unsuccessful experiments with isolation economics. That one is a tightly controlled communist model and the other a shambling democracy makes no real difference. Regardless of the political system, the economics don't work encumbered by too much government and divorced from the global marketplace. The once mighty Soviet Union imploded trying to make centrally controlled, communist economics work. France and Germany, slow to respond to competitive efficiencies, struggle with high unemployment, low corporate profits, burdensome taxes, labor instability and reduced prospects for the future. In a long-running embarrassment, Japan tries to dig out from the jumble of protective trade policies, tangled banking practices and unsustainable social contracts that leave the once proud economic juggernaut on shaky ground. Canadian taxes and the expensive social contracts they support often get the nation's industrial complex bypassed in the global marketplace and produce a "brain and capital drain" that no country can long afford. On the other hand, free-market proponents like the U.S., Singapore, New Zealand, The Netherlands and Ireland continue to illustrate the competitive advantages to be gained by a healthy mix of tolerable taxation, prudent banking practice, deregulation, privatization, flexible work provisions, the introduction of new technology and a healthy domestic consumer base.

Notwithstanding recent setbacks caused by the Asian-born currency crisis, unimpeded trade and commerce moves closer to fruition every passing year. It is obviously a superior framework for conducting business, or so many countries would not have abandoned alternative systems to join the global marketplace as free-enterprise practitioners. But this decidedly robust economic system is a two-edged sword. It cleaves on the positive side, and cuts with the negative. The more entangled and interdependent the economies of the world become, the more a financial wound to one quarter staggers the whole. What goes up in the free-enterprise system often comes down. No artificial props allowed. No protection from the consequences of bad business practices. You can't have it one way, then another when things don't suit you.

Message for Government – Compete. Help the private sector create wealth. Wealth means liquidity—cash to do things. Russia wallows in one failed attempt after another to right its economy because there is not enough homegrown liquidity to make the right things happen. The problem is endemic to other less-developed economies as well. With the creation of wealth, a nation's money supply grows, credit is extended by the international community and direct investment from abroad increases. All together, it drives economic activity. But it starts with a willingness to compete. How well a nation's economy competes in the global marketplace determines the vibrancy and quality of the workplace. Healthy workplace, healthy economy; ailing workplace, ailing economy.

Help the private sector create wealth. Wealth means liquidity—cash to do things.

And competing successfully today is not the same proposition it used to be just a few years ago. The International Institute of Management Development (IMD), based in Lucerne, Switzerland, analyzes and ranks

Most Competitive Nations — April 13, 1999

1. USA	18. Taiwan	35. Brazil
2. Singapore	19. Austria	36. Mexico
3. Finland	20. New Zealand	37. Turkey
4. Luxembourg	21. France	38. Korea
5. The Netherlands	22. Belgium	39. India
6. Switzerland	23. Spain	40. Slovenia
7. Hong Kong	24. Israel	41. Czech Republic
8. Denmark	25. Chile	42. South Africa
9. Germany	26. Hungary	43. Colombia
10. Canada	27. Malaysia	44. Poland
11. Ireland	28. Portugal	45. Venezuela
12. Australia	29. China	46. Indonesia
13. Norway	30. Italy	47. Russia
14. Sweden	31. Greece	
15. United Kingdom	32. The Philippines	
16. Japan	33. Argentina	
17. Iceland	34. Thailand	

Source: International Institute of Management Development (IMD)

the competitive environments nations create for their business communities to operate in. Nations manage their affairs in the face of what the IMD calls the Four Forces of Competition:

- *Proximity versus Globality* – Domestic consumption of the nation's product balanced with the sale of goods abroad and the consumption of goods from abroad. A nation must have a strong domestic market, but it cannot be an island unto itself.
- *Attractiveness versus Aggressiveness* – Creating national appeal that attracts direct foreign investment and jobs balanced with aggressive investments abroad and exports. Attractiveness generally creates jobs, aggressiveness income. Germany, Japan and South Korea have followed the latter course, Ireland, Thailand and the UK the former.
- *Assets versus Processes* – A reliance on natural resources for income (Brazil, Kuwait) balanced with transformation processes that add value to products and services (Japan). This distinction

marks the difference between inherited wealth and created wealth.
* ***Individual Risk versus Social Cohesiveness*** – Individual risk, deregulation and privatization (the Anglo-Saxon Model) balanced with the preservation of social cohesiveness (the Continental European Model).

The effectiveness with which these complex forces are reconciled with the strengths and weaknesses of any given country results in the quality of the nation's workplace—good and prosperous, bad and unsupportive, or somewhere in between. It's complex and elusive stuff. What works today may not work tomorrow. Enlightened economic policy set in concrete may prove dead weight with the shift in little-noticed trends. Germany, Japan and Korea, for example, climbed to lofty economic heights in recent years by pursuing a policy of aggressive foreign investment and exporting (Aggressiveness versus Attractiveness). The strategy created tremendous cash flow but hurt job growth. And for years, all three countries have suffered as a result. Attractiveness as a place to invest and produce is in tune with the times. How quickly the pendulum swings. The key to success in the global marketplace is diligence and flexibility like never before.

In light of today's integrated economic order, governments everywhere must strive to see themselves as the global marketplace sees them. If, after such an analysis, any nation concludes that the marketplace has better options than to deal with the domestic business establishment, the country's leadership might want to examine the forces of competition that are causing the problem. Are taxes oppressive vis-à-vis the competition? Is control of the money supply weak? That will spook investors and employers for sure. Labor costs out of line? Who needs it when there's a better deal down the road? Is the movement of labor too restrictive? Don't expect major employers to get excited about your country when there is some question about labor supply. Is the lack of skills and education turning off investors? Social unrest causing problems? Is government policy too meddlesome, unresponsive or ineffective? Of course, recognizing the problem is only part of the solution for a country's leadership. Hard decisions have to be made to improve a nation's standing in the global marketplace. Open markets, hard money, tough bankruptcy laws, wealth creation incentives—the longer these things are deferred, the more painful the cure. So, where to start?

Ask first, what is the proper role of government in today's workplace? Logic and common sense say that it is to adjust to the winds of economic change rather than trying to bind those changes in regulatory tethers that won't hold. The marketplace won't be manipulated and tampered with very long. The Organization of Petroleum Exporting Countries (OPEC) first learned that lesson back in 1973 with the Arab Oil Embargo (back before there was a real global marketplace). The marketplace adjusted to the high prices and heavy-handed tactics with energy efficiencies, increased exploration and unheard-of new sources of supply. Throughout most of the 1980s and 1990s, the marketplace was awash in a glut of oil, and OPEC's control over that basic commodity was mostly a distant memory. Of course, "big oil" was back at it again in 1999 and 2000. Outrageous prices, economic dislocations, manipulation of the marketplace. It was a poor strategy in the 1970s, and it is a poor strategy today. The marketplace will adjust.

There is another question governments should answer when assessing their prospects in today's global marketplace. How do I get mine? How does government make the global marketplace work to the benefit of the state and its populace? Without some great natural source of wealth like oil, nations must rely on the labor and ingenuity of their people for the good life. The dictates of wise macro-management say "maximize the effectiveness of your wealth-makers and everything else will take care of itself." Ironically, world-leading pay scales and expensive social safety nets do little for the effectiveness of a nation's wealth-makers (Individual Risk versus Social Cohesiveness). The workplace can't perform

Without some great natural source of wealth like oil, nations must rely on the labor and ingenuity of their people for the good life.

if the business goes elsewhere. Obstacles to the timely reduction and expansion of the workforce, for example, drive employers elsewhere and diminish the jobs that produce the wealth of individuals and nations. Instead of maximizing effectiveness, the opposite occurs. And the good life slips away. This is not to say that a nation's wealth-makers should go poor so as to be effective in the global marketplace. But it is to say that people and nations cannot live beyond their ability to attract business and perform at a price that will keep the business coming back. In this sense, every nation must do essentially the same thing to make free-market economics work. They have to be competitive, produce and deliver efficiently, provide for flexibility in the workplace, break down the barriers to employee mobility and move fast. Every nation has certain strengths it can employ in the global marketplace. And there's wealth enough to go around. The trick is to answer the question, "How do I make the system work for me?"

Message for Labor – Get with the program. Things have changed for the labor movement just as they have for employees, employers, government and labor exchange services. In the global marketplace where the "virtual corporation" flows around obstacles, organized labor has to reinvent itself. This is not the 1950s where the "quality of life within a region could often be calibrated to the competitiveness of its largest employers," reminds Working Partnerships USA and the Economic Policy Institute. Back then, the U.S. auto industry was concentrated in southeastern Michigan. Production was dependent on local and regional labor, a fact that enabled the United Auto Workers (UAW) to negotiate "lucrative contracts which helped to move hundreds of thousands of southeastern Michigan families into the middle class." Booming car sales meant plenty of jobs and healthy tax revenues, and the entire area grew and prospered. What was good for General Motors may or may not have been good for America, but certainly it was good for Detroit, Lansing, Grand Rapids, Flint, Pontiac and other towns in the region. But today, employers can be quite competitive outside a region and prosper as a result, with little calibration to the local or regional market. GM, Ford and Daimler Chrysler AG now build automobiles throughout the world, where costs are cheaper and the quality just as good. The game changed. A model of trade unionism designed for Henry Ford and Frederick Taylor is as unworkable as it is unattractive, caution the researchers at Working Partnership USA. Change the game, and the rules change. Labor can no longer pine for more and better jobs on the one hand, then drive away just what it's seeking with noncompetitive wages, benefit and job security demands on the other. Not when the effect is to get the nation's

> In the global marketplace where the "virtual corporation" flows around obstacles, organized labor has to reinvent itself.

wealth-makers bypassed in the global marketplace.

If competitiveness is the name of the game in commerce today, then organized labor needs to contribute as a legitimate team player for a nation's economy to score well. It's a country's employers, employees, labor representatives, government policymakers and labor exchange services arrayed against the world. Literally. Those nations that best utilize all their players win, those that don't don't. The team structure of old won't get the job done (i.e., organized labor and government paired off against employers, with employees standing idly on the sidelines and labor exchange services yipping about the fringes). Nowadays, employers and investors can take their balls and go elsewhere to play. And the game ends for the locals.

The only way for national economies to grow in the world today is to be competitive in the global marketplace, both as a place to work and as a supplier of goods and services.

The only real answer to unemployment and prosperity is economic growth. The only way for national economies to grow in the world today is to be competitive in the global marketplace, both as a place to work and as a supplier of goods and services. Anything else is wishful thinking or worse. So how does organized labor best serve its membership in a business world where free-market economics is clearly the winning ticket and protectionist welfare states are not? Try this:

1. Use the free-market system to organized labor's advantage. The power and influence of unions employed to advance national competitiveness in the global marketplace pays big dividends for all. Dutch unions can tell you all about it. Specifically, labor needs to pursue and/or support local, state and national legislation that "maximizes the effectiveness of the area's wealth-makers." This includes initiatives to:
    *   Open markets to competition.
    *   Ease the burden of social security costs for employers so that they are more competitive in the global marketplace.
    *   Deregulate the labor market so that the benefits of flexible forms of employment can be brought to bear on productivity and job creation.

157

- Smooth the processes of commerce so that efficiencies and response time are improved.
- Foster teamwork and cooperation among the key players in the workplace: employers, employees, government policymakers, labor exchange services and organized labor.
- Provide for the transportability of employee benefits so that the flexible workforce can go about its business protected from the exorbitant costs of illness, injury and retirement.
- Clear away barriers to the movement of human skills, talent and labor so that the workplace is truly fluid and efficient.
- Develop tax policy that attracts business, capital and needed workers or, at least, doesn't drive them away.

As a coordinated package, tailored to the special circumstances of each nation, these things would do more than any other action or series of actions to raise the level of the general economy and organized labor right along with it. More on this later.

2. Organized labor would serve its membership well by basing union demands on the ability of the economy to attract business so that the workforce gets to show its stuff. Ultimately, unions cannot rise on actions that lower the depth of the economy. Like government, organized labor has no wealth but that provided by its members. Help to grow the economy. And take your rewards in profit, not in principal.
3. Prepare union membership for the flexible workplace. Skills enhancement and cross-training are natural services that organized labor can provide. Instruction in what it means to be working in the global marketplace would be a good place to start. Training in self-managed career development would go a long way in preparing members for the flexible workplace. Develop systems and marketing expertise for matching union skills and labor with employers' needs in the marketplace.

Deregulation moves to the front, and protective government policy falters.

The theory behind laissez-faire enterprise is that business, unencumbered by government interference, will create more competition, provide a higher level of service at lower prices and generally spawn a boom in commercial activity with all its attendant benefits. While there are tough penalties for failure built into the free-enterprise approach to business, it's hard to argue with the results when things are done right. British Telecommunications PLC proved the point in 1984 when the nation's deregulators cast the giant, sleepy monopoly into the private sector and opened the gates to competition so that the theorems of Adam Smith might take root and grow. Ever so gingerly, the newly privatized leviathan struggled to regain its feet, burdened by a protectionist mentality, the weight of 240,000 employees, a bureaucratic paunch of considerable girth and the discomfiture of first one competitor and then, in 1991, a growing horde. But BT began to get the picture and act. It started to upgrade technology, downsize the labor force, respond to the demands of the marketplace and move fast. By 1994, the firm had gone from the only telecommunications company in Great Britain to just one of 120. By then, however, BT was a player and competed quite nicely, thank you. By the spring of 1998, the company's earnings were better than ever, and shareholders were delighted. More importantly, the privatization and deregulation of the British telecommunications industry created an explosion of new businesses, new jobs, higher pay, improved telecommunications services, lower customer costs and heightened prospects for the future. More than 150 new companies ultimately rushed into the British telecommunications market, many of them entrepreneurial ventures headed by former BT employees. Industry analysts see nothing but continued growth for the industry in the foreseeable future. "The verdict from the UK is as clear as a fiber-optic link," reported the Dow Jones News Service in April 1998. "Telecom deregulation can create more jobs than it wipes out. Although competition initially may force old-line companies to reduce costs by firing thousands of workers, improved phone service and lower rates eventually trigger rapid growth in telecom traffic and open up opportunities for all sorts of new players."

Deregulation has had similar results elsewhere in the world. In the U.S., AT&T cut deeply into its workforce throughout the 1990s, yet total telecommunications and cable employment had risen 9 percent by 1999, according to DRI/McGraw Hill. The airline industry deregulated in the 1980s and experienced a surge of growth. The U.S. electric utility industry is still working through deregulation. Results so far are mixed. But one thing's for sure: ideas and competitors never before imagined are tearing into the old monopolistic order, remaking the industry time and again in an effort to deliver the best product at the best price across the width and breadth of the country. Consumers, business and the nation's workforce can only benefit in such an environment.

As the world got smaller and more competitive, it was inevitable that the financial community would have to step out from behind long-standing protectionist government policy. Some countries took the action on their own, others were prodded into the move. Lured by the prospects of growth and profit, U.S. banks moved boldly in 1998 after decades of confinement imposed by interstate branch banking laws. "No outside competitors allowed" was the basic message of state chartered banks. Until the 1980s, that's the way it stayed. But banks couldn't grow well in such an environment. Mutual funds, brokerage firms and credit card companies began to cut into traditional bank business. And, with the advent of the global marketplace, few U.S. banks could muster the resources to capitalize on the opportunities presented. So the protective walls of regulation began to come down. In April 1998, it was announced that NationsBank would merge with Bank America to form a $62.5-billion megabank. Bank One and First Chicago NBD agreed to a $30-billion marriage. Not long after, Wells Fargo and Norwest paired up to create a $34-billion business. More consolidation followed, right up through the summer of 2000 with the announced merger of Chase Manhattan and J.P. Morgan & Co. For the first time ever, the notion of an American "national bank" began to have some meaning. It was inevitable that the merger mania would spread across national borders. Germany's Deutsche Bank was the first to make the move into the U.S. market with a deal to acquire Bankers Trust of New

> *As the world got smaller and more competitive, it was inevitable that the financial community would have to step out from behind long-standing protectionist government policy. Some countries took the action on their own, others were prodded into the move.*

York. Merged, the two represent the largest financial institution in the world and a multinational juggernaut. The January 1999 announcement that Spain's first and third largest banks would merge started a fresh wave of consolidations in European banking. The French took a run at creating the first trillion-dollar bank, only to be foiled by national regulators. Japanese banks began to merge in hopes of repairing their competitiveness in global financial circles. Mexico moved to introduce more openness in the nation's financial institutions, including foreign ownership of banks.

Prodded by the realization that there is no safety in regulatory barriers to competition, Canadian banks launched an ambitious merger effort in 1998. At the time of the first big U.S. bank mergers, 90 percent of all Canadian banking activity was controlled by just six banks. And the government protected them from takeover and meaningful competition, and ensured that they never went broke. In this protectionist cocoon, however, growth was slowed and global strength eroded. "The longer we wait [to merge], the more marginalized Canada is becoming," said Royal Bank's finance chief Peter Currie to newspaper reporters in April of that year. "Canada can't think it's an isolated market, immune from all those dynamics" driving the megamergers. Shortly after those words were spoken, Royal Bank of Canada announced a merger with the Bank of Montreal, a major development in the global banking community. Other banks moved to pair up quickly. But the Canadian government failed to see the fears and opportunities that prompted the merger efforts, and killed the initiatives. Time will reveal the wisdom of that decision as Canadian banks sit in status quo while the competition in the global marketplace adjusts to change.

There are those like the French and Canadian finance ministers who worry that the deregulation of key industries like banking may lead to fewer suppliers of essential services that will result in higher prices for consumers or, worse, public bailouts if these giants run into financial trouble. Certainly, there is concern when so many eggs are placed in so few baskets. But the very nature of truly competitive business environments is that new competitors find every crack and opening left by the big and very big. In the financial community where I live in Atlanta, Georgia, for example, mergers and consolidations have raged since 1997. Yet, at the close of 2000, there were 587 financial institutions in the state,

As long as government policy keeps the marketplace open so that competitors can challenge the establishment for a piece of the pie, the ratio of risks to rewards is apt to remain in tolerable balance.

according to the *Atlanta Journal-Constitution*—70 more than four years earlier. Competition and the heady growth it helped create opened doors for those 70 new players that didn't exist before. As long as government policy keeps the marketplace open so that competitors can challenge the establishment for a piece of the pie, the ratio of risks to rewards is apt to remain in tolerable balance. If competition diminishes in an open market, demand grows for a better deal. And a market niche is born. Entrepreneurs move to fill the demand of the new market, forcing the establishment to match the competition or lose business. So goes the natural balancing mechanisms of the free-enterprise system. But it takes a lot of nerve, agility and staying power to survive in this realm. When business is good, everyone loves the free-enterprise system. When excesses and miscalculations bring on tough times, many want to retreat behind protective walls. Such was the case in the aftermath of the financial collapse of the Tigers of Southeast Asia in the last years of the 1990s.

To pump life back into these once vibrant economies, the International Monetary Fund (IMF) forced the banking establishments in Thailand, Indonesia and South Korea to deregulate in 1998 and to open their doors to external competition in exchange for desperately needed cash. The intent of IMF's actions was to replace "crony capitalism" and favoritism with good old-fashioned merit as the criteria for making loans. Faced with successful competing banks, the privileged families and chaebols that historically controlled the wealth of the nations would have to clean up their acts in order to survive. It was believed that, in time, due diligence and sound financial analysis would become the order of the day. Bank security would improve. Consumers would return to the banks with their savings. Foreign investors would notice. Capital would again flow into the workplace. And the economies would begin to grow, and jobs as well. That was the logic. Though subsequent events proved the thinking more or less correct, prominent figures at the height of the crisis in 1998 felt that the IMF approach was too heavy-handed. Maybe it worked in strong, developed economies, the sentiment went, but in places like East Asia, Russia and parts of South America, the financial situation had deteriorated far beyond the ability of any kind of "tough love" to correct. Protectionist sentiment crept back into the lexicon of economists and government officials. In September 1998, Malaysian Prime Minister Mahathir Mohamad proclaimed "the free market a disastrous failure" and threw up barriers to capital flow in and out of the country. At the same time, Russia refused to pay portions of its foreign debt. Some Latin American countries toyed with the notion of restrictions on the flow of money across borders. Newly elected German Chancellor Gerhard Schroeder spoke favorably on the subject. France did as well. Restrictions on the flow of capital—certainly the volatile short-term variety—came in for a great deal of security and some correction of the most blatant abuses. But things didn't progress far down that road. Quite simply, business, jobs and a better standard of living follow the flow of money. And East Asia, South America and Europe, if not Russia, have benefited too richly too recently to turn the clock back on themselves any longer than absolutely necessary. Killing off free-markets and the global capitalist system is not the answer to the financial shocks that reverberated around the world at the end of the 1990s. It's learning what it takes to compete successfully in the global marketplace in good times and bad, and sticking with the program. Deregulation is a critical piece of that formula.

Message for Government – Deregulate. When government steps into the economic arena with regulatory initiatives, a couple of things happen, neither of which are especially good for the workplace. The volume of regulation grows and the size of government increases necessarily. Eventually, commerce begins to clash with protective government policy. Free enterprise becomes less free, open markets less open, the competitive edge dulled. When the regulation begins to affect the bottom line, well-heeled employers start looking for greener pastures elsewhere in the global marketplace. Investment from abroad begins to dry up. Jobs, and the wealth they create, decline. A certain level of government regulation is necessary, of course. But too much starts an economic deterioration that inevitably hurts the

> . . . the bigger government gets, measured by its expenditures, the less growth the economy experiences.
>
> – Results of a study by Professor James Gwartney for U.S. Congress's Joint Economic Committee

163

Organization for Economic Cooperation and Development (OECD)		
• *Australia*	• *Czech Republic*	• *Germany*
• *Canada*	• *France*	• *Iceland*
• *Finland*	• *Hungary*	• *Japan*
• *Greece*	• *Italy*	• *Mexico*
• *Ireland*	• *Luxembourg*	• *Norway*
• *Korea*	• *New Zealand*	• *Spain*
• *The Netherlands*	• *Portugal*	• *Turkey*
• *Poland*	• *Switzerland*	
• *Sweden*	• *United States*	
• *United Kingdom*	• *Belgium*	
• *Austria*	• *Denmark*	

workplace and, soon enough, the populace in general. In an equally deleterious way, the size of government gets in the way of economic growth. That's a phenomenon revealed a few years ago by Professor James Gwartney and two associates at Florida State University. Reporting on a study prepared for the U.S. Congress's Joint Economic Committee, Gwartney presented convincing evidence that the U.S. and other nations need to develop serious, long-range strategies to reduce the size of government for the sake of economic prosperity. The gist of the study is this: the bigger government gets, measured by its expenditures, the less growth the economy experiences. Conversely, the less government spends, the more the economy grows. Using statistics from 23 member nations of the Organization for Economic Cooperation and Development (OECD), Gwartney's group found a striking relationship between the size of government and economic growth. As the size of the U.S. government expanded between 1960 and 1996, for example, the growth of real gross domestic product (GDP) steadily fell. "Even though the U.S. economy is now moving into the eighth year of an expansion," noted Gwartney in a 1998 *Wall Street Journal* article, "the growth of real GDP during the 1990s is only about half of what it was during the 1960s and well below even that of the turbulent 1970s." The same phenomenon is seen in all OECD nations. Government expenditures as a percentage of GDP rose on average from 27 percent in 1960 to 48 percent in 1996. Over the same period, the average economic growth rate fell from 5.5 percent in the 1960s to 1.9 percent in the 1990s. When government spending was less than 25 percent of GDP, OECD countries realized an average real growth rate of 6.6 percent. As the size of government rose, growth steadily declined—all the way down to 1.6 percent when government spending exceeded 60 percent of GDP. But for those nations whose governments grew least, economic growth suffered the least. In the U.S., Britain, Ireland, Iceland and New Zealand, for example, the government grew less than 15 percent between 1960 and 1996. And the average economic growth rate for those nations was just 1.6 percent lower in the 1990s than in the 1960s. But the governments of Denmark, Finland, Greece, Portugal, Spain and Sweden expanded by 25 percentage points or more from 1960 to 1996. And the average growth rate for those countries fell by 5.2 percentage points. In Gwartney's study, the negative impact of bigger government on economic growth held true across 60 nations representing diverse economic systems. Clearly, excessive government spending retards economic growth, but many politicians seem oblivious to the relationship, he concludes.

Message for Labor – Deregulation and privatization can be held up as enemies of the working man and woman with some effect in threatening economic climates. But opposing these trends doesn't do much for union membership, and it doesn't do anything to develop jobs. Indeed, regulation and government intrusion exacerbate the problem. Those businesses, industries and economies that sort out these problems the quickest return to profitability the quickest. Might it not be wiser for organized labor to join with employers and policymakers in a concerted effort to shorten the duration of poorly performing economies and lengthen the life of healthy, job-creating economies? With the creative forms of workplace flexibility now widely practiced throughout the world's developed economies, surely organized labor can find new and better ways to protect workers in poor-performing economies and enrich them on the rising tide. Take the lead in opening the economy to competition, internally and externally. Respond to the challenge with added value, flexibility, technology, special training that provides employers a competitive edge, and other tactics that keep the business coming to the nation's workforce. Base union demands on a careful analysis of what it takes overall for your economy to compete with outside interests. Organized labor can compete against nearly all comers. It will lose more frequently without protective regulation, but it will also win more. And the winnings, in the long run, will far exceed the losings. The reverse is just as certain in a highly regulated workplace—the losses may be less frequent—but so will the wins. And the former, over time, will far outweigh the latter.

Labor flexibility is winning; fixed labor costs are not.

Flexible work arrangements that enable employers to expand, contract and reallocate labor for greater efficiency are paying off in improved bottom-line results. And the job market improves consequently. Even diehards like Germany are getting the message. Technically, there is no such thing as "temporary" employment in the German workplace. By law, all just-in-time workers are employed full-time with full benefits. The only way employers can end relationships with workers they no longer need is to give them "suitable notice" and a cash indemnity. It is an expensive, inflexible effort to provide job security that drives up labor costs, reduces competitiveness and increases unemployment. As Manpower CEO Mitchell Fromstein noted in a speech before the 1998 Staffing Industry Executive Forum, "The countries with the most rigid labor laws are the countries with the highest unemployment rates. And the countries with the most flexible labor laws have the lowest unemployment rates. I suppose one could draw the conclusion that flexibility produces employment—and that would be exactly right."

Faced with this reality, Germany's government began to relax enforcement of some of the more stifling rules and succeeded in taking a percentage point or so off the unemployment rate of 11-12 percent by mid-year 2000–still excessive, but a good indication of what a little flexibility in the labor market can accomplish. Other tightly regulated European economies haven't been as tepid as the Germans in loosening the bounds on flexible work arrangements. When the global marketplace began to turn elsewhere for what it wanted in the mid-'90s, and the unemployment rate bulged, policymakers in Spain, Britain and The Netherlands reassessed their work. Employers simply were not adding workers, even in good times, because labor laws made it so difficult and expensive to dismiss them when business slowed. The conclusion was inescapable:

clear away the barriers to flexible work arrangements. As these nations busied themselves with the task, the results gradually became apparent. A net increase in jobs was registered for the first time in a decade. Employment in Spain in 1997 was up 6.2 percent from 1994. In The Netherlands it was 6.9 percent, and 4.0 percent in Britain. By contrast, Germany, with its restrictive labor laws, registered a 3.3 percent decline in employment between 1994 and 1997. It didn't take long for Sweden, Italy and France to see the light and to move to relax their labor constraints. Staffing agencies began to boom throughout most of Europe, and a growing number of governments began to allow companies to hire personnel on short-term employment arrangements. In this new environment, employers began to lead a quiet revolution to improve Europe's competitiveness—like Sweden's Saab Aircraft and telecommunications giant Ericsson. Under the nation's newly relaxed labor laws, they can hire needed skills through a staffing organization, then release the person when the job is over. No pink slip required, no severance bonus or hassle from a labor union. And staffing employees—people like Mikael Lindburg who has made aircraft engines for Saab one week and microwave ovens for Ericsson the next—like the flexibility very much. "You can change your profession every month," he remarked to a *Wall Street Journal* reporter in 1998.

In that speech at the Staffing Industry Executive Forum, Mitchell Fromstein characterized the U.S. workplace as the only "totally free labor market unencumbered by government regulations." Then he hoisted a warning flag. "One danger, as we move forward in the global society, is that the countries with rigid economies and high unemployment levels will introduce more flexibility—because they have to. But the freest labor market in the world, the U.S., will tend to become more rigid through judicial decisions and possible changes in the labor laws if it doesn't understand what it has and how it functions."

Just such a development occurred in August 2000. Achieving by regulatory reform what Congress would not give, unions were granted the right by the National Labor Relations Board (NLRB) to include temporary workers with permanent employees in bargaining and organizing activities. While a major coup for organized labor, the ruling is widely viewed by employers and labor exchange organizations as potentially threatening for the workplace. The concerns were well expressed by Edward

Whatever the outcome of the NLRB's action, an obstacle that didn't exist now lies in the path of flexible, innovative work arrangments.

Lenz, General Counsel of the American Staffing Association (ASA). "The long-term danger is that business could be deterred from using temporary employment arrangements, and that would be damaging to workers, damaging to business and damaging to the economy," he said. "If you reduce labor-market flexibility, you'll increase unemployment. That's the price."

Whatever the outcome of the NLRB's action, an obstacle that didn't exist now lies in the path of flexible, innovative work arrangements. Just how much the American workplace will be affected by this decidedly European development is beyond judging at this juncture, but it is the wrong direction for the "freest labor market in the world" to be traveling.

The mention of flexible labor usually conjures up images of just-in-time workers employed in increasingly imaginative ways. But labor flexibility doesn't end there. Permanently employed core staff is increasingly salted with regular part-timers, job sharers, telecommuters and those who work various flextime schedules or compressed work weeks. The mix of flexible work arrangements includes family leave, educational sabbaticals, phased retirement, voluntary time and other twists on the old nine-to-five workaday routine. In some fast-paced professions where the hours are long and travel commonplace, employers go so far as to provide their breadwinners concierge services like laundry pick-up and delivery, pet and plant care, grocery shopping and other timesaving conveniences. Where seasonal demand brings a crush of long hours—tax time, for example—many employers compensate with shorter hours in slack periods. The list goes on and on, all of it born of the recognition that employees have lives outside work that had better be accommodated or business will feel the effect. "A burned out, disaffected employee will not produce as high a quality of work, focus full attention at work, be as responsive to customers, go beyond core-job requirements, or take on new responsibilities to the extent that a satisfied, committed employee will," writes Barney Olmstead of New Ways to Work, a nonprofit organization specializing in workplace issues. "And," he added, "programs to resolve worker stress or pay for disabilities resulting from fatigue or stress can be expensive."

What's interesting about this widespread adoption of flexible forms of employment is that business is benefiting, in most cases, by catering to the individual lifestyle needs and desires of its employees. The old notion that employees had to leave their personal lives at the door of the workplace before entering is being replaced by a commitment to individuals that is not only morally admirable but good for business too.

In the beginning, flexible work arrangements were considered an accommodation. More and more, the concept becomes mainstream human resource policy and practice. Nevertheless, very few organizations have designed HR policy from the start with "labor flexibility" as a guiding principle. This must change in a world where global and technological reliance calls not only for virtual corporations but virtual employees.

For a flexible workplace to succeed, certain essentials are required, say the experts at New Ways to Work:

1. Visible support for flexible forms of labor from top management.
2. Published guidelines for managers and employees to follow.
3. Promotion of the concept internally and externally so that everyone understands the program.
4. Team efforts throughout the organization to advance the concept and refine the processes.
5. Training of managers so that the initiatives are properly carried out.
6. Tracking and evaluating the process to determine effectiveness and corrective measures.

To this list, I would add three other essentials:

1. The creation of a regulatory environment that fosters the growth and development of flexible labor usage.
2. The adoption of the concept by organized labor.
3. Preservation of the basic rationale underlying the emergence of labor flexibility—cost reduction.

Message for Government – The emergence of flexible labor is not something government needs to protect its constituents from. The flexible workforce is a valuable asset to the business community, to those millions of workers who specifically want flexible forms of employment, to those who would have no jobs if not for the just-in-time needs of employers, and to the larger society that knows no artificial barriers to earning a living. Organized labor's claim that the growth of the flexible workforce means the decline of permanent jobs fails to acknowledge the impetus of competitive pressures on the development, the earnings potential of *FlexLife®* careers or the real reason behind its opposition—the growing difficulty of bolstering sagging union membership. Timothy Bartl of the Labor Policy Association, representing more than 250 of the largest corporations doing business in the U.S., notes that public policymakers need to remember a few basic points when fielding organized labor's arguments against flexible forms of employment:

1. What labor refers to as "contingent workers" are actually the gamut of just-in-time employees, and they do not constitute a "permanent underclass of workers forced by employers into insecure arrangements."
2. The current body of U.S. labor law already protects flexible workers. Far from "legal orphans," as labor claims, flexible workers are protected under the same laws that protect permanent workers—14 major labor and employment laws in all.
3. Employers are not converting full-time jobs to "nontraditional jobs" against the wishes of employees. A typical nontraditional position "is not a descendent of a permanent, full-time position," writes Bartl in his book *America Wants Flexible Work.* "More often than not it is a new position created by the employer to meet a need that traditional employment does not address."
4. Flexible work enables employers to adapt to rapidly changing market conditions and, thus, helps ensure job security for employees. The adaptations employers go through nowadays are not produced by corporate greed but by market reality. "In virtually all industries, companies that attempt to do business the same way they were doing it even five years ago are doomed to failure," Bartl writes.
5. In the modern workplace, employers and employees alike often need employment arrangements that fall outside the realm of traditional permanent work. "In the vast majority of situations, those needs are matched to the advantage of both parties."

In light of these observations, Bartl concludes, "It would be a tragedy if policymakers were to misinterpret a handful of situations where there is a mismatch and attempt to craft policies that would force employers and workers back into the traditional box." The traditional box—that is exactly where employers and just-in-time personnel would find themselves if recent legislative initiatives had become law. In 1994, legislation was proposed in both houses of Congress that would have forced employers to pay the same health and pension benefits to part-time and just-in-time personnel that are paid to full-time permanent employees. One proposal, the Contingent Workforce Equity Act, even dictated that just-in-time personnel be paid the same wages as the permanent workforce. Thankfully, these efforts didn't get far in Congress. Certainly, just-in-time personnel need health and pension benefits no less than permanent employees, but forcing this expense on employers reduces the principal motivation for using flexible employees to begin with—the ability to cut costs as needed. In many cases, it would be easier just to hire permanent employees—which was the intent of the proposals from the start. The rightful source of health and pension benefits for just-in-time personnel is the third-party labor exchange service that matches the employee with employer. Staffing agencies, especially, are not shying away from that realization. Fully 77 percent of U.S. staffing agencies with annual sales in excess of $50 million offer health benefits to their staffing employees, the National Association of Temporary and Staffing Services (NATSS) found in a 1997 survey. The impetus for this development is market-driven. To get and retain good assignment personnel, staffing agencies are having to do more to attract them. Employee benefits, including 401(k) contributions and stock options, are a natural evolution of the flexible workplace. As for tying the pay of just-in-time personnel to the level of the client workforce or the union scale, if it applies, this denies employers the right to negotiate the best deal for themselves and assumes that the marketplace is incapable of setting the pay scale for needed just-in-time skills and labor. Nothing could be further from the truth. Independent contractors and long-term

> *Fully 77% of U.S. staffing agencies with annual sales in excess of $50 million offer health benefits to their staffing employees. . . .*
>
> – 1997 Survey
> National Association of
> Temporary and Staffing Services

171

staffing employees earn more on average than permanent employees because that's what the marketplace is willing to pay. And the just-in-time personnel are still a good buy compared to permanent employees.

Another proposal recently introduced in the U.S. Congress urged the federal government to replace all temps with permanent employees and required the Federal Office of Personnel Management to provide health, pension and life insurance benefits to just-in-time workers. That would have worked against the flexible workforce, cost taxpayers more for the same or less service and reduced the points of entry for those looking for a job with the federal government. California Representative Tom Lantos submitted a bill to the 105th Congress that would have prohibited government and defense contractors from cutting costs by using independent contractors. Part of the motivation behind the proposed legislation was to ensure that contractors didn't escape the cost of employment taxes by classifying legitimate permanent employees as independent contractors. There is nothing wrong with that. But when legitimate independent contractors pay their own self-employment taxes or a labor exchange organization does it for them, isn't it a bit ludicrous to ban the use of just-in-time employees when all that's needed is a clearer definition of "independent contractor"? Throwing the baby out with the bath water is shortsighted in the extreme. These kinds of initiatives, coupled with the very real actions of the National Labor Relations Board that provide for the unionization of temporary workers, lend substance to the fears many harbor of creeping regulation of the U.S. workplace.

So, the message for government on the subject of flexible employment is this:

- Break down the barriers to the efficient use of just-in-time skills, talent and labor.
- Facilitate the growth and development of the flexible workforce so that it is good for employers, employees and the society at large.
- And don't lose sight of the real strength of flexible labor.

Barriers

For employers, employees and the national economy to extract the greatest benefit from flexible forms of employment, government needs to prepare the way by eliminating barriers to their development. Consider the following:

1. Clear the legislative books of laws that restrict, confuse or muddle the flexible use of just-in-time workers. This includes inconsistent standards for distinguishing just-in-time workers from permanent employees and inflexible provisions governing the design of benefit plans for the flexible workforce. There is nothing but gain for all parties in a fluid, flexible workplace where employers conduct business in the context of clear, unmistakable rules, and flexible workers of every kind obtain the benefits best suited to their needs and resources.

2. Simplify distinctions in the various forms of employment. Private firms like Marks & Spencer of the United Kingdom show the way for government by throwing out the concept of full-time and part-time workers all together. For several years now, everyone at M&S is either a permanent or temporary employee. All permanent staff get the same benefits package whether they work 10 hours a week or 45 hours a week. The benefits are simply adjusted on a pro rata basis to the hours worked. Similar measures spread throughout advanced economies as the flexible workforce grows.

3. Provide for transportable employee benefits. The job security of old may be a lost cause for a growing number of employees, but traditional employee benefits need not be, and ought not to be. At a minimum, provide the legislative framework for health insurance and pension plans to be attached to the individual wherever in the workplace he or she may move. "Medical Savings Accounts" (MSAs) are a move in the right direction (see below), as are transportable pension plans. There are a variety of ways to provide the flexible workforce with basic health insurance and pension protection without heaping unnecessary costs on employers or taxpayers. The key players in the workplace—business, government, organized labor and labor exchange services—just need to get their heads together and make it happen.

4. Don't forget the needs of the flexible workforce when weighing the merits of Medical Savings Accounts (MSAs). With the growing ranks of flexible, self-employed workers, affordable health insurance coverage becomes a constant challenge. Staffing agencies have responded to the needs of just-in-time workers, but other options must be developed. The MSA is a logical addition to the all

too short menu of possibilities. Ideally, it would enable employees to acquire good health insurance coverage with high deductibles that cost less and protect against the worst of medical setbacks. The MSA would pay all or most of the deductible. Employees and/or employers could fund the MSA with tax-exempt contributions. This would not only reduce the cost of health insurance, it would foster cash accumulation by working men and women. Moneys from Medical Savings Account not used would be allowed to accumulate and accrue to the benefit of the individual or family. This is a tool that could go far in improving the "employment security" of a great many people.

5. Open the way for labor supply to flow to wherever there is labor demand. Ultimately, this includes improvements in immigration procedures and practices, especially where skills or labor are involved that employers want and are ready to pay for.

6. Continue to eliminate physical and psychological barriers to the employment of the "chronically unemployed." Join in creative partnerships with employers, labor exchange services and labor unions to turn this under-used resource into an asset. Sweeten the pot where necessary to provide incentive and defray the cost of training and preparation. Much has already been done in this regard, but the possibilities have hardly been exhausted.

7. Interject some flexibility into legislation that governs the design of employee benefits. In the U.S., for example, it is impossible for staffing agencies to tailor a benefits plan to the needs of part-time retail workers that differs in any appreciable way from the plan offered high-powered information technology specialists. By law, both types of workers must get the same plan, though the circumstances of the two may vary considerably. This kind of inflexibility inhibits innovation and cooperation between staffing agencies and their customers that might split the benefits obligation, including costs, between the two parties. Other possibilities never get beyond wishful thinking in the current legislative environment. A truly flexible workplace cannot be so inflexible on the very basic inducement of employee benefits. Costs get distorted, pushing benefits beyond the reach of too many of the flexibly employed. Too often, benefit plans fail to address the needs and desires of

flexible workers and, thus, lose their relevancy. Most importantly, the growth of the flexible workforce is stymied.

Facilitate

Eliminating or lowering barriers to the efficient use of flexible labor would be an important first step for government. But it needs to go further. Consideration should be given to joint-venture efforts that address the whole range of issues affecting the healthy development of the flexible workforce. The logical joint-venture partners would be some combination of employer, government (local, state, federal), organized labor, labor exchange services and even foreign governments on issues like migrant workers. Partnerships born of any such cooperative efforts might want to adopt as public policy some of the practices that have proven so effective in the private sector. Doing so would not only facilitate a healthy expansion of flexible forms of employment, it would help forge a well-coordinated "national team" to take on the competition in the global marketplace. Here is a sampling of the kind of flexible labor strategy practiced in the corporate world that might make good public policy:

1. Continued training throughout a person's career, right up to retirement. This is imperative if the workforce is to remain motivated and productive and employers are to have the skills, talent and labor needed when needed.

2. Elimination of seniority-based pay. It is fraught with basic inefficiencies and hidden costs, especially at the end of employee careers. The effect in former bastions like Japan and France is that employers find it difficult to keep older employees because they cost too much. In the place of seniority, performance is the rightful measure of an employee's worth. There is nothing discriminatory about this. With their experience, time on the job and accumulated competencies, older workers have a natural leg up on younger employees in the vast majority of cases. Where the skills of older workers fail to measure up to that of newcomers, or the job market for certain capabilities requires the payment of premium wages, employers should not be put in a situation where they must pay solely for a person's longevity. The losers inevitably turn out to be the entire workforce as productivity and competitiveness decline and business goes elsewhere.

3. Pension payments based on employees' pay rather than end-of-career compensation. This is a complex issue that can result in the stifling of an employee's advancement as he or she nears retirement age. A pension calculated on a person's average pay is probably a fairer basis for retirement compensation, at least from the employer's point of view. The average retiree, however, would receive less in pension payments. What's fair is probably what is most sustainable, given the competitive environment in which the employer operates.

4. Gradual retirement. The more flexible the workforce and the faster the pace of business, the more sense gradual retirement makes. It provides employers the opportunity to retain needed skills after an employee's retirement age, to make room for new employees or to build flexibility in the workforce. It provides employees a way to extend their earnings beyond normal retirement age or to retire early without the complete loss of income and benefits. The advantages of this approach are many, even in those economies where the Anglo-Saxon Model of flexible labor usage predominates.

5. Redefine employment. A redefinition of basic employment probably needs to be formulated. Is it the elusive "traditional permanent job?" Is it full-time employment via a succession of short-term job assignments managed by a third-party agent à la *FlexLife®*? Is it part-time work for all citizens of an age and ability to work? Perhaps employees and the workplace in general would be better served with an official redefinition of what so many people do in so many different ways.

6. Somewhere in all this, child-care must be made accessible to those mothers who would work if affordable, quality accommodations for their children were available. To the extent that employers need the skill and labor of these women, some part of the cost of child-care is business's to bear. To the extent that society pays severely for poorly tended children, some part of the cost of child-care is government's to bear. To the extent that mothers and their families can pay, they should pay. But to leave the costs solely to them, especially when there is but a single parent, is to rule out effective child-care for far too many and, thus, to rule out gainful employment. There is too much money in the system, and too much economic incentive all around not to provide child-care to those who

would work if the service were available. All that's required to make it happen is a little creative financing.

Remember

Lastly, government should not lose sight of the primary value of flexible forms of labor—their contribution to economic competitiveness. It is important to remember this as the definition of "flexible labor" takes on broader meaning in the global workplace. The driving force that launched employers on the remaking of the traditional workforce is the potential for reducing costs, competing more effectively and increasing profits as a result. That's what started the modern trend to flexible forms of employment. But other motivations have emerged, most notably in Europe. The first approach, called the Anglo-Saxon Model by economists, is most associated with the U.S. and other fast-growing economies like Australia, New Zealand and Ireland. As used in these nations, flexible labor implies a rapid contraction or expansion in personnel costs in order to get—or remain—competitive. There is no hiding the reality of what's involved. During periods of contraction, people get downsized out of jobs. Income stops. Unemployment insurance is limited both in

The driving force that launched employers on the remaking of the traditional workforce is the potential for reducing costs, competing more effectively and increasing profits as a result.

amount and duration. Health insurance benefits may be lost. Pension contributions cease. Even when new jobs materialize, there is no promise of job security. For unprepared employees, there is pain and stress. The bottom line for employers is that "head count" goes down. Payrolls shrink. Local, regional and/or national unemployment rates may go up. But, if employers downsize wisely, a certain nimbleness is acquired, the ratio of cash to expenses improves and the ability to compete in the open market rises. Bottom-line results get better. Growth ensues. Additional skills and labor are required. Hiring picks up, not always for traditional permanent jobs, but, increasingly, for gainful employment that can be parlayed into attractive *FlexLife®* careers. The unemployment rate shrinks. Prosperity returns. And overall growth continues. Depending on how well business stays in competitive trim, it's possible for sustained economic growth to continue for extended periods of time. Witness the

U.S. economy since 1993. Some economists go so far as to suggest that a new economic era is upon us, one without the historical booms and busts of old. Be that as it may, the U.S. economy well illustrates the effectiveness of the Anglo-Saxon Model of flexible employment.

The European Model is most evident in France and Germany, though not limited to those countries by any means. As employed in these workplaces, labor flexibility takes a different tack. Driven by organized labor and compliant governments, labor flexibility here does little or nothing for employer competitiveness in the global marketplace. Instead, the objective is to reduce the unemployment rate, compensate for a lack of real economic growth and reconfigure the workforce (shift older, higher paid workers into government-subsidized retirement and fill the vacancies with younger, less expensive replacements). High wages and benefits, expensive social contracts, inflexible labor rules, shortened workweeks and inflated taxes all conspired to turn away cost-conscious business and reduce economic growth throughout the 1990s. In France, for example, gross domestic product (GDP), adjusted for inflation, did not exceed a 2-percent average annual growth rate throughout the 1990s. Germany performed only a little better. (It takes in excess of a 3-percent annual growth in GDP in both countries to cut into their unemployment rates.) Consequently, job growth failed to keep up with job demand. Eager young job seekers showed up at the doors of employers in ever increasing numbers only to find the jobs locked away by well-ensconced older workers in a seniority-biased workplace. Unemployment, especially among the young, rose inexorably. Not since 1984 has the unemployment rate in France sunk below 9 percent. The last time German unemployment was below 8 percent was 1993.

To help address the unemployment problem, the governments of France, Germany and other EU members, prodded by organized labor, encouraged older workers to take early retirement. The objective: to clear positions for younger job seekers. The inducements to retire were—and are—so attractive that senior workers rushed to take the offer. In 1998, for example, employees 55 years of age or older with Siemens AG, Germany's largest electronics and engineering firm, could cut their working hours by 50 percent and still receive 82 percent of their full-time wages. Health insurance stayed in force and pension contributions continued. The French insurance company AXA waived regular work hours for its workers 55 years old and over and called on them as needed. (Employees must have been with the company 15 years and have the requisite number of years required to retire.) The employees received 65 percent of their full-time salary and retained their status as active members of the firm. They retained all employee benefits but did not have the right to take another job. If needed, these "retirees" could be recalled to full-time status. But only for the same or similar job held before retirement and a pay rate 100 percent of their full-time earnings. Pretty attractive stuff.

The net effect of this "job creating strategy" was to reduce the "occupational life" of the national workforce. By 1997, less than 60 percent of the active male population 55-59 years old held jobs in France and The Netherlands, according to the International Society for Work Options. Less than 20 percent of the men in the 60-64 age bracket held jobs. The rest are essentially retired and quite comfortable financially. The figures are only a little higher in Germany and the UK. Such a deal! It all seemed quite ingenious, especially for the workforce. Then employers began to feel the crunch of skills and expertise lost prematurely to early retirement. And the little matter of costs began to rear its ugly head. Retirement, it turns out, isn't cheap. And business, through corporate-funded pension and insurance plans, foots most of the bill. The rest comes from taxpayers. So the cost of doing business rises, as do taxes to help subsidize the expense of retirement. And national competitiveness suffers on both accounts.

Policymakers started to look around for a new strategy, and found one—gradual or phased retirement. Instead of working full time one day, and retiring full time the next, why not ease employees into retirement gradually? Pay them reduced wages for reduced hours worked. Contribute proportionately to pension plans. Cover "retirees" with health insurance during the phase-out period. Push phased retirement with the workforce in lieu of early retirement. And spread the retirement process over one to ten years, whatever is mutually agreeable to employee and employer.

The work-hours and jobs freed up by this phased departure of full-time employees can be filled by newcomers to the job market. Job creation? You could call it that, but the claim is a bit dubious. The strength of gradual retirement programs lies in other areas. Phased retirement proves to be an excellent strategy for not only reducing the working lives of employees (early retirement occurs gradually rather than abruptly) but for extending them as well (employees work part time after retirement). And it is very "flexible." Any number of variations are possible for phasing employees out of jobs so that replacements can be brought in. Sweden, Finland and Austria adopted phased retirement as national policy in the mid-1980s. Denmark, France, Germany, Luxembourg, Spain and Italy followed.

Phased retirement proves to be an excellent strategy for not only reducing the working lives of employees (early retirement occurs gradually rather than abruptly) but for extending them as well (employees work part time after retirement).

All this is very creative and serves a high-profile agenda—employment. No doubt there is much in the European Model of labor flexibility that can be put to good use elsewhere in the global workplace, including Anglo-Saxon countries. Nevertheless, the European model is not rooted in a strategy that addresses economic competitiveness. It's mostly about "having your cake and eating it too." "Yes," proponents seem to say, "the nation suffers from high unemployment and grows very little. But the workplace doesn't have to bite the bullet and get competitive because the government spreads the available jobs over more and more people with flexible schemes of employment." Ultimately, this approach to flexible labor doesn't work. Labor costs are just not competitive under this scenario. Employers and capital go elsewhere for the competitive edge they need. Economic growth declines even further. Unemployment and underemployment increase. And trouble brews. A case study conducted by the International Association for the Study of Insurance Economics (the Geneva Association) makes the point. A major French bank developed a trend-setting gradual retirement program for its workplace that moved 600 older full-time employees to part-time status in 1994-95. The program cleared the way to add 300 new recruits, many of them new to the workplace. There are some legitimate pluses in this kind of maneuver, certainly for the retirees. New blood (and cheaper) rejuvenates the workplace. Retirement "exits" from the company are staggered. The rise in employer pension/retirement insurance costs is slowed. Partial retirees prove to be excellent trainers for new recruits, so productivity doesn't suffer. Part-time work is shown to advantage, opening the workforce to other kinds of flexible employment arrangements. And there is no addition to the local, regional or national unemployment rate. But, there is little, if any, actual cost savings for the employer and nothing to improve the organization's competitiveness outside its immediate market niche. Look at the numbers: 600 full-time employees took partial retirement, replaced by 300 full-timers. There is a net gain here of employees, not a reduction. Where before there were 600 employees, there are afterwards 900 employees. Any way you slice it, the bank added to its "head-count." With the added personnel, HR costs rise rather than fall. Total labor costs after the launch of the gradual retirement/job creation program could hardly have made the firm leaner and more competitive in the marketplace. And minus that, where's the savings or profit in the action? Job creation is good—when it's born of economic growth. Making one job into two gets to be very questionable, especially when a nation's wealth-makers start taking home smaller paychecks.

Partial retirees prove to be excellent trainers for new recruits, so productivity doesn't suffer.

By any name, flexible labor costs have to mean legitimate bottom-line savings and increased competitiveness to be worthy of the term. If the use of flexible forms of employment is simply a way to reduce unemployment or to compensate for a lack of real economic growth, then it is a ruse. There are not meaningful bottom-line savings to be had for employers. Competitiveness is not served. Employers end up in the social safety-net business and, soon enough, won't be able to pay the bill and survive.

Message for Labor – With the terrific volatility in the workplace due to technological innovation, telecommunication advances, interdependent economies and capital movement, organized labor does itself no good working against the best interests of job creation and competitiveness. Businesses and industries and entire economies come and go too fast these days for organized labor to play adversary with the very source of jobs they so desperately want. Flexible labor simply has to mean more than innovative ways to maintain payroll at current levels. It has to provide for real cost reduction when necessary for employers to adjust to changed conditions. The benefits of flexible labor for employees cannot materialize in a workplace that requires overtime pay after eight hours on the job, for example. Where's the incentive for employers to provide flextime to employees who may want a long weekend by working four 10-hour days instead of five eight-hour days? The benefits of flexible labor won't take root in a regulatory environment that prompts employers to terminate just-in-time workers after six months in order to avoid pension and training obligations stipulated in certain European employment laws. Organized labor has lost no relevance in the modern workplace. Its basic mission remains the same—good jobs for the most people. But its strategies, tactics and "service line" are in drastic need of overhaul.

Lean-and-nimble is winning; ponderous-and-slow bring up the rear.

Fast is a fleeting term in the new millenium. Last year's super-hot personal computer (PC) is this year's clunker. Market leadership is here today, gone tomorrow. Thriving businesses disappear overnight, swallowed up by merger and acquisition, never to be heard from again. Foreign competitors, pushing products and services you never heard of, gain market acceptance with increasing speed. Coca-Cola did it in China in a decade. Ericsson and Nokia did it in the U.S. in a couple of years. Merrill Lynch did it in Japan in a matter of months. In that development lies a telling story for any organization or country professing to compete in today's global marketplace.

The appeal of Japan for securities brokers at the end of the 1990s resided in the nine trillion dollars in personal savings mostly just lying around in low-interest bank accounts. The country's aging population clamored for a better return on its money but didn't trust the homegrown brokerage industry. Brokerage firms, banks, insurance companies and other financial institutions were often family affairs in Japan. Capital from one organization feeds another. Cross-guarantees of debt among family (chaebol) members was commonplace. Public disclosure and accounting standards didn't force an admission of these actions. So a seemingly attractive firm could have much less cash and much more debt than investors realized. And a misstep by one could bring down the rest. It was a situation that bred little public confidence in the country's securities industry.

"Outside" securities brokers who would come to the Japanese people with quality reputations, high standards for disclosure and ready access to investment opportunities around the world would surely be well received. But, historically, Japanese policymakers had held foreign competitors at bay. There matters languished until the summer of 1997 when the currency crises in Thailand, Malaysia, Indonesia and South Korea began to come home to the Japanese financial community. No banking establishment had lent more to the Asian Tigers than Japan. None had more to lose. And lose Japan did. And because capital and debt wound back and forth through the chaebols, the losses reverberated throughout the country. These difficulties, piled on top of huge losses still on the books from bad real estate deals in the early 1990s, finally began to unravel the protectionist policies that had dominated Japanese commerce since World War II.

The government began to deregulate, tighten government oversight and open the nation's markets to foreign competition. But Japan is still Japan. Fifty years of practice and thousand of years of tradition do not turn on a dime. And things were moving fast. There were crises and scandals born of crises for the government to tend to. Problems sprang from every shadow. Foreign competitors hovered nervously at the door to the country trying to make sense of the situation. In this environment, Merrill Lynch moved nimbly and decisively. In July 1997, a small advance team of savvy non-traditionalists began to survey the field, looking for an opportunity to put the company in the retail brokerage business in a big way. There was no big corporate nerve center orchestrating moves, just a few nervy guys on cell phones and laptop computers making things happen. Nothing promising caught their eye at first. Then, on November 24, 1997, an opportunity presented itself. Yamaichi Securities Co., Japan's fourth-largest brokerage firm, shocked financial markets worldwide by announcing that it was closing its doors because of crushing losses after 100 years in business. All sorts of merger schemes and bailout possibilities were bandied about to keep the organization afloat. But Merrill Lynch saw the situation differently. There sat 7,500 experienced employees and a national network of branch facilities, all of it getting ready to disband and shut down. Why not step into the breech, hire as many of the employees as needed, put Merrill Lynch's name on the door and sell the company's widely respected line of retail brokerage services? It was certainly a bold notion and no small gamble, even for an organization of Merrill Lynch's timber. Few companies anywhere had ever tried to establish such a far-flung retail organization so quickly, much less in tradition-bound Japan. But the time was right. And the company didn't flinch. The advance team moved quickly to clear the way for the initiative with Japanese officials. By the end of February 1998, the new company had taken shape, complete with a freshly appointed president. Never mind that Merrill Lynch Securities Japan, Ltd., had no employees, no head office and no branches except on paper. A couple of glitches nearly killed the deal early on, but an opening date was finally set: July 1, 1998.

When the doors at Merrill Lynch swung open to the Japanese public, no foreign company was more deeply ensconced in the country's financial services realm. And it was all the result of a corporate culture that understood what it takes to excel in the business world. Credit must also be given to Japanese policymakers. Had the situation with Yamaichi Securities occurred a year or even months earlier, a lot of skilled employees would have found themselves unemployed in a bleak job market, the country's diligent savers would still be looking for reliable access to the securities market and Japan's general malaise would have been another degree or two worse. There are critics aplenty of the Japanese economy. But policymakers there may well prove a lot of skeptics wrong with a steadfast deregulation program and a new lean and nimble approach to the global marketplace.

Opportunities like that which catapulted Merrill Lynch deep into the Japanese consumer market abound in the global marketplace. But it is no place for the meek or the slow. Indeed, if Japanese policymakers had been further along in the re-engineering of the nation's economic system, Yamaichi Securities may never have met its end, or a domestic firm might have been in a position to seize on the opportunity afforded by the firm's demise instead of Merrill Lynch.

Message for Government – Create a regulatory/economic environment where the lean and nimble can perform at their best, and behold a general improvement in business and job growth as the whippets score big and the sluggards trim down and psych up to get into the game. Provide the parameters for the private sector to operate at optimum effectiveness—that's half the challenge for government. The other half, as pointed out by Professor James Gwartney of Florida State University, is to keep the size of government well below 25 percent of Gross Domestic Product (GDP) so that the nation's wealth is not diminished by the cost of public services. Lean and flexible government, strong in all the right places, out of sight and out of mind everywhere else—there is a pretty good formula for serving well a national constituency.

Message for Labor – Fear not the pace of events. Beneath the big money, deal-making, technology, negotiations and general swirl of events, there are employees, the workforce that provides the glue and propulsion of enterprise. Without the requisite skills, talent and labor of employees, business ventures are a shell, a concept. People add the value. In Japan, Merrill Lynch had all the capital, know-how and clout it needed to do what it wanted. The government was cooperating. The market was there. The timing right . . . the only thing missing was the people needed to launch a nationwide retail brokerage business. Merrill Lynch might still be waiting for an opening had the unfortunate dissolution of one company not delivered into the hands of the other the people needed to complete the picture. In the often chaotic state of modern business, the best way to keep your bearings is to focus on the workforce. If it possesses attractive skills, the forces of commerce will converge on it; without those skills, torpor will follow. Therein is a message for organized labor: monitor the workforce you represent. If its skills are slipping, shore them up. It's in everyone's best interests that you do.

Employee mobility is winning; labor constraint is not

Basic to the successful match of employee competencies with the skill, talent and/or labor needs of employers is the ability of the one to access the other. Employees need to be able to get to work, whether that be down the road, across town, upstate or over international borders. When the workers can't get to the job, the job has to go to the workers. Thus do employers move operations wherever necessary to close the distance to the workforce needed to perform most productively. One way or the other, the match of employee and employer usually requires some degree of mobility. Part of the requirement deals with the means of transport. Government has a responsibility to provide, as much as possible, the basic infrastructure necessary to move employees effectively and efficiently to the workplace. For the most part, developed economies do a fair-to-good job on this front. But there's much yet that can be done. The societal pay-back from a comprehensive transport system, high-tech and low, that eliminates barriers to the workplace is too impressive to be ignored.

There is another side of the mobility issue that is not as cut-and-dried as the devices of transportation. It's politics, fear, ignorance and selfishness, cobbled together in amorphous obstacles thrown willy-nilly into the global workplace. Encumbered by these stumbling blocks, the modern workplace is far from the fluid, efficient environment that it could be. National prosperity suffers as a result. Unskilled workers stream from pockets of poverty to pockets of prosperity where employers have too little use for them and the social safety net intended to care for taxpayers is depleted by needy foreigners. Skilled workers are often barred from going to where the best jobs are, and employers pay the price for the lack of available competencies. Kuwait couldn't function if it were not for a host of foreign workers.

Government has a responsibility to provide, as much as possible, the basic infrastructure necessary to move employees effectively and efficiently to the workplace.

Yet so many in a small land raises security fears. Heavy immigration to Denmark, the quintessential welfare state, has raised concern among Danes for the integrity of the nation's schools and the system of public assistance. Germany has worried that the influx of eager, low-paid Polish workers would drag down the highest wages in the world. Hong Kong long turned away boatloads of Vietnamese for fear that they would take jobs from the locals. "Skilled" migrant farm workers from Mexico and Central America are vital to U.S. growers and low consumer prices, but inadequate accommodations and social services for these people while in the country create an embarrassment. Major employers around the world spend tens of billions of dollars every year recruiting and hiring needed personnel—and still come up short in certain key industries. In the Information Technology (IT) field, for example, more than half a million jobs went unfilled in continental Europe in 1998. In the U.S., the Information Technology Association of America put the shortfall of skilled engineers and other technology workers at 346,000 as of March 1998 and over half a million in 1999. The figure is expected to grow to a couple million on the near-term. There are capable workers elsewhere in the world, but immigration quotas bar their employment. Not only do corporate earnings suffer with this kind of labor constraint, but technological advances are sidetracked, job creation is quelled and, ultimately, the competition gains the upper hand. "Skilled immigrants create new jobs for native-born Americans," reminds an exasperated T. J. Rodgers, CEO of Cypress Semiconductor Corporation in Silicon Valley, California. In a newspaper column, he noted, "The claim that skilled H1-B immigrants take jobs from Americans is preposterous. Did Hungarian immigrant and Intel CEO Andy Grove take some 'real' American's job, or did he help to create 50,000 high-quality jobs? . . . America's loss [immigrant skills] is our foreign competition's gain. Our need for engineers has driven us to start R&D centers anywhere we can find engineers—currently, in England, Ireland and India. We're forced offshore to fill the jobs we cannot fill here— a fine way to 'protect' American jobs."

Message for Government – Resolve legitimate national and local labor concerns within the context of a fluid workplace, one that lets market demand set the quotas. Job creation and the benefits that come with it are too closely tied to a sufficient supply of skills and labor to tamper with the flow of this basic commodity. The case is well-made by T. J. Rogers. Pointing to his own firm, he quantified the statement that "engineers create jobs." Of the 2,771 employees that comprised the company's 1998 workforce, 470 were engineers. Each engineer, thus, created a job for five other people who made, administered and sold what the engineer developed. Thirty-seven percent of the company's research and development engineers were immigrants—typical in Silicon Valley, he wrote. Had Rogers' firm been prohibited from hiring those immigrant engineers, there would have been 860 fewer jobs available at Cypress Semiconductor. Four of the company's 10 vice presidents were immigrants. Chairman of the Board Pierre Lamond is French-born and -educated and a founder of National Semiconductor. His venture capital firm, Sequoia Partners has provided capital to 200 Silicon Valley companies with a total market value of $175 billion and 150,000 employees. Cypress director Eric Benhamou was born in Algeria, grew up in France and was educated in the U.S. Later, he became CEO of 3Com Corp., the leading Internet infrastructure supplier with 100 million customers and 13,200 employees. "The conclusion is clear," Rogers noted. "Our immigrant executives, directors and engineers have created thousands of new American jobs." And high-paid jobs at that. The average employee at the company's San Jose headquarters, excluding the executive team, earns $81,860 a year, including benefits. The immigrant executives he cited all earn six-figure incomes. "Whose pay are they holding down?" Rogers asked rhetorically. "With 0.4 percent unemployed in the [IT] field, and record-low unemployment in the broader U.S. economy, where are the out-of-work Americans displaced by foreign talent?"

A free flow of labor would also be a big help in Russia. The horrendous economic problems gripping the country at the end of the century would be substantially improved with a loosening of restrictions on the movement of the labor force, believes Alexei Bayer, an expert on the Russian economy and president of the New York-based consulting firm Kafan FX Information Services. "The real solution for the wage crisis gripping Russia is not to find money in the budget to pay workers of bankrupt enterprises," he wrote in a newspaper editorial, "but to find ways to employ them productively elsewhere. This will require eliminating or easing many current restrictions on mobility, including internal passports, Moscow's residence permit system and the labor book, a detailed work record kept by primary employers." Free the initiative, creativity and productivity of the workforce—that's Bayer's message to Russia, and it's a good one for every other nation. But jobs and competitiveness and productivity are only part of the motivation for unrestricted labor flow. There is the old-fashioned value that immigrants bring to any society. New blood, thoughts, perspectives and traditions are enriching in their own right—despite initial fears in some of the populace. In the recession years of the early 1990s, for example, segments of the U.S. populace fell into a frenzy of anti-immigrant sentiment led by witch-hunting politicians and intellectuals. They preached that immigrants—particularly Latinos— were a permanent underclass that would either stay on welfare forever or take American jobs for wages no self-respecting citizen would tolerate. These people would be an economic burden on the rest of society, and it would only get worse, they said. California politicians were particularly vociferous on the subject and pushed hard in local, state and federal legislatures for draconian limits on immigration.

Yet, in 1998, the picture was quite different from that forecast. In a calming measure that America's Latino middle-class is quickly closing the income gap on other Californians, Axiom DataQuick Information Systems found that nine out of 10 homeowners in heavily populated Los Angeles County had Latin or Asian names in 1997. Eight years earlier, there was but one Latin name in 10 on Axiom's list. Let it be remembered that homeowners bear the principal tax burden for local government and rarely show up at the welfare office. Far from stealing jobs from Americans, the people named Garcia, Lee (an Asian name), Rodriquez, Lopez, Gonzalez, Martinez, Hernandez, Kim and Perez are helping the California economy grow at the lowest unemployment level in decades.

If more immigrants were allowed into the U.S., there is every reason to believe that the economy would grow even faster. Certainly, the Information Technology (IT) field believes that. And west coast fruit growers have been so concerned about finding good agricultural workers that they recently pushed a pilot program to bring in 20,000 from Mexico and elsewhere. New York State suffers from labor shortages due in large part to an immigration bottleneck created by those overzealous politicians of an earlier era. Newly nationalized Latinos turned out for the 1996 presidential election at a greater rate than other citizens, reported the polling firm of Political Data, Inc. And, like other Americans, they can't be counted on to march to any one drummer's tune. Four out of 10 newly nationalized Latinos polled after California's vote on Proposition 227 voted against bilingual education. When you get right down to it, witch hunting among a nation's foreign-born citizens gets to be pretty fruitless. America's experience proves them to be nothing less than an asset. The same is no doubt true, more or less, in most of the rest of the world.

> *If more immigrants were allowed into the U.S., there is every reason to believe that the economy would grow even faster.*

Message for Labor – "Protecting jobs" inevitably results in the loss of jobs. That's the recent history of the labor movement. It's only by the creation of jobs that employment security—not necessarily job security—is acquired. Where job creation requires the skills or labor of foreign workers, so be it. That is the only policy that will work for organized labor over the long run.

Education and skills-enhancement
are winning, and unprepared labor isn't.

Some nations do a better job than others in connecting young people to the workplace and making their education relevant to the real world. The U.S., with 57 million youngsters enrolled in public schools in the fall of 1998, is not yet one of those nations. Major American employers, especially in technical fields, have written off the secondary school system as a bust when it comes to preparing young people for the demands of the workplace. The problem was expressed at a 1995 symposium on workplace options in Berlin, Germany, and hasn't gotten much better since then. Steve Trippe of New Ways to Work said that the K-12 educational system in the U.S. serves just two groups of kids: those that go on to college and top athletes. Only about 25 percent of high school graduates go to college. "The U.S. is the only industrialized nation that lacks a comprehensive and coherent system to help its youth acquire the knowledge, skills, abilities and information about the labor market necessary to make an effective transition from school to work," Trippe explained. "Seventy-five percent of high school students enter the workforce without four-year college degrees. Many high school students don't possess the basic academic and occupational skills necessary for the changing workplace or to pursue further education."

That is a terrible indictment of public education in the U.S. and a real threat to the nation's competitiveness in the global marketplace. It's a situation that cannot continue if America is to maintain its position on the world stage. Pressed by the lowest unemployment rate in 25 years, employers are beginning to take matters into their own hands. They lobby state and federal officials to make the public school system more relevant to the workplace and have gotten more involved in local schools. In Irving, Texas, for example, AMR Corp., fearing a travel/reservation agent's shortage, began licensing its Sabre reservation system to area high schools in 1996. Students use a computer terminal in a replica travel agency and book simulated flights to various spots around the country and world. Upon graduation, they have the skills to land a job in the travel industry, and employers like American Airlines are glad to get them. Boeing Company developed the Manufacturing Tech Prep program in Wichita, Kansas, to train local high school students to work on the company's assembly line for two semesters, starting in their junior year. With that preparation, the kids have an excellent shot at a good job when they graduate. Many companies are lending personnel to public schools to tutor skills like math and reading. Better employees result, wherever they may ultimately work.

State and local governments are starting to get the message. Henry County, Virginia, located in a rural part of the state, suffered debilitating plant closings in recent years as employers like DuPont phase out old, inefficient operations. To attract new employers, the county launched an innovative advertising campaign and set about improving the skills of the workforce. Patrick Henry Community College in Martinsville developed a curriculum that helped match graduate skills and education with the local job market. And the county put $280,000 a year into an expansion of adult education classes in the public schools. Just to make sure the momentum wasn't lost, Henry County committed to spend $362,000 per year to give every child in the fourth and eighth grades a laptop computer to keep through high school. In Indiana, a state-funded program called Business Modernization Technology trained high school students to be machinists. Employers, offering $10 per hour starting pay, stood in line for the graduates. Nationally, Congress passed the School to Work Opportunities Act in 1994. Among other things, the program provides subsidies to school districts for establishing partnerships with business. By June 1997, the number of partnerships between high schools and business had soared 270 percent. A lot is going on to address the problem of America's educational shortcomings, particularly as they relate to the workplace. But far too many of these actions are reactive, uncoordinated and likely to disappear if the job market ever slows.

Message for Government – Education is its own justification and does not necessarily have to relate to the development of specific job skills. But the practicality of the matter is that people have to trade their skills and labor for the means to live and prosper in modern societies. For all practical purposes, there is no other way for the masses of people. Since secondary education is mandatory in the U.S., and since so much of the "new blood" available to employers each year comes out of high school, isn't it about time that a linkage is made between public education and the workplace? The answer must be yes, but getting the job done is a monstrous undertaking. The answer is not more money.

America invests more in public education per child than any of the 23 nations that comprise the Organization for Economic Cooperation and Development (OECD), except Switzerland and Austria. Yet, the U.S. ranks near the bottom in achievement, reports Chester Finn of the Fordham Foundation, a Washington, D.C.-based education reform organization. And the problem cannot be rationalized away on the basis that so many children come into the public school system from poverty, broken homes and poor parental support, he contends. Those conditions are not unique to the U.S. Quite simply, the record shows that American public schools are the least efficient in the industrialized world. More computers and grander facilities are not going to correct the problem. The secondary school system's very approach to education must be redesigned on a new philosophy—relevance for all who pass through the system.

Message for Labor – Call for an overhaul of the nation's public education system. Demand greater respect for the needs of the workplace in the development of curriculum. Join with curriculum developers in adding "career paths" to the menu of educational offerings. What are history and math and economics and languages without a backdrop of labor and skills application? Michelangelo negotiated a contract to paint the Sistine Chapel, turned out for work every day, delivered his product more or less on time and gave value for value received. Albert Einstein didn't just think and hypothesize and noodle all the time; he held down a regular job in the Swiss patent office, then later toiled in the classroom at Princeton University like other hardworking professors. Education and skills enhancement are not foreign to organized labor. Any concerted effort to develop better job skills in the nation's youth would be a great service to the nation.

"Competitive taxation" is winning; confiscation of personal and corporate earnings to support expensive social contracts is losing.

With no source of operating capital but the wealth of its people, democracies have no alternative but to tax in order to do the public's bidding. That being the case, it behooves constituents to, (1) make sure government is spending public money well and (2) limit what they want in government services. Cradle-to-grave security, for example, is very expensive. To deliver it, government needs more taxpayer money than, say, a neighboring country that demands less social security. The greater security is fine, so long as the electorate doesn't mind forfeiting more of its earnings in taxes to acquire the benefit. Countries like Denmark, Sweden, Switzerland, Canada and Uruguay have long opted for this course. In relative isolation, the welfare state has much to recommend it. But in the global marketplace, the cost of a welfare state begins to cut into job creation and tax revenues because business pays an extra premium—higher taxes—on top of the other costs of production. That neighboring country where the populace demands less social security now becomes a more attractive place to work and to do business because fewer earnings disappear in taxes. Jobs and skills flow from the high-cost economy to the lower-cost economy and, in the long run, the populace that demanded less security to begin with enjoys more security as a result of their fiscal conservatism. Simplistically, that is the message for government today. Look what happened in Canada in the last half of the 1990s. A great many of the best and brightest took their skills and labor across the border to the U.S. where taxes are a lot friendlier. More than 26,000 Canadians obtained NAFTA visas in 1996 compared to 2,600 temporary work visas granted in 1989, reported professor Don DeVoretz of Simon Frazier University. It represented a brain-drain that troubled many. Somewhere in those numbers could have been Canada's Bill Gates, DeVoretz laments. Sweden, longtime welfare state, spent 46 percent of GNP (gross national product) on welfare in the last years of the 1990s, more than any other country. Overall, public spending was 63 percent of GNP. The income taxes required to deliver those public services took 59 percent of the pay of people earning as little as $30,000 a year and obliged employers to pay up to 41 percent of employee earnings to social security and pension plans, reported the *New York Times* in 1998. Proposed reductions in social services by a concerned national government were received by the populace like "swearing in church," said an opinion research pollster. Given those numbers, is there any question why Sweden began to slip vis-à-vis the competition? From the fourth-highest per capita income ranking in the world, the country sank to 15th place. Swedish industrialists pointed to the high personal income taxes as a major impediment to competing successfully in the global marketplace.

Ericsson, the nation's largest and most successful private employer, threatened to move its headquarters to Britain where the "business climate" is more favorable. Throughout the country, people long for a restoration of the old Sweden, the one that was among the three or four richest nations in the world. But that is not apt to happen, not with the costs and the consequences of so thorough a welfare state.

Message for Government – Reign in the services provided your constituents to at least a "competitive level" or lose the earnings base and brain power necessary to sustain economic growth.

Message for Labor – Taxation that drives employers and skills into the arms of other economies does local labor unions no good whatsoever. Government services spawned by pressure from organized labor pose risks and need to be carefully appraised for the negative consequences that arise from a diminution of competitiveness and a resultant flight of capital, jobs and skills.

Hard money is winning; unsustainable fiscal practice staggers to finish.

Speaking before the U.S. House of Representative's Committee on Banking and Financial Services in September 1998, renowned international investor George Soros reminded his listeners that financial markets, "far from trending towards equilibrium, are inherently unstable. A boom/bust sequence can easily spiral out of control, knocking over one economy after another." It is urgent, he said, that financial authorities, nationally and internationally, recognize this. Nothing less than the survival of the global capitalist system that generated so much prosperity throughout the world in the 1990s is at stake. Soros believed that the system was "coming apart at the seams." He cited as evidence the collapse of the Indonesian economy which wiped out 30 years of gains in living standards, the "total financial meltdown" of the Russian economy, stock market declines throughout Asia more severe than the great Wall Street crash of 1929, a flight of capital from Brazil that sucked out 50 percent of the value of publicly traded corporate stocks and raised interest rates to 40 percent, a sobering 3.3 percent decline in Japanese economic activity in the second quarter of 1998, the roiling of American stock exchanges and a growing credit crunch throughout the global marketplace. In this environment, Soros feared that the global capitalist system and the free trade that spawned it could be abandoned, turning the clock back to isolation economics where every nation was an island unto itself. Malaysia, he noted, opted out of the global marketplace in September of 1998 when it shut off financial markets to foreigners in an effort to halt the departure of critically needed capital. And the U.S., faced with cheap imports from every corner of the earth, debated whether or not to raise trade barriers, an action that surely would have touched off reciprocal steps by other countries. It was not a pretty picture he painted, and few economists argued with his premise.

To get the gyrating global capitalist system back into equilibrium, people like Soros believed that two things had to happen:

1. Market discipline by the community of nations that make up the global marketplace had to materialize. This means real, hard currency pegged to known, reliable value; sound fiscal policy in boom times and bad, even when it slows growth and recovery; and universally accepted bookkeeping practice that is open to review. It means no large public debt, and government spending that doesn't sap capital from the private sector.

2. An "international federal reserve" that serves as a lender of last resort and, ideally, provides checks and balances for the global capitalist system had to be developed. Part of this solution already exists in the form of the International Monetary Fund (IMF). But there is no institution in existence that oversees and intercedes in global financial markets as do federal reserves in the U.S. and Germany, for example. Such a body will have to be created sooner or later if the global capitalist system is to endure. The IMF is simply inadequate for the task, but it is all that the world's financial markets have at present. And, despite critics, it is indispensable, contend experts like Paul Krugman of MIT. Writing in the *New York Times*, Krugman asked, "If we need a domestic lender [Federal Reserve] of last resort to deal with domestic financial crises, doesn't the globalization of financial markets mean that now, more than ever, we need a lender of last resort to cope with international crises? . . . To hobble the IMF in the belief that world financial markets will take care of themselves

195

is to gamble the stability of those markets on a speculative theory—a theory that even most of the theorists think is refuted by the lessons of history."

Message for Government – The message for government on the matter of fiscal and monetary policy is twofold:

1. Run a tight ship, one that will hold up in the often stormy seas of the global marketplace. Create and maintain a solid, verifiable fiscal and monetary foundation for the operation of the private sector. Pursue strategies that keep purchasing power high and incentives to invest and grow at all levels. This may necessitate painful steps now and then—like currency devaluations, a short-term loss of competitiveness, culling failed financial institutions and hurting investors in the process. . . . The trick is to be reliable, prudent and open. This won't insulate nations against bad economic times, but it will help eliminate surprises and expedite recovery. Business can plan and adjust when the way ahead is clear. Surprises can be killers, and investors just won't run the risks. Against this kind of backdrop, any promise displayed in a nation's economy can be pursued with confidence. That's the basic starting point for countries on their way to prosperity.

2. Contribute to the development of an international banking system that helps to prevent the kind of domino effect that rocked the financial community from Thailand to America at the close of the 1990s, devastating much of the global capitalist system in the process. No nation of any consequence is now immune to the fallout that results from poor banking practice anywhere in the global marketplace. It is in every nation's best interest to have an overseer, controlled by the cooperating countries, that can monitor financial activity across the globe, raise an alarm when situations get out of hand, and step in with mutually agreed upon corrective measures and emergency funding when necessary.

Message for Labor – Push the national government to build and maintain a strong, internationally competitive banking system. And support efforts to stabilize and manage the global capitalist system. Capital, from abroad or domestically generated, is flighty and will not be bound. Try as a nation may to stop it, money will find a way out if it detects a risk or poor return. So goes capital, so go jobs and, by extension, labor unions. Organized labor is a powerful force in all developed economies. As an ombudsman for the workforce, it can be a very effective protector of the capital engines that drive job creation.

The winners in the race for a more efficient and prosperous workplace are closely bunched. The losers continue to chase, and though they appear from time to time to be gaining, it is a cruel illusion. For the real losers in this contest are the billions of people around the world who struggle for security and subsistence in economic systems that cannot compete in the global marketplace. The fault is not the people's, but the powers that be who saddle the workforce to a losing horse.

Chapter Six

Playing the "labor exchange" for jobs and profit

Inventing "everyman's agent"

n the newly old workplace of traditional permanent jobs (TPJ), the typical job search was a several-times-a-career event with long periods of employment in between. For most employees, there was just no ongoing need for job placement assistance. Employers didn't much need help finding employees either. Plenty of takers normally applied. A host of incentives were extended to keep needed human resources on hand, full time. The typical HR department was a rather cut-and-dried operation. Recruit in the same old proven places. Cherry-pick from the abundance of qualified or nearly qualified job applicants. Serve up the standard benefits package year after year. Train those on the payroll. Keep the troops happy. . . .

Then, following the confluence of events precipitated by the recession of 1991-92 (see Chapter Four), things changed abruptly. More employees than ever found themselves seeking work regularly, either because traditional permanent jobs were hard to secure and people moved around, taking what they could get, or because newly evolved FlexLifers and other free agents eschewed traditional permanent jobs in favor of a succession of short-term job assignments. For the first time since World War II, job searching in the general workplace became a recurring fact of life for many. That posed a problem. Finding a job several times in a working lifetime doesn't take all that much time and know-how. An "in" here, a connection there, an interview or two, and the deed was done. But finding a job every couple of years is another matter altogether. It's time consuming, for starters. People usually don't get paid while looking for work. Furthermore, job openings and job seekers are not always known to each other, not without someone or something to match the two. Clearly, good and qualified people in growing numbers needed help finding work and employment security in a flexible job market.

With the churn of personnel, employers also had a set of new problems. In the beginning, downsizing meant quick relief from excessive operating costs. Then, as competition heated up, employers found themselves scrambling to get needed skills, talent and labor when needed but only as long as needed. They were faced with the challenge of generating enough employee loyalty to ensure the availability of needed personnel in the future, and managing the comings and goings of increasing numbers of just-in-time workers. And, with little consideration given to upgrading the skills of flexible employees, employers were not at all sure who would prepare the workforce for the jobs ahead.

Now, experienced, qualified workers are constantly in jeopardy of losing their jobs, not because of ineptitude or a poor economy, but because the workplace no longer favors traditional permanent jobs.

How quickly things change. Not so long ago, the idea of a third-party service to keep experienced mainstream workers gainfully employed was hard to imagine. Not so long ago, employers treated human resources as a fixed cost and excess personnel as a necessary evil. Not so long ago, the workplace was fairly predictable and easy to negotiate. Now, experienced, qualified workers are constantly in jeopardy of losing their jobs, not because of ineptitude or a poor economy, but because the workplace no longer favors traditional permanent jobs (TPJ). Forced by the competition, employers cut personnel costs and raise productivity but lose the security of on-hand skills, talent and labor to handle any contingency. Predictability evaporates. Uncertainty reigns. Jobs go wanting. Opportunities are missed. Employees and their families suffer.

Something is missing.

The old order has fallen away, and an effective catalyst to tie together the new flexible workplace has yet to materialize. That missing catalyst is an effective labor exchange mechanism that accomplishes two vital tasks:

- Matches the employment needs and desires of the general work-force with the skills and labor requirements of employers.
- Supports the flexible workforce in the same way that employers have traditionally supported permanent employees, i.e., with bene-fits, steady work, career guidance, training, etc.

Much of the componentry of this requisite labor exchange service already exists is some form or another, though not in any single provider. Let's look at the current offerings before getting into what's needed to improve upon the product.

Staffing Agencies

Staffing agencies are the dominant labor exchange service in the new flex-ible workplace and the best-positioned candidate to eventually fill the role of "FlexLife agent" for the average working man and woman. The staffing industry has long served as intermediary between employees and employers and, at $100 billion-plus in size, it has enough critical mass to eventually fill the demands of the workplace.

The New Workplace of Flexible Employment		
EMPLOYEE	**AGENT**	**EMPLOYER**
• Responsible for own career management	• A growing factor in the general workplace	• No longer responsible for employee career management
• Responsible for own training, value-added skills enhancement and career development	• Major contributor to employee's career man-agement, skills enhance-ment and marketplace preparation	• No longer responsible for value-added skills enhancement except where it's in the employ-er's best interest
• Loyalty withdrawn from employer and bestowed upon agent	• Helps provide "employ-ment security" for employees in lieu of "job security"	• Employee loyalty lost
• Agent loyalty gained for employer loyalty lost	• Employee loyalty gained for agent loyalty given	• Agent loyalty gained

Employers and employees are not solely dependent on the staffing industry for the all-important match of need and skill that is the starting point for getting things done, however. Driven by the rapidly changing workplace, other forms of labor exchange have emerged that challenge the staffing business. Indeed, the staffing industry may well find its prospects diminished if it languishes long in fulfilling its potential as "everyman's agent."

One-Stop Career Centers

The State of Massachusetts launched an initiative in 1997 to improve employment services for employers and job seekers. After a lengthy research process to gauge what its "customers" wanted, the state funded a network of one-stop career centers to serve as an interface between those with skill needs and those wanting jobs. By January 1999, centers existed in Boston (three), Springfield (one), Holyoke (one), Woburn (one) and Cambridge (one). And two new facilities were planned for Brockton. The Future Works Career Center in Springfield represents the best of services provided the workplace under the program.

- State-of-the-art technology to create and maintain a "talent pool" of resumes which can be matched to jobs through key-word searches.
- A point of contact where employers can call or fax job openings daily and employees can inquire about job possibilities. Hundreds of jobs posted daily on the career center job boards and on the Internet.
- Prescreening of resumes by company-designated account representatives who forward appropriate credentials directly to employers daily.
- Company-specific testing, reference checking and interviewing.
- Special recruitment fairs conducted for employers moving into the area.

Some of these services result in a fee for employers, but job postings and resume forwarding are free. On becoming a member of the center (no charge), job seekers are eligible for resume and job-search assistance and can submit resumes for open positions, talk with employers, join job clubs and meet with career counselors. No agents or employee benefits are available, but the center and the network to which it belongs are promising additions to the workplace.

In-House Employee Development Centers

To protect their own best interests, large employers like Carrier Corporation, TRW and Mobil Oil recently established in-house employee development centers to raise the skill level of non-permanent workers. These firms recognize that cost-consciousness can work against them if the flexible labor pool can't do the job when called upon. By helping to ensure the employability of people they will likely release on the short-term, these organizations protect their own best interests in the long-run. In-house employee development centers assist employees in designing professional development plans that match the company's objectives, projected career paths and future skill needs. If employees like what they see, an action plan is designed based on their career interests, goals and current skills. The plan is discussed with a supervisor and implemented. It may call for specialized training, some of which the organization will provide or fund, some that the employee must acquire on his or her own. With these action plans, employees gain a measure of control over their development within the scope of the company's mission. It's a shining example of the dynamics of the new workplace and excellent long-range planning on the employer's part.

Talent Alliances

Going a big step beyond in-house employee development centers are talent alliances that pool and develop flexible workers who move around on short-term job assignments within the alliance, yet stay employed full-time. At least, that's the objective. Firms like AT&T, DuPont, GTE, Johnson & Johnson, Lucent Technologies, TRW, Unisys and UPS see this as an effective way to have their cake and eat it too—save on labor costs when certain skills are not needed, but have them available and ready to go when need arises. It's an inter-industry approach to training, job matching and career counseling.

The Internet

The growing importance of the World Wide Web (www) as an employment matching service has been covered elsewhere in this book, but it deserves repeating here. For all the fanfare, the Internet provided only a small percentage of total jobs as of 1998—something like 2 percent. But the frequency of Internet use for recruiting grows exponentially.

And the skills and earnings level of positions filled via the Internet are way out of proportion to the actual number of hires. The potential of the Internet as a job conduit knows no bounds, not just in glamour occupations like Information Technology but in all fields, including *FlexLife®* assignments. Recently, one of Randstad's branch managers received a solicitation with her regular monthly credit card statement. For just $4.95 per month, a circular touted, the credit card holder could sign up for an Internet-based job search service. "Congratulations!" the letter read. "As a First USA Bank card member, you are eligible to take advantage of an extraordinary new service that can make a quantum difference in your career. . . ." This, from a bank.

Labor Unions

Many people might be surprised to see organized labor included in a labor exchange list for flexible forms of employment. It's not happening yet, but can it be far off? Organized labor, of necessity, is changing. The new workplace will pass it by if it doesn't. There are hints of things to come in the Information Technology hotbed of California's Silicon Valley. Working Partnerships USA, in conjunction with local community colleges and labor unions, launched a pilot project in 1998 that provides skills certification, job rights training and job placement for temporary workers throughout the area. The jobs are mostly clerical positions and there is heavy emphasis on the placement of welfare recipients. It's a modest start in the right direction. Opportunities exist for labor unions to become an important force in the development and growth of flexible forms of employment. There is no reason unions can't fill much the same role for their membership that staffing agencies fill for their assignment personnel. This includes skills enhancement, training in the management of a *FlexLife®* career, providing employee benefits and so on.

In-House Specialists

Increasingly, employers are supplementing traditional human resource operations with specialists who handle nothing but just-in-time personnel requirements. No longer an afterthought, the flexible portion of an organization's workforce is starting to get the attention and resources needed to maximize productivity and competitiveness.

The foregoing list of service providers indicates the lengths to which the workplace is willing to go to ensure a sufficient supply of skilled flexible labor now and in the future. But the labor exchange realm is still in the embryonic stage. What's needed to develop the concept to its logical conclusion? If the idea of a FlexLife agent for a large portion of the workforce is the way to go, what has to occur for it to happen? Here are some answers:

Develop and perfect the concept of the "**FlexLife®** *or everyman's agent."* Earlier we made the point that the mercurial state of the modern workplace is not to be feared—it's OK. The changes that have occurred, and the concerns they raise, breed their own solutions. The rise of the staffing agent illustrates the point. The principal reason there is little to fear from the new workplace is because there are staffing consultants and other forms of labor exchange to fill the void left by the dissolution of the old employer/employee relationship. Staffing agents reconcile the needs of both parties to the benefit of society at large. Without this labor exchange device, or something very akin to it, things would not be OK in the workplace. What sets the staffing agent apart from other forms of labor exchange is the remarkable singular product he or she offers—the match. After all is said and done, this is what staffing agents are all about: matching the skills, talent and/or labor needs of employers with just the right staffing employee capabilities. Because it takes place between the ears of the staffing agent, the match doesn't exist in tangible form, and must be created anew every time the agent does his or her job. The match can't be stored. You can't see it. When you boil down the process that results in a successful match, it's clear to see why it is one of the most individualistic, intellectual products in existence. And it's not an easy product to create and deliver, over and over again. This is why staffing agents are so important, and sure to become more so. Creating staffing agents

Upgrading the Labor Exchange

- *Develop "Everyman's Agent"*
- *Deal with whomever calls*
- *Upgrade the flexible workforce*
- *Eliminate barriers to benefits for just-in-time personnel*
- *Promote the appeal of flexible forms of employment*
- *Teach employers how to develop and manage a flexible workforce*
- *Improve worker mobility*
- *Develop new sources of skills, talent and labor*

from the growing pool of staffing industry "consultants" is not a big stretch in many cases. More or less, it would involve the following:

1. Improved education and training to increase the prospective agent's knowledge of the workplace in general, the flexible workplace in particular, the labor exchange universe and the skills required to be successful in the business. From this platform, the education requirements get more specific. Staffing agents, above all, must know the business and the needs and desires of the employers they serve, and the background, aspirations and expectations of staffing employees who represent the solutions to the employers' problems. For, ultimately, it is the client—employer or employee—that confers agent status on the staffing agent. What the client gives, the client can take away. Staffing agents don't yet take a course and get a license to act as an agent. That status is earned.

2. Industry standards that distinguish a staffing agent from others in the trade may need to be established, complete with testing and certification. The standard might include one's educational attainment, experience in the field, length of service in the industry, successful completion of a course of study and a passing grade on a test. The course of study and test would cover a variety of subjects but certainly should include the basics of the staffing business:
    *   Learning what it means to be a "Staffing Agent" and how the status is achieved.
    *   Building and maintaining a working database of assignment personnel that match the skill requirements of employers in the local market.
    *   Developing Web pages for *FlexLife*® careerists. Their skills are what staffing agents have to sell. What better medium to do that than the Internet.
    *   Defining the personnel needs of local employers so as to be a vital cog in their labor planning and management process.
    *   Developing and improving the reservoir of assignment personnel. How is it done? How do you keep them busy and on a career track that keeps them happy?
    *   Developing a winning presence in the local workplace and an understanding of why it is important.

- Going beyond the quest for profit with thoughtful community involvement. A good corporate citizen serves itself well just by the act of reaching out and contributing.
- Achieving a "house style" and corporate culture that breeds confidence in staffing employees and employers alike.
- The processes and procedures to respond reliably and promptly to the expectations of assignment personnel and employers. Prompt compensation for staffing personnel, for example; delivering just the right skills when needed for an employer's unexpected project.
- Understanding the big picture in the workplace. There is much to know about the staffing industry and the workplace in which it operates. And it all changes very rapidly. Failing to know or to stay current is to court failure.

3. Touting the concept of "Staffing Agent" in the workplace. Emphasize the special qualities of the role and the value acquired by those who employ the services of such a specialist. Set a high mark for the right to be called "Staffing Agent," and make aspirants stretch to obtain the status. Do this, and the marketplace will begin to demand the equivalent of everyman's agent. And the promise of *FlexLife®* will spread.

A successful staffing agent would need more than a handsome certificate and fancy professional designation at the end of his or her name. In the ever-evolving global marketplace, it makes sense to possess foreign language skills and the know-how to move staffing employees across national borders. Basic economics says labor supply will flow to labor demand so long as barriers don't block the way. Barriers can take the form of laws, differences in culture and language, distances, or poor communications between employers and employees. Whatever the case, staffing agents would need to be able to cut through the obstacles. In this environment, things like passport and "green card" administration may become routine in full-service staffing organizations. Internet expertise that matches employer needs with employee skills far removed from one another might well become part of the staffing agent's portfolio of competencies. With a fifth of the U.S. workplace operating as telecommuters, and the practice growing rapidly in developed nations around the world, staffing agents had better be prepared to advise both employees and employers on the fine points of the practice. A good grasp of the legal distinctions between just-in-time personnel and permanent employees would be needed to keep client employers out of hot water. Contract knowledge and counseling are other skills that staffing agents might be expected to possess as they step into the breach opened by the new rules of work.

Deal with whomever calls. While specialization is the norm in the staffing industry, turning away inquiries from job seekers because they don't fall in the bailiwick of a particular staffing agent or agency is poor business and undermines the concept of a staffing agent for every marketable competency. It happens all the time. An agency specializing in industrial workers tells other callers, "Sorry, we don't handle personnel like you." Worse yet, staffing specialists in large multifaceted staffing organizations field telephone inquiries from people whose skills don't match the specialist's interests and the callers get the brush-off. "Sorry, we don't handle those kind of skills"—even when another office elsewhere in the organization may.

Every organization and every person who claims to be in the staffing business owes it to their profession to deal with whomever calls, so long as they possess employable competencies and want to work. A referral directory should be standard issue at every staffing agent's desk. It should be organized by broad industry classifications, followed by a listing of typical jobs within each category. This would help position any caller

Referral Directory	
Industry / Skills	Referrals
LEGAL SERVICES • Lawyer • Paralegal • Court reporter • Typist • Researcher • Librarian	Downtown Office Bob Bridges (404) 239-0777 xxxx xxxx xxx Rent-A-Lawyer Leslie Kennedy (770) 439-2993 xxx xxxx xxxx x
LETTER SHOP • Machine operators	Machine Staffing Services, Inc.

by field of expertise. The next column should note in-house specialists who can service the caller, then local competitors that may be of assistance, including labor exchange services like One-Stop Career Centers and the Internet. Provide specific contact information for each referral.

Why go to such trouble, especially when there's no direct remuneration in it for the staffing representative or his or her agency? These kinds of courtesies come back to both parties in heightened image in the marketplace and referral business that can't be accounted for. They strengthen the image of labor exchange services overall, which also pays off in additional business. A good referral system, widely practiced, would help fill in the gaps in the emerging flexible workplace, resulting in increased business and improved status for staffing professionals. And the workplace becomes ever more friendly and enriching. Those are pretty good reasons why staffing representatives should never tell a caller, "Sorry, we don't deal with your kind of competencies."

> *A good referral system, widely practiced, would help fill in the gaps in the emerging flexible workplace, resulting in increased business and improved status for staffing professionals.*

Commit to upgrading the job skills and self-management know-how of the flexible workforce. In a rapidly changing workplace where the current state of the art in many professions has a half-life of 12-24 months, a resource as valuable as the flexible workforce cannot be allowed to molder. That means the entire workplace team has to chip in for the desired results, especially the staffing agent and his or her organization. The record shows that the staffing industry understands what it must do. Back in 1993, according to the National Association of Temporary and Staffing Services (NATSS), 29 percent of all temporary workers received more than 20 hours of training and 66 percent gained new skills. Three years later, the association found that "temporary-help" companies spent $260 million per year on training, reaching approximately 2.2 million people annually. In 1997, the figure rose to $720 million and 4.8 million people trained. Today, leading labor exchange services offer skills assessment and training for assignment personnel, particularly in the field of computer usage. Data entry, word processing, spread sheets and database applications are typical offerings. A growing number of labor exchange services offer training in math, reading, second languages, resume writing, interviewing, telephone etiquette and dressing for success. Many staffing organizations have developed computer software and distant learning programs via the Internet to train just-in-time personnel for specific client needs. A good example is Kelly Scientific Resources, a unit of Kelly Services, Inc. The firm launched the first in a series of Internet-based classroom training courses for scientific personnel in 1998. The program included instruction for those who worked with the U.S. Food & Drug Administration, blood-borne pathogens, the Occupational Safety & Health Administration (OSHA) and other clients with high-skill needs. "This will help us meet the needs of our employees to broaden their skill sets and progress them higher through their careers," said Senior VP Rolf Kleiner. Similar arrangements have sprung up between employers and staffing organizations to supply high-demand circuit-board assemblers, catalog sales personnel, directory assistance operators and other workers. In these cases, the staffing organization usually contracts to recruit, screen, hire and train a very specific workforce. Most of these people are placed in temp-to-hire situations where both sides get to evaluate each other before making a commitment to full-time employment. Upgrading the skills of the flexible workforce means that staffing agents must get heavily into the career management and guidance business. Where employers leave off—and nearly all do when it comes to just-in-time workers—labor exchange services need to pick up. For example,

Upgrading the skills of the flexible workforce means that staffing agents must get heavily into the career management and guidance business.

1. Staffing agents should be able to prepare career development plans in concert with the assignment specialist, and action plans to move the person from "A" to "B" to "C." The partnership of staffing agent and staffing employee needs a track to run on, a game plan that pays off for all parties. The career development plan helps provide continuity for the employee and serves as an individual baseline and reference point for the staffing agent to keep his or her charges on course. Employers reap the rewards of skilled personnel who have their act together.

2. Staffing agents must be in a position to grease the skids of mobility where necessary to match employer needs with just-in-time skills. TravCorp, a major medical staffing firm in Malden, Massachusetts, exemplifies the requirement. The company places nurses and other medical personnel in assignments for four to 26 weeks, provides a

full range of paid benefits and coordinates the staffer's living and travel arrangements while on assignment. It's a full-service approach that is sure to become more prevalent in the general staffing sector.

3. Besides skills enhancement, staffing agents and their organizations must groom assignment personnel in self-management (teaching just-in-time employees how to operate in the flexible workplace) and marketplace awareness (educational offerings that add to the "big picture"). Suzanne Smith of New Ways to Work reminds us that most of the flexible workforce doesn't know how to manage its finances and the independence of just-in-time employment. Her message for the just-in-time workforce is this: "Your wages, benefits and future are now in your hands. You have to learn how to negotiate the best deal for yourself and otherwise operate successfully." Operating successfully would include things like basic personal money management, tax planning, time management, the fine points of negotiating and health insurance options.

> . . . most of the flexible work force doesn't know how to manage its finances and the independence of just-in-time employment.
>
> "Your wages, benefits and future are now in your hands. You have to learn how to negotiate the best deal for yourself and otherwise operate successfully."
>
> – Suzanne Smith
> New Ways to Work,
> nonprofit organization

4. Staffing agents should keep abreast of educational and training opportunities in the community where staffing employees can hone their skills and develop new ones. These opportunities can be found in local community colleges, trade schools, union halls, corporate seminars, government initiatives and distance learning programs via the Internet. Because staffing agents are supposed to be experts on matters dealing with the flexible workforce, they should know what kind of educational opportunities are available and bring them to the attention of assignment personnel.

5. Staffing agencies and other labor exchange services might even go so far as to advance tuition moneys to dedicated *FlexLife®* careerists. Get the expenditure back with a commitment from the employee to work for the agency until the loan is repaid. If it's a fair deal, a *FlexLife®*

career could be upgraded and the agency's talent pool expanded as well. Agencies might fund scholarship programs from earnings or special events. Associations can lend a hand. At its 1998 conference, the National Association of Computer Consultant Businesses (NACCB) raised $500,000 from attendees for its training initiative, the Open Door Education Foundation. Enlightened employers who recognize the need for a skilled reservoir of just-in-time workers may be induced to contribute to educational funds. Funding for legitimate work-related education is obtainable; all that's needed is the initiative. And that needs to come from labor exchange specialists.

6. Labor exchange services might design and sponsor training and educational programs in the local market with community colleges, trade schools, high schools and government agencies. Progressive employers are always on the lookout for better-trained personnel. Municipalities, counties, states and regions benefit from the availability of skilled workers. They attract industry which creates jobs, provides tax revenue and improves prosperity.

7. Staffing agents must put "their people" in job situations that match their "workstyles" and enhance their skills, income and prospects for the future. No one should know the assignment specialist's prefences and competencies better than the agent. Those competencies are what the agent has to sell. Part of that selling job is to "stretch" the person's skills with more demanding assignments without putting him or her in too deep. It makes for a healthy, positive situation that keeps just-in-time employees happy, strengthens the fiber of the workplace and increases the value of the staffing agent.

8. Finally, the staffing agent must stick with his or her pool of assignment personnel in good times and bad. Economies ebb and flow, and, with them, employment security. But people need jobs whatever the state of the gross national product. Thankfully, *FlexLife®* careerists are just as valuable, if not more so, in poor economies as in good ones. In hard times, employers will contract to the smallest core staffs possible, relying on just-in-time workers for a larger share of the workload. Many women drop out of the workforce to bear and raise children, then return. Staffing agents should be ready to pick up with these people right where they left off. Frequently, assignment personnel take full-time jobs. That

doesn't mean their agents should lose touch. Things change. Former FlexLifers may opt again for the lifestyle. Whether a lengthy illness, sabbatical or relocation—staffing agents should stay in touch and "be there" when called on.

Ultimately, *FlexLife®* careerists are responsible for their own professional development (see Chapter Three). But the staffing agent is best positioned to guide and counsel. In the final analysis, staffing agents must be part psychologist, counselor, trainer, prognosticator, motivator, confidant, financial analyst, strategic planner and trusted advisor. They take the hopes, aspirations, skills and abilities of people and find matches that work for all parties. And they do it day in and day out. The responsibility for developing the flexible workforce falls logically at the feet of the staffing industry and other labor exchange services. And the pressure grows to do more.

Work to eliminate barriers separating the flexible workforce from the security of health insurance, retirement provisions and the other traditional benefits provided full-time workers.
When it comes to benefits for the flexible workforce, labor exchange services are obliged to take the lead—whatever the issue. People ought not to have to stay in a bad job situation just to retain their health insurance and other benefits. It's not good for the employee or for the workplace. Just-in-time workers must be able to move from one job assignment to another or between labor exchange services without an interruption in their benefits. This would seem axiomatic in the world of flexible employment—but it isn't. Labor exchange services can help change this situation in several ways:

1. By pushing more aggressively to develop innovative benefit packages specifically tailored to the *FlexLife®* careerist and other just-in-time workers. Particularly important are better, more transportable health insurance and pension plans. Staffing agencies employ well over two million just-in-time workers on any given business day. What the industry sees fit to do for its own reverberates throughout the rest of the workplace.
2. By promoting the concept of flexible, transportable benefits for

just-in-time workers with client employers. The more employers understand the situation, the more they are apt to be advocates.

3. By developing and pushing clear, precise recommendations for legislative initiatives to right the wrongs in the current body of law that blocks or hinders sensible benefit provisions for just-in-time workers. Individually, staffing agencies already offer a wide range of benefits to their assignment personnel. Health insurance and vacation and holiday pay are the most common benefits offered. A 1997 poll by the National Association of Temporary and Staffing Services (NATSS) found that 53.7 percent of respondents offered health insurance coverage. Nearly 80 percent offered vacation and holiday pay. And many firms provided 401(k) retirement plans and stock purchase options. Forced by the competition to attract and retain quality assignment personnel, agencies are even beginning to pay part of the costs of staffing employee benefits. MacTemps of Boston, Massachusetts, for example, pays 60-100 percent of health insurance costs, 100 percent of dental and disability coverage, and contributes $0.25 for every dollar placed in a 401(k) plan. And the staffing employee is 100 percent invested immediately.

Promote **FlexLife®** *and the other forms of flexible employment with the public and the flexible workforce.* People know the pain of downsizing, outsourcing, re-engineering and so on. They experience firsthand the uncertainties and insecurities endemic to the modern workplace. But they are not well informed on the alternatives to traditional permanent jobs (TPJ) and the lifestyles they dictate. As a public service, if for no other reason, the staffing industry and other labor exchange operations need to convey the positive side of the decline in traditional permanent jobs. Employers would take a lot of heat off themselves if they joined in the effort. Labor unions have much to contribute on this point as well. Overall, the workplace would benefit greatly with a new roadmap for navigating the future. If the public learns through institutional advertising and other programs that the alternatives to a stifling, all-consuming permanent job are surprisingly attractive, we may witness a surge of people opting to manage their own careers in some *FlexLife®* mode or another.

Why aren't staffing agencies out on college campuses recruiting graduates to pursue *FlexLife*® careers built on their course of study? A better promotion and selling job needs to be done with those who comprise the flexible workforce as well. Low-paid temps, part-timers and others of the genre need to understand that the business has a lofty upside. With hard work, a well-conceived career development plan, and a dedicated agent, they can obtain good, reliable earnings and an attractive lifestyle too.

Teach employers how to develop and manage a flexible workforce and maximize the investment in just-in-time employees. Just how far can employers go with flexible forms of employment in reducing the size and cost of the core staff? To what extent can labor exchange services share HR functions once borne solely by employers? How do you set up labor alliances where a group of employers share a pool of just-in-time workers? What are the benefits of such a thing? Why go to the expense of training temps, of all things? What kind of flexible employment arrangements might work best for companies A through Z? The possibilities for reducing labor costs while ensuring needed skills and labor are many, but they have to be compiled, researched, verified, packaged, presented and implemented. That job logically falls to the community of labor exchange services. Matching employee skills with employer needs may be the crux of the business, but it is not the end of the story, not by a long shot. The very scope and size of the flexible workforce, the comings and goings of so many people—these things create management challenges that few employers have ever experienced. Who better to help develop a flexible workforce management system for employers than staffing agencies? Any such system must encompass the following:

1. Clear lines of responsibility. In advance, determine which party provides employee benefits, if any, and how training responsibilities will be split. Hash out risk management details, recruitment and selection strategy and how performance will be monitored. Establish the employer's "interface" with just-in-time workers—greetings, orientation, supervision, termination, replacement and so on. And set up lines of communication that keep the process flowing smoothly.

2.   Detailed proposals on the best practices in the flexible workplace for just-in-time employee training programs, benefit packages, talent alliance creation, recognition and reward systems and other issues specific to short-term job assignments.

3.   Agency-provided HR services for just-in-time personnel as an option to employer-designed and -implemented models.

4.   The administrative process required to employ, pay, insure, monitor and manage just-in-time personnel on an ongoing basis. This includes proper compliance procedures to meet all legal requirements.

5.   The particulars of supervision and management so that just-in-time workers are able to perform more quickly and effectively while on the job (see Chapter Four).

Make it easier for just-in-time employees to go where the jobs are. When Fokker nv, the aging Dutch aerospace giant, began to succumb to competition in the mid-'90s, Randstad Polytechniek of The Netherlands set up shop in Seattle, Washington, to match employee skills from the dying business with employer needs at the Boeing Company. On paper, it looked like a slam-dunk: skilled, reliable Dutch engineers, newly unemployed with no comparable work anywhere in Europe, and the world's largest aircraft maker prepared to pay top wages for what it needed. But, as events unfolded, fewer Fokker personnel than expected elected to capitalize on the Boeing opportunity. The ties to home and family and familiar ways were too strong for many people to venture off to faraway Seattle. Cultural differences were too big a hurdle for others to cross. From the perspective of Holland's generous and secure social support system, the American attitude about job security and taxation was a bit unnerving. The program was successful enough—over 30 former Fokker engineers took assignments with Boeing, and the way was paved for similar exchanges later on. But, in retrospect, many at Randstad wish the company had done a better job of easing the transition for our Dutch countrymen. We should not have left them on their own with unfamiliar details like filing quarterly estimated tax returns. They had never been exposed to this practice before, and it became a concern. Payroll deductions were confusing. A little advance planning and training would have avoided the problem. America doesn't provide for the extended vacation and time-off provisions enjoyed in Europe, and more could have been done to prepare the Dutch for this lifestyle adjustment. The Boeing Company corporate culture might have been better conveyed. Language training and support could have received more emphasis. The Seattle-area Dutch community might have been better utilized.

There are good ways to make distant assignments more palatable, and every effort needs to be made by staffing organizations to examine the issues and plan for the eventuality. The workplace before us will require more and more assignment personnel to move from wherever they happen to be to wherever they need to be. Think for a moment about that massive General Motors expansion program described earlier. The kinds of skills necessary to build state-of-the-art automobile factories in China, Argentina, Malaysia and the Philippines are not available in those countries. GM brings in the skills from around the world as needed. Doesn't that suggest in-house travel agency services? Some large staffing organizations have developed this capacity for their managers, but the need could well extend to the movement of just-in-time workers to distant job sites.

Continue to develop and bring into the workplace those previously excluded. U.S. law requires that employers not discriminate in their hiring on account of disability, sex, age and other criteria. But it took the labor shortages of the last half of the 1990s to finally open the doors to any and all able-bodied people who wanted a job. In this development, the staffing industry is due a great deal of credit. But the work of developing previously untapped or little-used sources of skill, talent and labor has only begun. The most fertile ground lies under the following:

- People with disabilities.
- Older workers.
- Welfare recipients and other chronically unemployed.
- Women with young children.

People With Disabilities

In the U.S. alone, there are well over six million unemployed people with disabilities who are ready, willing and able to work. Interestingly, many of the physical workplace barriers to the employment of these people have been removed by federal and state decree; it's "attitudinal" barriers that still block the way. According to a recent Lewis Harris survey, fear, prejudice and an overall lack of understanding on the part of employers are the biggest barriers to the workplace for people with disabilities. The good news is that fear, prejudice and ignorance are susceptible to enlightenment. And that's what the staffing industry needs to be doing—enlightening employers. It's happening here and there, but the effort needs to be an industry-wide priority. For the staffing business may be the single best vehicle for developing this long-neglected pool of workers. One new study, *The Emerging Role of the Staffing Industry in the Employment of Persons with Disabilities* by Peter Blanck at the University of Iowa, concludes that the staffing industry provides a "vital link" to the permanent employment of persons with disabilities. The study tracked 10 disabled workers who sought jobs through the temporary employment giant Manpower Inc. Nine of the 10 employees were placed in job assignments within 10 days of applying at a Manpower office, reported *Staffing Industry Report* in July 1998. Six of the 10 moved from no employment to permanent employment. Nine of 10 were placed in an industry or job in which they expressed interest, and the placements were consistent with their job skills. Nine remained in the workplace from the time of their first job assignment and earned above minimum wage. Based on these findings, the study by Blanck determined that Manpower "effectively and promptly transitions people with disabilities from unemployment to employment."

We at Randstad learned about people with disabilities firsthand with our involvement in the 1996 Paralympic Games as an Official Supplier of staffing services. So impressed were we by the experience that in August following the games, Randstad launched a program specifically designed to put individuals with disabilities to work. It's called No Limits! and is built on the following:

- *Training and education* – There are a lot of misperceptions about hiring people with disabilities. One of the biggest relates to the cost of accommodating them. On average, it takes less than $100 to accommodate an employee with a disability. The company tries to get this sort of information disseminated where it will do the most good. Another point stressed in the program is the good sense of employing people with disabilities. They are proven to be reliable, hard-working and productive. We developed a brochure entitled "No Limits! No Excuses or Barriers" and a lighthearted video tape to help employers focus on the person and the skills he or she possesses rather than the disability. These kinds of things help open employers' doors to disabled staffing personnel. After that, performance carries the day.

- *Consulting* – To prepare the way for the employment of people with disabilities, the company's staffing consultants meet with employers, tour their facilities, help determine where the disabled can be employed to advantage and train the existing workforce in how to interact with these people. Perhaps there is telecommuting work for the homebound? Maybe the Internet could serve as an effective conduit for the performance of certain tasks? Some simple training might make jobs available that were thought to be off-limits. You don't know until you ask and probe. Counseling on compliance with the Americans with Disabilities Act (ADA) is another consulting service the company provides.

- *Skills assessment* – Staffing consultants assess the skills of those they place in various staffing assignments. The objective is to match the person and his or her skills to the job so that employee and employer win. Adaptive devices like closed-circuit television (CCTV) and TeleType (TTY) are brought into play to assess the capabilities of people with disabilities. Some situations may call for a communications specialist to "sign" with a hearing-impaired applicant. Or there may be applicants who need help in filling out the written portion of an application—whatever it takes to get a good sense of the person's on-the-job capabilities.

- *Job placement* – Ultimately, Randstad is in the job placement business; that's how we justify our existence. So, like any other assignment, No Limits! is about identifying skilled, effective employees and matching them with rewarding job opportunities. The emphasis is placed on what a person can do—not on what he or she cannot do. People with disabilities are a valuable resource for employers. Using them is just smart business. The more the staffing business can get across that message, the better it will be for the workplace in general.

Older Workers

American Baby Boomers, 76 million strong, are moving into retirement age, disinclined to retire and, in many cases, unable to retire. And, for the U.S. workplace, it's a good thing. The nation's economy would simply grind to a crawl without the energy, skills and labor of so large a segment of the overall workforce. Europe's Boomers represent a different problem—mass retirement there would severely strain an already burdened tax base. Japan shares some of both problems. Keeping older workers as gainfully employed as they want to be fits the needs of far too many not to be taken more seriously by the various labor exchange services. One indication that the job is not being done well can be found in a 1998 survey conducted by the National Council on Aging. The gist of the study is that employers value older workers highly but often do not know where to find them. More than 80 percent of 240 firms polled responded that workers 65 years of age and older are thorough, reliable, stay on the job longer, are flexible and willing to change, and do not take time off for health reasons. Nevertheless, 61 percent of the respondents reported that the inability to find these workers is a significant barrier that precludes more being hired. The staffing industry, in particular, should take this as a personal affront,

More than 80% of 240 firms polled responded that workers 65 years of age and older are thorough, reliable, stay on the job longer, are flexible and willing to change, and do not take time off for health reasons. Nevertheless, 61% of the respondents reported that the inability to find these workers is a significant barrier that precludes being hired.

– 1998 Survey
National Council on Aging

and move systematically to correct the problem.

Tracking and cultivating retired and retirement-aged workers is only part of the requirement. Older workers have certain limitations in what they can do and what they are willing to do. Accommodations have to be made. Who better to develop employment regimens that suit older workers than the flexibility experts in the staffing industry? Flexible employment arrangements are a must in this segment of the workforce. Telecommuting may have a big role to play. The Internet could open up exciting possibilities for employer and employee alike. Computer training and *FlexLife*® instruction are needed. Where are the programs to adjust the workplace just enough to keep older workers on the job in a way that's good and comfortable for them?

Welfare Recipients

Across the U.S., new welfare laws are taking away incentives not to work and pushing people into the workplace. There are some exciting success stories, enough to illustrate the possibilities when it's in everyone's best interest to develop effective solutions. Though heavily involved in these initiatives, the staffing industry still does not plumb effectively the labor pool represented by welfare recipients. There is every reason to correct this oversight.

Women with Young Children

Yes, nearly half the U.S. workforce is composed of women. But that is hardly the extent of women who would work if they felt that they could. A great many of these women have young children and no good way to care for them when working out of the house. A job-holding husband doesn't necessarily solve the problem. In most developed economies, it often takes both parents working just to make ends meet. And in the U.S., there are nearly as many divorced mothers of small children as there are women employed in the workplace. To hold down a job generally means day care for the children. And that can get expensive— $400-$1,000 a month in major markets, as much as rent or a mortgage. Even for two working parents, the expense can be prohibitive; for a single parent, it is usually impossible. Somewhere, some way, sooner than later, the workplace must solve the problem of child care in a way that satisfies the basic tenets of good and decent absentee mothering. A little imagination goes a long way here. A San Antonio, Texas, day care center offers take-home food for harried parents who rush from work to pick up a child, then rush home faced with the need to feed a hungry family. Some day care operations have mounted cameras in their nurseries and tie them into the Internet. Parents can log onto the World Wide Web at the office and literally "look in" on their child during the work day. How unrealistic would it be for employers—even labor exchange services—to set aside day care facilities on-premises, staffing it with a revolving shift of those parents who use it? Mom or Dad brings the child to work, deposits him or her in the company day care center, then goes down the hall or upstairs to clock in. Somewhere during the day, the employee reports for a one-or-two hour stint as a day care assistant. The person can make up the lost time by coming in earlier or leaving later—an easy enough commitment when stops at the old day care are no longer required. Staffing agencies might consider compiling "best day care practices" from around the world and sharing them with local employers, government agencies, labor unions, churches and competitors. As an economic resource, mothers with small children are invaluable; as an economic liability, poorly tended children are a huge drag on society. There is benefit and liability enough for the workplace to move child care to the top of the priority list. The staffing industry and other labor exchange services have major roles to play in this effort because any solution will require flexibility, human resource expertise, employer training, matching skills and so much more of what "staffing" is all about.

The advent of the staffing industry and other forms of labor exchange, and the promise they hold for both employees and employers, does not lessen the pain of losing a job to downsizing or, in the case of employers, launching a program of personnel reduction. But the options for both parties are certainly increased by the prospects of another approach to working and living. Over time, as older generations adjust to the new standard of employment, flexible work may well become more appealing for the mainstream workforce than traditional permanent jobs (TPJ). So much of how this unfolds depends on how effectively the labor exchange industry fulfills its potential. The challenges are many. But the goal and the ways and means are clear. Those of us in the business need to fix our eyes on the target and not be distracted. Not only will the industry prosper by doing so, society at large will benefit as well.

Chapter Seven

Taking *FlexLife*® to the bank

Parting shots

Great theory, developing reality—but what happens when you take *FlexLife*® to the friendly local banker for a loan? There among the financial institutions is the real test for flexible forms of employment as a career and lifestyle. So far, this audience just doesn't "get it" when it comes to the new flexible workplace. For a successful FlexLifer in, say, the materials handling field to sit down in front of the typical loan officer, pass across his or her *FlexLife*® resume and ask for a new car loan or mortgage is to cause consternation at best and rejection at worst. What's the problem? The FlexLifer earns an attractive income. A succession of quality job assignments has kept him or her busy except for a break here and there—time off elected by the FlexLifer. Letters of recommendation from former employers laud the applicant's capabilities and work habits. The full range of employee benefits is provided by the individual's staffing agency. The person's skills are in demand, assuring employability, and the future is bright. What more can the banker want?

Well, it would help the banker immensely if the FlexLifer simply fit the age-old profile of a "good credit risk." Forget the income and the skill level and the employment security and the drift of the workplace. Why hasn't this person worked for a single employer for the last five or ten years? Where's the stability in this guy's employment record? Why does he or she bounce around so much? What's this six-week break to study anthropology? And what the hell's *FlexLife®*?

Industries that grew up in a world of traditional permanent jobs (TPJ) naturally developed models for lending, insuring and investments based on the world they knew. That world, it turns out, is dissolving, and a new one rises in its place. But how many in the financial establishment have changed the way they determine a person's credit worthiness, job stability, earnings potential and the other criteria that go into the decision to grant a loan or enter into an installment agreement? How many pension planners and insurance providers have recognized the need for new and innovative benefits to fit the modern workplace? The answer is "not many." Until the financial community catches up with the times, the growth and development of the flexible workplace will be hindered—to the detriment of a great many more people than the flexible workforce. If, indeed, flexible employment arrangements are the wave of the future, then employers and society at large need a vibrant corp of *FlexLife®* careerists ready, willing and able to live the life to its fullest. This includes financial services tailored to the lifestyle.

FlexLifers and their ilk throughout the workplace are consumers too. They need cars and houses, credit cards, investments and money for the kids' college tuition just like anyone else. And for the keen-eyed financier, these people are an excellent market niche. Employment security is every bit as good as job security. There is a wealth of new business in the ranks of the flexible workforce for those institutions that redraw customer profiles to match the changing marketplace. And it is business that will surely grow. No doubt the financial community will come to see opportunity where most in the business now see risk. Perhaps the sentiment and insights expressed in this book will help the cause. That would be reward enough for the time and effort put into *Don't Get a Job, Get a Life!*

These are exciting times in the workplace, wherever in the global marketplace you may labor. Never has the workplace been so big, so fast-paced, so promising, so fearful, so confusing, so breathtaking. There is no putting this genie back in the bottle. National economies, big and small, weak and strong, are much better off learning to live with this amorphous monster than they are trying to hide behind protectionist barriers and socialist forms of government. To retreat from open-market global capitalism because it bites back when mishandled is a terrible mistake for the family of man. No other system of commerce has ever served so many people so well for so long. And it's just a newborn. The promise of the global marketplace is hardly fulfilled, nor is its final shape yet decided. The excesses and sharp edges that produce financial havoc in vulnerable economies will be smoothed inevitably with practice and time. In this system, the "have nots" can compete with the "haves" because employers persist in seeking the best labor value, wherever in the world that may be. So long as that remains the case, and so long as employers downsize and "upsize" as market conditions dictate, it may not matter what governments do in the short run to adjust to the vagaries of the global marketplace. In the long run (never very far down the road in today's workplace), every economy will have to move to some form of open-market global capitalism in order to survive. Against these dynamics, the workforce has no choice but to adjust with a more flexible attitude about employment and a deeper conviction to "get a life" in the midst of so much job-related turmoil. Thankfully, there is *FlexLife*®. More and more, it is something that employees and employers alike will be taking to the bank with assurance.